Evangelism Now

Evangelism Now

U.S. CONGRESS ON EVANGELISM —
Minneapolis, Minnesota 1969

OFFICIAL REFERENCE VOLUME: Papers and Reports

Edited by Geo. M. Wilson

WORLD WIDE PUBLICATIONS
1313 Hennepin Avenue
Minneapolis, Minn. 55403

Published by World Wide Publications, 1313 Hennepin Avenue,
Minneapolis, Minnesota 55403 U.S.A.

Library of Congress Catalog Card Number: 78–145660
Manufactured in the United States of America

U.S. Congress on Evangelism

STATEMENT OF PURPOSE

1. To witness to the central fact that the Gospel of Jesus Christ has power to save people in this age, and that faith in Jesus Christ is the way of salvation for all.

2. To find anew the Biblical basis and strategy for evangelism through the urgent proclamation and teaching of the Gospel to each generation by a worshiping, witnessing, and serving church in which all believers once again declare boldly their faith in the risen Lord.

3. To teach believers how to do evangelism in the power of the Holy Spirit.

4. To experience a spiritual awakening within the church by the power of the Holy Spirit.

5. To challenge the powers of darkness, spurring the churches to stimulate believers everywhere to mount a vigorous attack upon the forces producing misery, inequity, emptiness, discrimination, and other evils in our society, and to lift, wherever possible, the spiritual and temporal burdens of man.

6. To encourage the church to develop and use modern and effective means for reaching people with the Gospel in all its relevance.

7. To demonstrate practical Christian unity through witness to the world that Jesus Christ is Savior and Lord.

8. To confess together past failures; to assess together opportunities for evangelism presented by a burgeoning world; and to strengthen one another in the common task of reaching out to that world for Christ.

9. To reaffirm that Jesus, the Lord of the church, is the Lord of history at whose return "every knee shall bow and every tongue confess that Jesus Christ is Lord to the glory of God the Father."

THE EXECUTIVE COMMITTEE OF THE U.S. CONGRESS ON EVANGELISM

Dr. Billy Graham	Honorary Chairman
Dr. Oswald C. J. Hoffmann	Chairman, National Committee
Rev. William Berg	Author and director of the black light drama
Rev. Paul P. Fryhling	Chairman of the Executive and Program Committee
Dr. C. Philip Hinerman	Chairman — Evening program
Dr. Mel Larson	Chairman — Publicity Committee
Dr. Carl Lundquist	Chairman — Morning program
Dr. Victor Nelson	Executive Secretary
Dr. Conrad Thompson	Chairman — Participation Committee
Mr. George Wilson	Treasurer and Chairman of Arrangements

NATIONAL COMMITTEE

FOREWORD

In the Fall of 1966, the world then, as now, stood at the edge of a precipice. In Berlin, where East meets West, 1,000 delegates from over 100 nations met for the World Congress on Evanglism. More than 200 persons from these 100 countries presented papers at the World Congress in Berlin where His presence and power were felt by the delegates in Berlin's Kongresshalle. These papers were presented in two volumes under the title: ONE RACE, ONE GOSPEL, ONE TASK.

From Berlin back to their native lands went Emperor Haile Selassie of Ethiopia; two converted Auca Indians of Ecuador; students of Ghana; pastors from Yugoslavia . . . church leaders and laymen endued with power from on high went back to their own countries. The blessings and inspiration from the eight days in Berlin in 1966 led to many national Congresses on Evangelism throughout the world.

In the fall of 1967, a Lutheran pastor in Minneapolis asked if there were any plans for a U.S. Congress on Evangelism. From Dr. Conrad Thompson's question grew several prayer sessions with delegates from the Twin City area who had attended the Berlin Congress. Out of this came the U.S. Congress on Evangelism in Minneapolis, Minnesota in September, 1969. Five thousand delegates from nearly all the states attended.

A committee of pastors and laymen was headed up by Dr. Oswald C. J. Hoffmann, Chairman of the National Committee, and Dr. Billy Graham, Honorary Chairman. Dr. Paul Fryhling of Minneapolis was Chairman of the Executive Committee. An honorary Committee of 100 from Minnesota, headed by Governor LeVander, tendered an invitation for the Congress to meet in Minnesota.

"Much is given — much is required," taken from Luke 12:48 became the motto of the Congress. Evening sessions, 45 workshops, the morning Bible Hour led by Archbishop Marcus Loane of Australia and Dr. Harold Lindsell of Washington, D.C., and the regular sessions made up the week-long program. Friday's Youth Night saw 18,000 young people crowd out the Minneapolis Armory and overflow into the City Auditorium. At the closing meeting on Saturday night, Dr. Oswald C. J. Hoffmann shared the platform with Dr. Billy Graham. Dr. Hoffmann gave a resumé of the Congress and Dr. Graham gave an evangelistic appeal to the 22,000 people at the

Metropolitan Sports Center. Hundreds of decisions were made that night. (An additional 25,000 listened to the message by public address system in the parking lot outside, and metropolitan police estimated some 80,000 people never got off the freeway.)

Now we present the papers from the U.S. Congress on Evangelism in this book entitled EVANGELISM NOW.

Truth is ageless. The mission of the church is changeless. Methods may change, but the goal is the same. In this spirit, the U.S. Congress on Evangelism met more in the formation of an institute rather than a conference. A layman wrote in his evaluation of the Congress, "God rolled out His plans for all who had eyes to see. He gave a brief preview of how things will be. Those who had eyes to see knew they were seeing Jesus Christ in action. Those who had ears to hear knew they were hearing the Son of God. The Holy Spirit blew through the assembly while the delegates joined hands and prayed."

This interdenominational U.S. Congress on Evangelism focused largely upon the relationship of evangelism to the day's social issues.

And that is what this book is all about. EVANGELISM NOW discloses the spiritual temperature of this generation and seeks to analyze obstacles retarding successful evangelism. This volume supplies some of the answers. Reading these addresses will challenge the thoughtful and will expand the spiritual horizons for all who seek to serve.

EVANGELISM NOW witnesses to the central fact that the Gospel of Jesus Christ has power to save people in this age, and that faith in Jesus Christ is the way of salvation for all.

Geo. M. Wilson

TABLE OF CONTENTS

ORIENTATION AND WELCOME

Dr. Billy Graham

I'm going to ask that we stand. I'm going to ask that all of us together repeat the 23rd Psalm and then repeat the Lord's Prayer together.

"The Lord is my shepherd; I shall not want. He maketh me to lie down in green pastures: He leadeth me beside the still waters. He restoreth my soul; He leadeth me in the paths of righteousness for His name's sake. Yea, though I walk through the valley of the shadow of death, I will fear no evil: for thou art with me; thy rod and thy staff they comfort me. Thou preparest a table before me in the presence of mine enemies: thou anointest my head with oil; my cup runneth over. Surely goodness and mercy shall follow me all the days of my life: and I will dwell in the house of the Lord forever."

Shall we pray. Our Father which art in heaven, hallowed be thy name, thy kingdom come, thy will be done in earth as it is in heaven. Give us this day our daily bread, and forgive us our debts as we forgive our debtors, and lead us not into temptation, but deliver us from evil. For thine is the kingdom, and the power, and the glory forever. Amen.

We will now have the posting of the 50 State flags and then we will be led in singing by our song leader tonight, Dr. Jim Davis, former Director of Music at the Moody Bible Institute and now Director of Music at the First Covenant Church. Then that will be followed by the leading in the opening prayer by the Chief of Chaplains of the United States Navy, Rear Admiral James Kelly.

(Everyone sang "The National Anthem")

REAR ADMIRAL JAMES KELLY: Let us pray. Almighty God, teach us how to pray. Visit tonight in the presence and power of your Holy Spirit. You have given to us the unspeakable gift of Jesus Christ and have placed upon us, your followers, the glad burden of being your evangelists. Grant to each of us gathered here a renewed dedication to the task of proclaiming the good news of the Gospel of your Son, the Lord Jesus Christ. May we find at this Congress a renewed zeal in communicating your unchanging truth in a changing world. May we discover and remove those things in ourselves and in our environment which impair the productive offering of the Gospel. May we see again clearly the heart of our Christian task, the creating of new life through your Word. Help us to learn ways to confront the bewildered with the fact of Christ,

DR. BILLY GRAHAM, Founder and President, The Billy Graham Evangelistic Association, and Honorary Chairman, U.S. Congress on Evangelism.

to give to the confused the creative word of the Cross, and to reclaim the disenchanted and disillusioned by the glory of the resurrection.

Keep before our minds, O God, and in our hearts, the private and social ills which cry out for the healing of your love. Make us particularly mindful of the painful fruits of war. We remember and commend to your special care these faithful servants of freedom who are prisoners of war, missing in action, wounded or dying. May they be treated with mercy and humanity and may they bear their burdens and fears in the strength of our Savior.

Throughout the deliberations of this Congress, grant us the patience to listen, the grace to share, and the wisdom to explore; and in all things support us, Lord God, by the presence of Him who is the light of the world and who overcomes every darkness. In the name of the Lord Jesus Christ we pray. Amen.

Mr. Graham: Our next speaker I could introduce in many ways — as a prominent attorney, as an educator — because he's a former professor of speech at the University — as a civic leader — now a political leader — but I'm going to introduce him tonight as the son of a Lutheran clergyman whose Christian faith has been a dominant factor throughout his life. For 10 years he was Chairman of the Commission on Christian Higher Education of the Augustana Lutheran Church. He has served as secretary of the National Lutheran Council for three years. Four years he served as president of the Minnesota Lutheran Brotherhood. He is the Governor of the State of Minnesota who was elected by one of the largest majorities of any Governor in this state's history. We welcome tonight a warm friend of the church, a warm friend of the Gospel, the Governor of the State of Minnesota, Governor Harold LeVander. Let's give him a warm welcome.

Governor LeVander: Thank you, Dr. Graham, distinguished guests on the platform, and distinguished guests from every corner of the United States. It's a very special personal pleasure for me tonight to welcome the United States Congress on Evangelism to Minnesota.

This is truly an inspiring experience for our state to see 5,000 or 6,000 people drawn together by God's will, to be sent forth with His Word. Minnesotans genuinely appreciate the chance to serve as your host during this week, and on their behalf I warmly greet you and thank you for coming to Minnesota.

You have chosen an appropriate meeting place. Minnesota has a rich and varied religious heritage. We are fundamentally a religious people and we are proud to have the national headquarters of several denominations here in Minnesota including yours, Dr. Graham. And furthermore, Minnesota will treat you well. The quality of life that you will enjoy here has been compared with all other states by the Yale professor, Dr. John O. Wilson, and Minnesota ranks second in the nation. We are very proud of that achievement and very aware that it happened because of the exceptional quality of our people. Certainly a strong religious tradition has shaped our people's character. Indeed, I think you've come to the right place. You've also come at the right time especially, speaking personally. Perhaps since I spent a third of my lifetime in a parsonage my views may be a little colored, but last week I attended the National Governors' Conference in Colorado. There were 49 Governors in attendance and scores of Federal officials and representatives of local government, to discuss problems that have baffled our country for years. The recommendations that were finally adopted called for some fundamental changes in some of our presently inept social programs, such as welfare and housing, yet no one there had the audacity to suggest that these government-sponsored measures could cure all ills. Such a prediction would be folly.

Each day that I sit in the Governor's chair, confronted with never-easy and never-ending problems, I am increasingly convinced that our people's concerns are not going to be solved simply by more money or more guidelines or more time. What we need is more personal character.

If the seemingly unsolvable is going to be solved, it will come from a deep and active commitment on the part of most Americans to follow Isaiah's command when he said, "The Spirit of the Lord is upon me. He hath anointed me to preach the Gospel to the poor. He hath sent me to heal the brokenhearted, to preach deliverance to the captives, and to set at liberty them that are bruised."

When our people are renewed and sustained by Isaiah's philosophy that God's Spirit must move us, then we've got a chance to resolve some of our social problems. And when we realize that we honor our fathers by serving our brothers, no matter how tough it is, then we'll be building a better tomorrow. When we recognize that basically it's the individual's relationship to individuals that counts, we'll start making some headway, and when our people appreciate Benjamin Franklin's observation when he said, "If it be true that not a sparrow can fall to the ground without His notice, how can we hope to see a new empire arise without His aid?"

The first United States Congress on Evangelism has come to the right place, at the right time, and for the right purpose. Your aim to summon people to know, to experience and to serve the Gospel is urgently needed. Your aim to summon people to take action is required.

A recent magazine illustrated that fact when it related an anecdote about Harry Cohen, the former head of Columbia Pictures. Cohen once bet an actor a hundred dollars that the actor couldn't recite The Lord's Prayer. The actor accepted the bet and then began, "Now I lay

me down to sleep. . ." Cohen tossed him $100 and growled, "I didn't
think you knew it."

Even more indicative of the spiritual shallowness too often found
in our nation is the common complaint that life is purposeless, meaningless and absurd. We need to introduce to these aimless and faithless
people the reasons for living, and we can do it with a message — with
a message that doesn't sound like the pronouncement of a political
party or the propaganda of a Madison Avenue publicity bureau, but
with a message brought by a humble carpenter's Son to a doubting
and self-satisfied people. The message which brings a changeless Christ
into a changing world.

May I congratulate you on choosing this theme. We live in an
age that worships change, and we often admire it just because it's
new. But you have reminded us of the basic changeless message,
"Love one another, do unto others as you would have them do unto
you, and honor thy father and thy mother that thy days may be long
in the land that the Lord God giveth you." You have re-emphasized
that despite our mechanics and material super-sophistication the
simple message of Christianity still provides the reason for an understanding of life. Nowhere was this more apparent than in our greatest
and most dramatic technological feat, the landing of man on the
moon. Few people know that while Astronaut Buzz Aldrin was preparing to land on the moon, he was also preparing himself. In his
own words he said, "When we knew we were going to be on the moon
for awhile I unstowed these communion elements and put them on a
little table I had in front of the abort guidance system computer. I
requested air to ground silence and then read some passages from the
Bible and then celebrated communion."

When *we* meet the great crises of our lives, or are about to experience an untested situation, do we pause first to read a passage of the
Bible and to take communion? If this Congress on Evangelism can
stimulate others to meet each new challenge by first a communion with
God, it will have fulfilled a mighty purpose.

My best wishes to you as you spread the Great Command and the
good news. "Rise up, O men of God, have done with lesser things,
give heart and soul and mind and strength, to serve the King of
kings. Rise up, O men of God, His kingdom tarries long, bring in the
day of brotherhood, and end the night of wrong."

Mr. Graham: Thank God for public officials that believe and publicly
acknowledge not only their faith in God, but our dependence upon
Him. The next item on the program is introductory remarks by Billy
Graham and I assure you that they will be very brief.

I want to take this opportunity to welcome all of you very in-
formally to the Twin Cities of Minneapolis and St. Paul, and have

you take note that the Twins are on top and are planning to go to the World Series and win it, and everybody from Baltimore said, "Amen."

Many people wonder why my headquarters are in Minneapolis. They ask me because they know that I live in North Carolina and they say, "Why do you keep your headquarters in Minneapolis?" I came here the first time about 23 or 24 years ago, and there was an enterprising young man running for mayor of Minneapolis. I happened to meet him in the swimming pool at the Y.M.C.A. and during our conversation I said, "I notice a word all over town. It says, 'Minne-haha.'" I said, "What does that mean?" And he told me about an old Indian word and then he laughed and he said, "Well, of course, we in Minneapolis think that Minnehaha means 'Minne' for Minneapolis and 'ha-ha' for St. Paul."

And many people think that this Congress is held here because this is our headquarters. That is not true. This Congress did not originate with me or with members of the organization that I'm associated with. A group of men came back from Berlin to Minneapolis. They were pastors and church officials here in Minnesota, and they came back here with a great burden that there might be a Congress in the United States on evangelism, similar to the World Congress held three years ago in Berlin. Dr. Conrad Thompson, Dr. Paul Fryhling, Dr. Victor Nelson, and all of these men came back. They began to meet and they began to pray together and finally they contacted Dr. Oswald Hoffmann and me and they said, "We feel burdened to have a Congress on Evangelism sometime in the next three or four years. If we decide to have it and if we promise to do all the work and all the planning, will you men participate?" I said that I would be delighted to accept an invitation as a speaker, but I soon found they were not too anxious to have me as a speaker. They said, "We want you to be the Honorary Chairman." Well, I've been Honorary Chairman of a number of things and I wasn't sure about my schedule and my plans. I said, "I will help in all I can, and will support it but I'm not sure I ought to do this, because I was Honorary Chairman in Berlin and I think it ought to be somebody else."

Well, they contacted Dr. Oswald Hoffmann in St. Louis and asked him if he would be Chairman and finally he said, "Yes." And then he called me long distance to Europe and he said, "Billy," he said, "I will be the Chairman if you will be the Honorary Chairman." And I said, "Ozzie, I will be the Honorary Chairman if you'll be the Chairman and do the work." And that was the agreement and that's how it came about. I've had absolutely nothing to do with the planning, the program, or any of the things that have gone into this Congress. This has been the work of a dedicated group of people who have worked hard and carried a heavy burden, who don't want the spotlight.

All they want to see are the fires of evangelism spread throughout this nation with a new urgency.

The question has been asked, "Why have a Congress on Evangelism in the United States this year?" I remember Bob Bilheimer, Associate Secretary at that time of the World Council of Churches making a statement in which he said, "If the World Council of Churches should make a definition of evangelism it would split the World Council." He said, "Evangelism is the most important item facing the agenda of the World Council."

We are living in a period of revolution — social revolution, political revolution, technological revolution, a student revolution — and the great question that comes to all of us in this room tonight is this, "How can we make the Gospel relevant in an hour of turmoil, unrest, frustration, and revolution?" Is the Gospel irrelevant? Should it be changed? Should it be adapted to this modern era? These are the questions that I find clergy, and seminary professors, and students are asking everywhere. Has the old Gospel lost its ancient power to transform life and society or is it still relevant, is it still powerful, is it still the power of God unto salvation?

We are witnessing a revolution in morals. Anybody walking down Times Square in New York as I've done recently, or walking down North Beach in San Francisco as I did day before yesterday, or walking through Westwood Village just off the campus of U.C.L.A. as I did two days ago, cannot help but see that morals have changed. Anyone looking at a news stand, or watching television, or seeing the motion picture ads in the newspaper, knows that a tremendous revolution is taking place.

There's a revolution in theology. We've even gone so far as to hear a group say that God is dead, and some clergy today say that they no longer believe in a personal God. We're seeing a revolution in church structures, a revolution in the Roman Catholic world, in the Greek Orthodox world, in the Protestant world, in the Russian Orthodox world. A tremendous change is taking place in church structures, and no one can predict what the next 25 years will hold in church life throughout the world.

There's a revolution in music, in methods. We now have jazz communions, beat music — some of it good — but the question comes to us, "How far should we go? Where do we draw the line? Where do we lose that sense of worship and reverence, in our desire to communicate and to be relevant?"

Social activism is now being called "evangelism." And I'm told in letter after letter that I'm not doing the work of evangelism unless I'm in a picket line, or in a demonstration. Is that evangelism? That's going to be discussed in this Congress.

In a conference on evangelism a few weeks ago, in a great church conference, young people were asked to volunteer to fight wars of liberation in Latin America and this was called the most evangelistic thing you can do. Is that evangelism?

Now there are going to be many things said from this platform this week that you're not going to agree with, and I'm not going to agree with, and that's the way it should be. We ought to have some shocking statements that will wake us up out of our lethargy and our indifference, and make us think and pray and search our souls.

I want to sit here with an open mind and listen to other people's point of view. There are some things that my mind is closed to, and I don't believe anybody can ever change it. The content of the Gospel is unchangeable as far as I am concerned. That was settled a long time ago. There's going to be dialogue and debate and discussion, listening to papers read and sermons preached, and when it's all over, what should we be looking for? I pray to God that we're not looking for another organization, because out of this conference is not going to come another organization, at least not one that's been planned by us here. But let us pray that there will be inspiration and information, but most of all a new dedication in our personal lives.

I believe, ladies and gentlemen, that we need, in the church today a new Puritanism, a new discipline in our personal lives. We need to know what it means to be separated from the world and separated unto God again. The night-club is now in our homes, the burlesque is now in our homes. We've become more and more tolerant to it all. How much has it robbed us of our spiritual power? We have to ask ourselves this week honestly. Our problem today is not so much personnel and money, our problem today is the power of the Holy Spirit. I'm convinced that the evangelist is not a man, the evangelist is the Holy Spirit, using men.

We are praying that this week there will be a step toward renewal. We are praying for a new urgency in evangelizing of our "turned on" and "turned off" generation. We are praying that there will come here this week a new unity among us, a new fellowship among us, and let us say to all the denominations of America that evangelism is urgent, that America has become a vast mission field that needs to be evangelized as much as Asia, or Africa, or Latin America.

The hippies and the students have been preaching to us. They've been crying out for an experience. They say, "We want to 'turn on,' we want to 'tune in,' we want to 'drop out.' " That's Biblical language. They're taking drugs, and sex, and substituting them for the experience that every one of us should have in Christ. They're searching, they're asking us questions. This week it is my prayer that we'll not only raise questions but we'll give answers, authoritative answers, based upon the Word of God.

KEYNOTE ADDRESS: GET WITH THE LORD, AND GO WITH HIM

Dr. Oswald C. J. Hoffmann

I don't know how to begin except by saying you wonderful men, Billy Graham, Governor LeVander, Archbishop Loane, Paul Fryhling, Chaplain Kelly, all you people of the Executive Committee and the National Committee who are here on the platform, all you people who have come here in order to address this meeting, some of whom are also upon the platform, and then probably most of all, all you people who are out there because you've got a heart for the Lord and that's the only thing that could possibly have brought you to this place. You have come for such a time as this.

We have come here from 50 states, 10 foreign countries and from 93 denominations in the United States. It was an inspiring thing to hear you people stand up and sing "The National Anthem" of the United States. I have the feeling on occasion, that is at athletic events and similar occasions, that this sort of thing is done simply "pro forma," but I had another feeling tonight. That was, that you people here in this place meant it, and there was something in the quality of your singing that gave me that impression.

You came for such a time as this, and I couldn't think of any better passage from Holy Scripture to read to you as a motto — not so much as a text but as a motto — for the beginning of this conference than the first verses of the Epistle to the Hebrews. I'm going to read it to you in my own uninspired translation.

"At various times and in various ways, in times past, God spoke to our fathers through the prophets. At the end of these days He spoke to us in His Son whom He made the inheritor of all things, through whom also He made the ages; who being the brightness of His glory and the character of His very substance, upholding all things by the word of His might, and having provided purification for sins, He sat down on the right hand of the Majesty on high."

At various times and in different ways God spoke to our fathers in times past by the prophets but in these, the end of days, He spoke by His Son.

There isn't much time, my friends, and that's why we're here.

This is no time to fool around. The time has come to "get with" the Lord and to go with Him.

There *has* been fooling around.

DR. OSWALD C. J. HOFFMANN, Speaker on The Lutheran Hour, St. Louis, Missouri, and Chairman, National Committee, U.S. Congress on Evangelism.

Our world has been playing around with secularism and the idea that people can "make it" without God, leaving Him entirely out of their calculations — forgetting His power to pass judgment — rejecting His mercy — paying Him lip service but offering Him no real respect from the heart — defaming His Name by word of mouth, by bitterness of action, and hopelessness of attitude.

The Church has been playing around. There has been a good deal of struggle for power in the church, forgetting what the Lord Himself said, "Among the nations, men lord it over one another. It shall not be so among you." When will the church learn?

There will be no politics played here, no one going to try to lord it over you — no organized movement to take over the churches — no partisan spirit — no bitterness — and no pretensions. Just respect for God, gratitude for His mercy made known to the world in Jesus Christ, and determination to do for Christ as He told us to do. "Go," He said, "make disciples of all nations, teaching them to obey everything I have commanded, and trust Me to see things through."

The Church has got sidetracked on all kinds of issues. Some are of major concern to all Christians, and some are minor — the kind that are solved automatically when the Church gets up a head of steam and starts rolling; or to use a more modern figure, when it starts up the engines and goes down the main runway to take off.

We are here starting up engines, to help the church take off — down the main runway.

We are just as concerned about the *major issues* of human life as anyone. When it comes to Christian unity, and the desire to improve human relationships on every level, we take second place to no one.

But we remember that the church will make little or no contribution to our world, if it does not do *its* "*thing*." That thing is to *take* the Good News of Jesus *to heart*, and then *to tell* people, by every means, of Jesus Christ; to bring to people wherever they are, under whatever circumstances, the Good News of Christ, the Savior of all men; and then to lead them by the power of the Spirit of God to the obedience of faith in Christ.

Jesus Christ is the Greatest and the Best. Everything else in the life of the church is second-best. He is the Head of the Body. Without Him the body is a corpse. With Him at the Head, sending impulses throughout the Body, the whole thing comes to life. It revives. It is renewed in strength. The Church lives by the Gospel — the Good News of *Jesus Christ*. Not by the law — no spiritual renewal in the law.

The Gospel is the product. It makes everything else go. Everything else is by-product — often good and valuable, sometimes indispensable, but still by-product.

1. If the Gospel is not at the heart of the Body, which is the Church, the whole thing dies. 2. If the Gospel is proclaimed in anemic fashion, the

whole thing becomes anemic. 3. If the Gospel is demonstrated only vocally and not vitally in the everyday actions of Christ's followers, the whole thing becomes a farce — *and the world knows it.*

It is a remarkable fact that the world often has seen what is wrong with the church before people inside became aware of what was happening. This is a practical world where people are not interested in frittering away time, energy, and resources on stuff that is obviously meaningless, purposeless, fruitless.

This is no time for fooling around. The time has come to get with Christ, and to go with Him.

"*Get with*" Christ. When young people talk about "getting with" something, they mean coming in out of the woods, or out of the rain, or wherever, to the world of reality where real things really are happening, and where other real things can happen.

Get with *Christ*. He is the One. He is the One who can make things happen. When Jesus Christ came, things happened — things that never happened before. That is what the writer of the Epistle to the Hebrews told his people (Hebrews 1:1–3). It is what we have to tell our people today. It is what we have to tell ourselves. Hence this Congress.

God has spoken — in His Son. World, listen! Church, listen! People, listen! This is what we are saying during these days to ourselves, and to everyone associated with us in the Christian enterprise! Listen to the Word of the living God! Listen to Christ!

The time has come to listen. The world is in a mess. High-sounding talk is not the answer to our problems. Fancy programs will not change things. Mere organizing and reorganizing lead down a dead-end street. Nothing else will do but to "get with" Christ, the living Son of the living God, crucified for the sins of our world, and raised from the dead to be the Son of God with power.

With great power gave the apostles witness to the resurrection. His men have always *told* people about Jesus Christ. In the *telling* they changed the world. His men always *followed* Jesus Christ. Following Him they led the world into a new age. "Awake from your sleep-walking," the apostles told their contemporaries, "and arise from the dead! Christ will give you light!"

Our world is on its way to a bad end. We are men, not mere animals, and we have to face the end. Glorious as the achievements of this century have been, they have not changed the basic tendency of our world to go downhill toward an inglorious end. The moon-walk, with all of its superb engineering, has not altered the world's destiny, in spite of all the optimistic statements it called forth at the time. Mankind is still estranged from God, men are still alienated from their fellows, and the world is still in a mess of its own making.

People don't like to hear this kind of talk. I don't like it myself. Most of us would prefer to be optimistic. At least, that direction points to some hope.

We are not saying that there is no hope. What we *are* saying is that the world's only real hope is Christ. This is not some idea of ours, giving us the opportunity to dominate others. We are in the same boat with everyone else.

"They" did it! What has happened to the world is something for which we ourselves must accept responsibility. God so loved the world that He gave His only Son. Either this happened when Christ came, or it did not. If it did — and we are persuaded with the apostles that God's Word is true — we cannot stand around idly as if nothing has happened. "Get with Christ," we say to the whole world and especially now to the United States. Get with Christ in the only way possible — with faith that He is the Son of God and Savior of the world. Get with *Him*!

Christ is with us. Christ is for us. No one ever accused Him of lack of concern for people, of being disinterested in people, of not having a heart for people. He was accused of a lot of things, but not of that!

People accused Him of lack of respect for existing institutions. They charged Him with subverting the people because He ate with the outcasts of society for whom the good church people of the time had no time. They said He misrepresented Himself and blasphemed God when He forgave the sins of people who came to Him for help. Oh, they accused Him of a lot of things, but never — never — of not having a heart for people who need to know God if they are to live.

One of His men said of Jesus that He saw the multitudes, the masses, wandering about as sheep having no shepherd. He could have thrown up His hands and said, as some of His followers unfortunately have done, "Isn't it too bad? All these people going wrong? What can one man do in the face of an impossible situation like that? I can't do anything — and even if I could, is it worth doing?"

Jesus saw the masses wandering about in chaotic search for some direction — any direction — from someone who knew what he was talking about. Seeing the people wander about with no sense of direction, no faith, no hope — Jesus was moved with compassion.

How little compassion there is in the world these days! How little compassion in the church! How little compassion in many families that call themselves Christian! How little compassion in human relationships, even when one or both parties to that relationship profess to be followers of Christ! How little compassion for the little people who have become convinced that they cannot make it on their own, but don't know where to turn.

How ready many Christians are to condemn the unfortunate, the dispossessed, the disenchanted, the retarded, the backward, in our highly complex and competitive civilization, and to offer the easy nostrum, "If only they 'get with' it, their lot will improve."

"Get with" WHAT, my friends? With political programs for the alleviation of poverty, that always seem to start out so glowingly and then peter out so ingloriously in the end? With the myriad organizations and agencies that contend with each other in a great business, expending millions of dollars, some helping people, others benefiting mostly themselves, and practically all of them overlapping one another on a grand scale? With the theological fads, maybe, that seem to come and go as they acquire — and then lose — their newsworthiness in the organs of public opinion? With the church, as it gropes to find its way between what it has been doing, and what it feels in its heart it ought to be doing?

This meeting has not been called to run down the church. Quite the contrary! We have come here to help build up the church, to help it live, and grow, and flourish — to give the church new reason for being, and new confidence in its mission to a stricken world. To the church and its assemblies, the congregations where Christian people come together for worship and work, we are saying, "Get with it."

Get with WHAT? Get with Christ, that's WHAT! Go with Him! This is no time to be fooling around. The time has come to "get with" Christ, and to go with Him. He is the Son of God, and the Savior of the world.

If you have come here with a personal fervor for Christ and a passion to help people, God be praised for His kindness to you in showing you how to go with Christ. If you have come here with a passion for Christ but little compassion for people, I pray that you will find something here — something great — that has heretofore escaped you. If you have come here with a burning feeling for people and little confidence that Christ is the answer to the world's problems — dealing directly with its deepest problem of waywardness and rebellion against God — I trust that here you will make the biggest discovery of your life.

Christ is with you, my friend. In all of His compassion, about which there can be no question on the part of anybody, He is with you. Get with Him, and go with Him.

Christ has died for you. He doesn't have to die again. He won't die again. Christ has risen from the dead. He is Lord. Nobody will ever take that away from Him. To His people, wherever they are, of whatever origin or class or condition, He says, "Go — I have been given all authority in heaven and on earth . . . Go, therefore, and make disciples of all nations . . . Make disciples of your nation."

Wouldn't it be something if we should take Him seriously, take Him at His Word, and go to other nations, all the while forgetting about our own nation? Or pick out some people as the object of our attention, and forget the rest? Or sock it to the old people, and forget about the young, the vital and volatile young people who are really looking for something — something great — that will challenge their enormous energies and give them hope for the future? Or give up on older people, just because they find it harder to accept a new idea than those of younger years, with fresher and more impressionable minds? Wouldn't that be something!

It would be something, I guess, but it wouldn't be much. It is that "not much" with which the church in these United States has been satisfied too long. The time has come to break out of the straitjacket we have drawn around ourselves. The time has come to get with Christ, and to go with Him — by every means that the modern world provides, by every means to save some, who will in their turn "live up" the saving Name of Jesus Christ as a witness for this generation and for other generations yet to be born.

This is a U.S. Congress on *Evangelism*. For some people the word "evangelism" has a bad odor. Some find it distasteful because they resent the very idea of personal commitment which the Good News of Jesus Christ commands, which it demands of a man. People can commit themselves to everyone and everything else, but not to Him!

Still others have a view of the church that makes it seem like a social club, consisting of first-class snobs *who want to make others over in their own image*. If that is evangelism, they tell us, you can have it. It demeans the church, and it degrades the people whom the church is trying to reach.

If we who are here have contributed in any way to false impressions regarding the meaning and purpose of evangelism, we must apologize. If we have given people the idea that our real object is to say to people, "Get with *us*," we here and now beg their pardon. In behalf of the Christian groups to which we belong, we say, "Forgive us. We meant to say something else and, apparently, we didn't say it very well. We have only one thing to say to you: "Get with Christ, and go with *Him*. He is everything to us, and He can be — He will be — everything to you."

We are here not to fumigate the church, but to invigorate it — with new life that the Spirit of God gives the church, in the Good News of Jesus Christ. It is not a sad thing that brings us here. It is a glad thing. Let the people of Minneapolis see the gladness of it on your faces, in your eyes, from your hearts — here at the auditorium, in the afternoon meeting places, at the places where you stay here in the city. Show your gladness in Christ to the people who came here with you, and to those who were here a long time before you came. Get with Christ right here, and go with Him.

Evangelism, as the New Testament describes it, is not child's play. "Do the work of an evangelist," said the apostle Paul to one of his young men. Evangelism is work, often hard work. Yet, it is not drudgery. How could work with and for people, not to speak about work with and for the Lord, ever become sordid and meaningless? Evangelism is instructive and enriching. It helps to develop the mature Christian personality of everyone sincerely engaged in it. If I may say so, it is fun in the best sense of the word. It puts a person in good humor, and makes him truly human.

At this meeting, I ask you to work hard, and to have fun doing it. Punctuality is the virtue of a worker, and doing his work happily is the finest quality he can contribute to it.

Our morning sessions will begin each day with the Word of God from the book God has given us, the Bible. That will be followed by a Word from God shared with us by people who have had rich rewards from following Christ. In the afternoon each day there will be at least thirty-two different meetings, where the Word of God will come from people who share their practical experience, and the various methods they have developed for doing the work of evangelism. In the evening will come refreshment of mind, body, and spirit through a Word from God in the form of music, drama, and other human expressions. There will be give and take throughout.

In all of it, the Word of God will come through. Help to make it so! Finally, on Saturday night, Billy Graham will address a public meeting, to which people will be invited who did not have the opportunity that you have of personal association, personal enrichment, and personal participation throughout this week.

All of us thank the Governor of Minnesota, and the people of this state, for furnishing the initiative that resulted in this congress of people from all over the nation. Thanks to the National Committee which helped to develop the plans for this assemblage, and to the executive committee for doing the enormous work to bring it about. Thanks to The Billy Graham Evangelistic Association for making available the services of Dr. Victor Nelson, the executive director of the U.S. Congress on Evangelism. Marcus Loane, thanks to you for coming to make this meeting what it is, a demonstration of faith, a confession of faith, a commitment to faith — a faith in Jesus Christ crucified, risen from the dead, and coming again. Get with Him — and go with Him.

STUDIES IN THE SCRIPTURES:
MEN ARE IN GRACE OR IN DISGRACE

Archbishop Marcus L. Loane

It is a very great privilege for me to be here this morning and to share in this Congress on Evangelism. I must first of all say how greatly I appreciate the very generous welcome and introduction which Billy Graham has just made on my behalf. I'm sure it would not be out of place for me to say that I would represent literally tens of thousands of our people in Australia who have shared in the crusades in the capital cities since 1958 in bringing greetings to this gathering, and in conveying their deep, prayerful and affectionate greetings to Billy himself. It's a great privilege to be here simply to represent so many who owe so much to the ministry of Billy Graham and his Team over the years in the country to which I belong.

The Bible readings for this morning and tomorrow morning come from the second and third chapters in the Epistle to the Ephesians; and this morning from chapter 2 and verses 1 to 9. In order to save time I will not read the passage but leave you to turn to it in your own Bible. Chapter 2 in the Epistle to the Ephesians.

I'm not going to say very much about the first three verses but merely refer to them by way of introduction to what follows, and my intention is to concentrate on verses 4 to 9. But we cannot look at verses 4 to 9 without taking into account the way in which this chapter begins. It begins with a graphic account of what men are like when they're left to themselves. The apostle says they are dead to spiritual reality as a result of the lethal control of sin. They are governed by the trends of fallen humanity. The pull of that power, which is at work through an invisible system of evil agencies, is always felt in their experience.

And the apostle identifies himself with his readers. What had been true of them had been no less true of himself. They had led the life of men who were ruled by the power of self. Whether or not it drove them to the grosser excess of outward and sensual indulgence, it made little difference, because they all stood exposed to the fact of the wrath of God. That is the message of verses 1 to 3.

Then in verses 4 to 9 he went on to say, "But such was the love and mercy of God" that they had been quickened from death and raised up in newness of life. And in virtue of their union with the ascended Redeemer they were now seated with Him in the heavenly stratosphere. And the divine

THE MOST REV. MARCUS L. LOANE, Archbishop, Sydney, Australia.

purpose in this work of mercy was that in the ages to come they might show forth all the wonder of His grace and loving kindness.

This is all summed up then as an act of God's grace in marked contrast with what they deserved from God's wrath. The grace of God and the wrath of God in this passage are seen as absolute opposites. Men stand either in grace or in disgrace. If they do not share God's favor, they must deserve God's wrath.

That is why the grace of God is both fundamental and preeminent in salvation and redemption. That great basic fact is true of every aspect of the saving work of God in the soul of man. It applies to the very faith by which men are brought into saving contact with Him. That faith, like everything else, is the gift of God. In other words, grace pulls away every stone on which man tries to sit when he thinks that he will boast in the presence of God.

Now let us look at each verse as it comes, beginning with verse 4. It was the guilt and plight of mankind that moved the heart of God and led to the mighty intervention of grace. "God, who is rich in mercy, for His great love wherewith He loved us." St. Paul, having referred to God, postponed the verb in this sentence while he paused to speak with ardent delight of His mercy and love.

One of the most tender combinations of language and ideas in the Psalms is found in the frequent mention of "loving-kindness and tender mercies." St. Paul took this combination and he set out to elaborate it in direct application to God's saving intervention in man's affairs. Jacob had once confessed his unworthiness in language that almost seems to anticipate this fact. He said, "I am not worthy of the least of all the mercies which thou hast showed unto thy servant."

David rejoiced in God as one who is plenteous in mercy. Micah declared that God "delighteth in mercy." And St. Paul caught up the thought of the Psalmist, and of the prophet, and rephrased their concepts in its finest setting as he spoke of God as "*rich* in mercy." And that mercy flows from a love that is so vast and free that it excels all the norms of man's love and transcends the power of words to express, just as we heard sung a little while ago:

"Love divine, all loves excelling; Joy of heaven to earth come down."

"I have loved thee with an everlasting love. Therefore with loving-kindness have I drawn thee," So God spoke to Israel.

St. Paul could only echo that great language in a phrase of superb simplicity. "His *great* love, wherewith He loved us." That was the sole, original motive for all that God has done for man. "For God so loved the world that He gave His only begotten Son."

The love of God reached down to the lowest level of our needs in order to save us through the action of Christ on our behalf. But God, even "when we were dead in sins, [has] quickened us together with Christ." God's great love for us when we were dead in sins led Him to make us alive with Christ. That is the same style of thought and phrase as a statement which the apostle made in the Epistle to the Romans. "God commends His love toward us in that while we were yet sinners, Christ died for us." The phrase here, "even when we were dead in sin," is caught up from verse 1 in this chapter. The only difference is that the pronoun is changed from the second to the first person. It is as though St. Paul resumed a thread of thought which had been laid aside for the moment while his mind raced off in pursuit of a tangent idea.

It is because men are dead in respect of sin that they need a new life. And such is the love and mercy of God that He quickens them in union with Christ, who was Himself quickened while He lay in the tomb.

The word "together" is used three times in this verse and in the next verse, in order to convey in English the effect of the prefix to three compound verbs which express the idea of union with Christ. In this case, the verb was apparently coined by St. Paul and it brings out the main concept with a luminous clarity. Men who were dead are made alive, and they are made alive because they become one with Christ.

Then an interruption occurs while he interpolates a few words in parenthesis "by grace have you been saved." But at this point he did no more than mention this great doctrine. He will expand it a little later in the course of this passage.

The next words elaborate what he meant by being "quickened with Christ." "He has raised us up together, and made us sit together in heavenly places in Christ Jesus." The letter had begun with a declaration in chapter 1, verse 3, that God has blessed us with all spiritual blessings in heavenly places in Christ. And the full meaning of that is now made clear by St. Paul's reference to the benefits of His resurrection and ascension. St. Paul referred to His resurrection and ascension as the special events which proved that one who was dead had been made alive. And he had already developed the thought that the mighty power of God had been seen in the resurrection of Christ from the stronghold of death and His exaltation to the throne of glory. Chapter 1, verses 20 and 21 spell this out.

Now St. Paul pursued the thought further in order to declare that what God had done for Christ He is willing to do for His people, as a result of their union with Christ. They must remain on the earth as long as they are in the body. But God sees them as they now are in Christ and in Him they are raised from the dead, and they are seated at God's right hand where Christ reigns in glorious majesty.

The phrase "in heavenly places" occurs five times in the course of this letter, but the Greek text has an adjective without a noun. The word "places" is not found in the text as St. Paul wrote it or dictated it. It is a special paraphrase. Perhaps it may even obscure the real force of St. Paul's meaning. The phrase may be uncouth and bare, but it shows that the full idea defies definition. St. Paul's magnificent concept was that while men are yet on earth, with Christ they are also in the heavenlies.

Then St. Paul set out God's magnificent design in words that lift our eyes beyond time to eternity: "That in the ages to come He might show the exceeding riches of His grace, in His kindness toward us, through Christ Jesus."

God's plan reaches beyond the great events of Christ's resurrection and exaltation. It reaches beyond the fact of our spiritual union with Him in this mighty experience. It reaches beyond this world to that which is to come. This is partly explained by St. Paul's later declaration in chapter 3, verse 10, that God had done all things "to the intent that now unto the principalities and powers in heavenly places might be known by the church the manifold wisdom of God." That would be the crowning display of His grace in all its exceeding riches.

St. Paul was quite prepared to do what we might not be so willing to do. He was prepared to strain all the powers of human language in order to convey the truth. If it were necessary he would violate the rules of grammar. If it were necessary he would coin a word where no word existed. And he alone, among New Testament writers, for example, made use of the superlative term which we find in this verse. Exceeding, "the *exceeding* riches of His grace." He used it twice in his second letter to the church of Corinth, chapter 3, verse 10; chapter 9, verse 14. He used it no less than three times in the course of this Epistle to the Ephesians, in chapter 1, verse 19; in chapter 3, verse 20, as well as in this verse.

And the "exceeding riches of His grace" have been expressed in His kindness toward us "in Christ Jesus." The same idea appears in a phrase in the Epistle to Titus which makes it clear that kindness means love in action. Titus, chapter 3, verse 4, "But after that the kindness and love of God our Saviour toward man appeared." The full impact of the whole verse is felt at once by a contrast with the tenor of the first part of this passage. In chapter 1, verse 19, we are told that the resurrection and exaltation of Christ were the supreme demonstration of the "exceeding greatness of His power." And now the union of His people with Him in this mighty experience is the supreme demonstration of the exceeding riches of His grace. The greatness of His power, the riches of His grace — they exceed the power of words to express.

Then we come to one of the most famous verses in the whole of Scripture, verse 8. And it is clear that St. Paul took up the word "grace" which he had just used, as well as the phrase which he had used in parenthesis a moment or two before, as his argument continued to unfold. "For by grace have you been saved through faith." The word "for" makes it clear that this verse is firmly linked with all that had gone before, and the definite article before the word "grace" helps to show that it referred to the grace which he had already foreshadowed. "But God who is rich in mercy," chapter 2, verse 4, is no less rich in grace (chapter 2, verse 7).

And what is grace? Grace is the free and boundless favor of God. Grace is the opposite of merit and the complement of need. And such grace is the ground of all God's actions for us men and for our salvation. Grace flows from the mercy of God and not from our human merit. Grace is like a king's largesse for the needy. Grace is like a royal reprieve for the guilty. Grace came where sin had come. It reached out its hand to man where he had fallen and it did this so that he might be saved. "By grace have you been saved."

We are told that we ought to find another word today to bring our language into more contemporary usage. But there are some words which must be spelled out in the same terms to every generation, because they are of such an intrinsic part of the message of the Gospel. And this word is one. Salvation is a word which implies the dual thought of danger and of rescue. Men are in danger of death and hell. They stand in need of the rescue of grace and God. No doubt the word was used in this context with the widest possible meaning. It was meant to cover the whole process of man's rescue from the results of sin, in all forms and aspects of sin.

The verb in its perfect tense was meant to express something present as a result of past action — something which is both an accomplished reality and a continuing process. It is by grace that men have been saved and are being saved. And the means by which this rescue is brought about is faith.

The next words in this verse are meant to define with a decisive clarity what is unique in this experience. By grace have you been saved "through faith; and that not of yourselves: it is the gift of God." There can be no doubt as to the primary emphasis of this statement, but a minor problem is posed by one detail. The key word "that" is a demonstrative pronoun in the neuter gender. To what does it refer? It may refer to the whole idea of a free salvation, set out in the verse as a whole. You have been saved as an act of grace and by means of faith, and that salvation is not of yourselves. It is the gift of God. That view derives support from the fact that the phrase "not of yourselves" is a parallel utterance with the phrase "not of works" in the next verse. And that verse must be read as an ultimate reference to the whole concept of a free salvation.

But the alternative of this is that it refers to the word "faith," and the clause as a whole is a fresh parenthesis. You have been saved by grace alone, in Christ alone, through faith alone, and that very faith is not of yourselves. It is the gift of God. The word "faith" is feminine in contrast with the neuter gender of the pronoun. But St. Paul used a similar construction elsewhere when he wanted to bring in a new thought which was meant to heighten all that had gone before. If the pronoun refers only to the special concept set out in the last words, it adds no fresh significance to the initial reference to grace. But if it is meant to take up the phrase "through faith," then it marks a distinct advance with the statement that faith itself must be seen as the gift of God. Salvation as a whole is an act of grace, and the very faith which makes it ours is a gift from God.

That allows us to read the verse as a whole with a richer insight into

God's great design for man in Christ. By grace have you been saved through faith and that faith not of yourselves. It is the gift of God. And this is important because faith is the one link in the chain which men have thought that they could forge for themselves. But St. Paul's words were meant to show that they can do nothing at all to win salvation as a recompense for virtue or merit. We may chase back the work of God in our lives as far as we can go in conscious recollections. We may suppose that the goal began with a moment of faith or trust or personal surrender or decisive commitment, but we need to inquire what lay behind that first conscious response.

Faith cannot be generated by an act of self-volition. A man cannot create true faith at will. Such faith does not depend on human understanding. It cannot be derived from mental effort. We cannot force ourselves to have faith in God. We're as much in need in this respect as in everything else. Faith can only originate in the soul of man by the gift of God. And St. Paul stated that in terms of singular interest in a practical connection. "Unto you it is given in the behalf of Christ . . . to believe on Him."

I must hurry to the end. The last phrase caught up the main theme in a final emphatic utterance. "Not of works, lest any man should boast." The last stronghold that man as a rule is willing to let go is the proud sense of independence which makes him suppose that he can make himself worthy. If that were true, even in the smallest degree, he would have grounds for self-glory and he would be free to boast. But St. Paul knew better. His own experience taught him that to boast was impossible.

The voice of the veteran Puritan, Stephen Charnock, may well be heard again: "What are a few tears but a drop to our sea of guilt? What are our petitions but as the breath of a child to the storms of our provocations? Our righteousness but as a mite to the many talents of our unrighteousness? Sinful duties cannot make an infinite and holy satisfaction."

Augustus M. Toplady proclaimed the same truth in words that are now part of our common Christian heritage. "Could my tears forever flow, could my zeal no languor know, these for sin could not atone; Thou must save, and Thou alone."

St. Paul wrote those words with calm and sober realism. He told his readers that by the grace of God and through the gift of faith, they have been saved indeed. And that has been true for men in all ages, once they have seen that the vast gulf between God and man can be bridged by Christ alone.

Such a discovery was made by John Charles Ryle when he sauntered into church one Sunday morning while the service was in progress. He felt depressed. He was so far oblivious of the world at large that he could never recall what church in Oxford it was. The prayers were read by a stranger. He forgot the text of the sermon. But he had come in and sat down just in time to hear the second lesson, and that was the second chapter of the Epistle to the Ephesians. It was read with uncommon earnestness. Two verses in particular were read with an impressive emphasis which he could not ignore. There was a pause between each phrase as though to let each new idea sink into his mind: "For by grace are ye saved through faith; and that not of yourselves: it is the gift of God: not of works, lest any man should boast."

Ryle must have heard those words often enough before, but their point had been dulled by the confused murmur of the world around. That morning in the silence of each fresh pause, the still small voice of God was heard. That voice spoke to his heart in such a way that it worked the power of faith with an immediate response to the grace and mercy of God. It was the simple hearing of those words of Scripture that led him to grasp the reality of salvation by grace alone, in Christ alone, through faith alone.

STUDIES IN THE SCRIPTURES:
BE STRENGTHENED BY HIS SPIRIT

Archbishop Marcus L. Loane

This morning we turn to the third chapter in the Epistle to the Ephesians, and I am particularly concerned with the closing paragraph from verse 14 to verse 21. However, in order to approach this paragraph in the context in which it occurs, it requires first of all a rapid survey of the chapter as a whole.

Verse 1 says, "For this cause I Paul, the prisoner of Jesus Christ for you Gentiles,". . . The cause which he had in mind as the chapter began refers back to verses 19 to 22 in chapter 2. This was the sovereign indwelling of God in His people. Now in chapter 3 he meant to say that this thought applies in a particular way to every Gentile convert. He would show them that the habitation of God in the church was equivalent to the habitation of Christ in their own hearts. So he began, "For this cause I Paul, the prisoner of Jesus Christ for you Gentiles."

But he got no further than this, just at this stage. The very mention of the Gentiles broke up his train of thought. His mind raced away at a tangent from the main theme and it was not until he reached the end of that passage that it became clear how he had intended to complete the first sentence. It is an interesting fact in the study of the Pauline letters to recognize that his mind was so agile that it often shot beyond his syntax. His mental process is sometimes clearer than his grammar. Many of his asides slipped into a sentence, then the sentence moved into a whole passage, and the passage itself owed its significance to some vital idea which all the time was subordinate to the primary argument.

So it was in this case. The word "Gentiles" sparked off this passage, a passage that dealt with the mystery, the great open secret of God, which was nothing less than the incorporation of the Gentile converts in the body of Christ.

Then in verses 7 to 12 he spoke more particularly about his own ministry. He, Saul of Tarsus, a man whose hands were once red with the blood of those whom he had persecuted, he, less than the least of all saints, had been chosen to proclaim among the Gentiles all the unsearchable riches of Christ so that angel beings would be led to marvel at the endless variety of the divine wisdom. And that takes up verses 7 to 12.

I sometimes wonder whether, as Gentiles, we are in a position adequately to appreciate what this meant for the apostle Paul. We are so accustomed to read the New Testament in our own English translations that the thought has grown familiar to us. We tend to lose the sense of wonder, and

THE MOST REV. MARCUS L. LOANE, Archbishop, Sydney, Australia.

surprise, and astonishment which this declaration of the grace of God for the
Gentile, on equal terms with the Jew, meant in that first Christian century.
In verse 8 of this chapter for example, we are caught up with the wonderful
phraseology at the beginning and end of the verse, "Unto me, who am less
than the least of all saints . . . the unsearchable riches of Christ."

But the truth is that in the eyes of the man who spoke these words, the
most remarkable thing in this verse was the reference to preaching the Gospel
among the Gentiles. I think that perhaps we can take this in better if we refer
for a moment to Acts, chapter 22, when he stood at the head of the staircase
of the Fortress of Antonia at the edge of the temple courtyard in Jerusalem,
and with the permission of the chief captain addressed the Jewish mob which
had been trying to rend him limb from limb. They listened to him in a
remarkable way even through the description of his own life until he came
to the point in verse 21 when he said, "The Lord said unto me, Depart: for
I will send thee far hence unto the Gentiles."

That was the end. They gave him audience unto this word, then lifted
up their voices and said, "Away with such a fellow from the earth: it is not fit
that he should live." They cried out and cast off their clothes and threw them
in the air. That was the reaction of the Jews to the idea of the proclamation
of the Gospel to the Gentile on equal terms as to the Jew.

And that is the thought that underlies the whole of the passage in the
third chapter of the Epistle to the Ephesians. But he goes on, in verse 13, to
say that he was content if he had to suffer in such a cause; and to suffer on
their behalf was in fact the glory of the Gentile converts. And then, but only
then, he resumed the thread of thought which had been laid aside with the first
verse. He brought the same clause into action in order to convey the fact that
he had returned to his initial purpose.

And so, in verse 14, he recovered himself as it were and went back to the
starting point, "For this cause. . ." Or perhaps we can best read it if we carry
over the words of verse 1 in full to verse 14 and read it like this: "For this
cause, I Paul, the prisoner of Jesus Christ for you Gentiles, bow my
knees unto the Father of whom every family in heaven and on earth is
named. . . ."

St. Paul never rises to a higher level in his letters than in the prayers
which they record. And none of his prayers is so rich or full as the soaring
intercession in this passage. All the circumstances surrounding it make it the
more remarkable. He was in prison quarters. He was handcuffed to a Roman
soldier. He was in bonds.

What was it like to bow his knees to the Father in those circumstances?
Did the pagan guard look on in scorn? Or did he listen in quiet wonder?
Perhaps someone like Tychicus or Epaphras may have come as a scribe. Did
the scribe, as well as the soldier, kneel at his side on the flagstone? Of course
we do not know, but he bowed his soul as well as his knees in the presence

of God as his Father. There was reverence here. The reverence that becomes a man who stands in the presence of his Maker.

But there was something more than this. There was confidence as well. The confidence that becomes a son who finds himself in the presence of a loved and loving Father.

It is impossible to preserve in English the close verbal kinship of the Greek text between the words that are translated as "father" and "family." A literal translation seems to imply that all fatherhood must be seen as derived from the Fatherhood of God. Perhaps a clue to the meaning is found in the earlier reference in chapter 1, verse 10, where he spoke of the spiritual oneness in Christ of the universal community, both in heaven and on earth. God is the true original Father who has given His name to the whole glorious company both in heaven and earth. And true family unity of both saints and angels is found in Him alone.

For as St. Paul says in chapter 4, verse 6, there is *"one* God and Father of all, who is above all, and through all, and in you all."

The first words of address were then followed by a series of three major requests. This is clearer in the Greek text than it is in the English, because each request is ushered in by a term that indicates a clear sense of purpose. Here is the first: "That He would grant you, according to the riches of His glory, to be strengthened with might by His Spirit in the inner man."

St. Paul's language shows that what he meant to ask for could be granted only as a free gift. But he asked that the gift should be both in the style and on the scale of God's unsearchable riches. He looked beyond their need to God's great and endless glory, and he asked that they might be strengthened with might.

This is like double-banking, words and ideas — twin ideas. Spiritual firmness and spiritual vigor. It was brought out by H. C. G. Moule in a delightful paraphrase, that He would grant you to be with power, made mighty. They would need that strength so as not to fear those things from which nature might make them shrink.

The one great agent in this process was the Spirit of God because He alone can penetrate the innermost depths of a man's moral being. His work, in other words, was to make them strong with a strength divine and the whole context points to the internal character of that strength.

St. Paul spoke of the "inner man" — deep down in the region of the innermost being, the region of the regenerate human spirit where new life is born, where it grows, where it comes to maturity. So God's Holy Spirit must strengthen man's regenerate spirit as an act of divine favor. And that was the burden of St. Paul's prayer, that He would grant you "to be with power made mighty by means of His Spirit in the inmost region of your being."

Then his next words explain why those Gentile converts stood in need of such an experience, and it was just the opposite of what we might have imagined such a reason would be. Why were they to be "with power made mighty"? Why were they to be strengthend with might by His Spirit? Was it so that they might shake the world? It was not. It was "so that Christ may dwell in your hearts by faith." That suggests that He was to make His abode within — not in just some passing experience, but in a sense that would be permanent and enduring.

And what St. Paul would have us to understand is this: it is indeed the work of the Spirit of God to make the Lord's presence within a deep reality. And what is more, His strength is needed in order to prepare the heart for the incoming and indwelling of Christ. It is hardly practicable to draw a firm line of demarcation between the work of the Spirit and the presence of Christ in this respect. One melts into the other, just as in the sequence of thought on another occasion, in Romans 8, verses 9 and 10: ". . . if so be that the Spirit of God dwell in you . . . if Christ be in you." The phrases are used virtually as though they were interchangeable, and it becomes impossible for us to say where one thought ends and the other begins. The Lord's presence within is a presence by means of the Holy Spirit, and this takes place, this is realized, by means of faith. Then why should men need such a strength in order to receive so great a guest? Is not this what we want beyond everything else? Shall we not welcome it more than words can say? There is no doubt that we need Him to dwell within, and that no words are adequate to express that need. At the same time, we have to recognize, as St. Paul so clearly perceived, that because of human weakness and sin we are prone to shut the doors of that inmost sanctuary.

Men sometimes do not dare to ask the Lord to come and dwell within as a matter of right. They know that they have in themselves something which seems to dread the thought of His absolute indwelling. Do we feel that we can trust Him with such sovereign possession? Do we ask ourselves how He will use His authority, if He is in supreme control? So we let Him into the porch, into the hall, into this room, that room, but our hand may be on the latch of the last door. And we need to be strengthened with might by His Spirit, so that we may open the door and so that He may come in.

The next clause which indicates purpose is difficult in construction, but the context makes it clear that the words at the end of one verse belong to the verse that follows. The verse reads like this, ". . . that you, being rooted and grounded in love, may be able to comprehend with all saints what is the breadth, and length, and depth, and height." The words "in love" are emphatic by position, and they are followed by two participles which combine the imagery of botany and architecture. One suggests the life that is derived, and the other refers to a building which is founded. Plants are rooted and buildings are founded. The same combination comes out in the Epistle to the Corinthians, "You are God's husbandry; you are God's building."

The roots are to go down, or the base is to be laid, in love, because St. Paul knew the danger of a faith which has no basis in love. So his prayer was followed by this sublime request — that they might be able to comprehend, that they might get strength to understand, the love of Christ.

And that points to a further landmark in their spiritual experience — something that calls for a mighty stretch of thought and faith. It was not an isolated experience. It was something that each was to share with all the saints, and the object of the comprehension was set out as the length, and breadth, and depth, and height. That four-dimensional imagery was perhaps meant to point to the visible universe in which the eye may rove east and west and up and down. Not that St. Paul meant each point of the compass to have its own special meaning. His one idea was that men should grasp the infinitude of that of which he spoke. And what was that? He did not say in this verse. The sentence was broken, but the context shows that it was the love of Christ. And so St. Paul began again in the next verse, "And to know the love of Christ, which passeth knowledge." Those words depend on the same verb which had governed the last unfinished utterance, and the sentence is so much clearer if that is kept in mind. "That you may be able to know the love of Christ, which passeth knowledge."

His prayer was that, resting on and rooted in that great love wherewith He loved us, they might go on to know more of the love of Christ.

St. Paul had once tried to declare what that love meant to him. "The Son of God loved *me* and gave Himself for *me*." He could only refer to it with a sense of wonder and awe, and it was that sense of wonder which led him to describe it in terms of majestic paradox. He longed that they should know the love of Christ, even though it will always transcend the very knowledge which it invites — a love which passes knowledge. The only comparable phrase is the comment on the peace of God which passes all understanding. The love of God is like the peace of Christ — it will always exceed our knowledge and experience, but will reveal itself in ways too deep for the mind of man to fathom.

"Amazing love, how can it be, that Thou, my God, shouldst die for me?"

The third purpose clause is the briefest of all, but it marks the climax of these petitions "that you might be filled with all the fullness of God."

The basic idea is that of a vessel which is linked with a source of boundless supply and which ought to be filled to its utmost capacity.

There was no real limit to this process other than the fullness of God Himself. The word "fullness" occurs four times in this letter and twice in the Epistle to the Colossians. The fullness of God has only one equivalent and that is found in the Epistle to the Colossians, chapter 2, verse 9. It refers to the totality of the divine riches, the perfection of character in the Godhead. It is not that finite human vessels can in themselves ever hope to hold the infinitude of God's gifts and graces. It is not that any single gift or any combination of such gifts will ever suffice. But all that St. Paul could ask for his Gentile converts in the way of strength, or faith, or love, is absorbed in the mighty concept of the wholeness of God.

St. Paul had stretched the powers of thought, and speech, and prayer to their limit, but he went even further in the words of the doxology that conclude the passage: "Now unto Him that is able to do exceeding abundantly above all that we ask or think, according to the power that worketh in us."

Those are words of triumphant ascription, "to Him that is able," because faith can rest on the ability of the omnipotent one to come to the aid of those who have no might. The three men who faced the burning, fiery furnace spoke for all the servants of God in their steadfast reply, "Our God whom we serve is able," and that truth stands in total contrast with the fact that man in himself is helpless. It refers to something that is infinitely beyond our own capacity. St. Paul tried to express it by his use of this compound superlative, "He is able to do exceeding abundantly."

God is not only unlimited in His resources, He is unrestricted by our horizons. He was able to do all that St. Paul had asked and do it on a scale of an exceeding abundant display of love. And then there was still an immensity of grace in reserve, and St. Paul could only express what was in his mind by saying that He could do "above all that we ask or think." He knew that he was carried beyond his depth, but he believed that God could do more than he even knew how to ask. St. Paul loved those great sweeping statements, but he qualified this one by saying that it was "according to the power that worketh in us": that is, the might that wrought in Christ when He rose from the dead, the power with which we are to be made mighty by means of His Spirit.

The great cumulative effect of so many superb ideas couched in superlative language comes to an end with the final words, "Unto Him be glory in the church in Christ Jesus throughout all ages, world without end. Amen."

He may have bowed his knees on the prison flagstones, but his spirit had scaled the heights to catch a vision of things beyond human sight. He had asked that Christ might dwell in their hearts by faith, that they might know the love of Christ, though it passes knowledge, and that they might be filled with the very fullness of God.

Would those Gentile converts in the Roman province of Asia feel that this was so far beyond their faith or hope that it could be nothing more than an idle dream? They might feel like that, until they heard the words of the doxology, and those words would tell them that all their dreams would fall short of what He is able to do. All that words could express would still fall far below the vast reality of God's boundless grace and favor. There is nothing too hard for Him to do, even though things might seem so far beyond our reach that we hardly dare to let our thoughts dwell on them.

He is able to do above all that we ask or think. It goes beyond articulate prayer or understanding. To pass from such words of Scripture to the daily experience of all the saints is like falling from the skies of glory. Yet, it is part of the object of grace that the men in whose lives the work of grace is done shall, in ages to come, show forth how great is His glory. And that will be seen both in the church as His body and in Christ as its head. Therefore, St. Paul shuts up prayer and doxology alike with the golden clasp of this loud, final "Amen." Even so, let it be.

STUDIES IN THE SCRIPTURES:
THE POWER OF PRAYER

Dr. Harold Lindsell

We have come to this Conference because of our interest in and concern about evangelism, and up to this point I haven't heard any definition of evangelism. I suppose we could use any one of the classic definitions but insofar as I am concerned, in my simple way, I like to think that it is the presentation of Jesus Christ to men as the Savior of the world. In doing the work of evangelism, you and I have some things that we need to do besides just witnessing and communicating the Gospel of Jesus Christ. We need to be in prayer. We need to have the fullness of the Holy Spirit. We need to live a life of love. Now you have heard the themes prayer, and the power of the Spirit, and the idea of love spoken about again and again. For the three mornings which we have together, I would like to concentrate on those three themes — the power of prayer, the power of the Spirit and the power of love.

This morning I will be speaking then on the subject of "The Power of Prayer." I am thinking in terms of power because we are power-conscious in our day. There is white power, there is the establishment power, there is black power, there is economic power, there is political power, there is the power of the hydrogen bomb, but when I read the Scriptures I discover that the Scriptures do not concentrate on these kinds of power, but speak about other kinds of power. For example in 2 Corinthians 10:4 the Scripture says, "The weapons of our warfare are not carnal, but mighty through God to the pulling down of strongholds."

When I think about the power of prayer, there come to mind immediately many Scriptures. James says, "Ye have not because ye ask not." Paul says, "Pray without ceasing." To Timothy he says, "I will therefore that men everywhere pray, lifting up holy hands without wrath and doubting." In Philippians he says, "Be careful for nothing but in everything by prayer and supplication, with thanksgiving, let your requests be made known unto God." In Matthew's Gospel, "All things whatsoever ye ask in prayer, believing, ye shall receive." Indeed, the Scripture says, "Man ought always to pray and not to faint." In 1 John, "And this is the confidence that we have in him; that if we ask anything according to his will he heareth us, and if we know that he hear us, we know that we have the petitions that we desired of him." Jesus said, "Ask, and it shall be given you. Seek, and ye shall find.

DR. HAROLD LINDSELL, Editor of *Christianity Today*, Washington, D.C.

Knock and it shall be opened." "Everyone that asketh receiveth, and
he that seeketh findeth, and to him that knocketh it shall be opened."

But perhaps the greatest words that come to me from all the
Scripture with respect to prayer are the words, "Ye have not because ye ask not." Now I know there are many people listening this
morning who wish they could be great evangelists like Billy Graham.
I know that there are some of you, and I may be numbered among you,
who wish they had a radio broadcast that went around the world like
the broadcast of Oswald Hoffmann. I can't be Billy Graham and neither
can you. I can't be Oswald Hoffmann and neither can you, but I say
to you there is a greatness that can come to all of us, but it is a greatness
that comes to us through prayer, for the Scripture indicates that
prayer is available to the least of God's saints. It makes no difference
whether you are young or old, or whether your position is one of
great heights, or one of great depths. It makes no difference whether
you are male or female, whether you are rich or poor. The greatest
power in the world that comes to the Christian is the power of prayer,
and it is available to all of us. There are two limitations, of course, which
the Scriptures place on prayer. The first: we know that it belongs peculiarly to the people of God. Sometimes I hear people say to a person
who is not a Christian, "Why don't you pray that God will save you?"
I never say that to an unconverted person, because the unconverted
person can pray all the days of his life but he will never get saved. The
Scripture makes it plain he's not to pray; he's to open his heart and
receive Jesus Christ, and then when he has done that, he can begin
to pray as a child of God.

The second reservation on prayer is the fact that it can only be
used for good and not for evil. You see you can use atomic energy
for the good of man or for the evil of man. You can use politics for
good or for evil. You can use all of the other powers of life for good
or for evil, but prayer is the only power, and the greatest power, that
can be used only for good. And with these reservations the Scripture
tells us that we ought to use this power which belongs peculiarly to the
people of God.

Now my purpose this morning is to extract from the Scripture
specific incidents which illustrate the power of prayer to the end that
you and I may not only understand the greatness of prayer, but also
that we may then reach out and lay hold of prayer and use it as God
intended that it ought to be used. What is amazing to me is that the
Scriptures are literally filled with a great variety of answers to prayer
which illustrates this fact: there is nothing having to do with my life
about which God is unconcerned. He is interested in the smallest detail.

I remember when I first went to college in the days of the depression. I had a fountain pen and I didn't have any money. I lost my foun-

tain pen on an airfield and I didn't know where it was. In the simplicity of my youth, because I was not nearly so sophisticated in those days, and because I had no money and could not replace the fountain pen, I prayed and I asked God to show me where the fountain pen was. I walked in a straight line across that airfield and in a pool of oil I found my fountain pen. Now you may say, "Well, what's a fountain pen?" The answer is it was of significance to a poor college student in the days of the depression, and God is interested in the least of the details concerning my life as well as the greatest. There is nothing beyond the confines of His love for me, and so I can pray about anything and everything. Indeed, the Scripture says, "In everything we ought to pray."

Now in 1 Samuel, chapter 1, you will find the incident of a woman whose husband had a second wife. Her name was Hannah. In her particular family situation the other wife had children, and the Scripture says Hannah's womb was closed. Now to understand it within the perspective of the ancient world, we must recognize that children were regarded as the gift of God, and if a woman did not bear children it was looked upon as a reproach, as though the blessing of God was missing from her life.

The Scripture says that this woman was agitated so that she was a weeping woman who lost her appetite, and her heart was sad. One day, we are told, she went up to the temple of God and she spoke to God, and in verse 10 of chapter 1, "she was in bitterness of soul, and prayed unto the Lord, and wept sore. And she took a vow, and as she vowed she prayed, "O Lord of hosts, if thou wilt indeed look on the affliction of thine handmaid, and remember me. . . and give me a . . . child" — I didn't read the reservation; she was a little more specific than I was because we have four children. My first one was a girl, my second one was a girl, my third one was a girl — and Hannah prayed and she said, "Lord, give me a boy." And Eli, thinking she was drunk, rebuked her. And yet Eli, speaking as the prophet of God, said "Go in peace and the God of Israel give you your petition."

And then the Scripture says, "It came to pass, when the time was come about after Hannah had conceived, that she bare a son, and called his name Samuel . . . because I have asked him of the Lord." Here was an answer to a woman's prayer. Here was God at work in response to the petition of His child.

Go over to 2 Kings, chapter 19, and you will recall that Sennacherib, king of Assyria, was one of the great monarchs of his day. He had sent a message to King Hezekiah. The substance of that message was very simple. He said, "I'm bigger than you are. I have an army that is greater than your army. Expect me to visit you and I am going to wipe you off the map." And when Hezekiah got the message, and he got it, he did not send to the Chief of Defense and ask, "How many bombs do we have, how many soldiers, how many intercontinental ballistic missiles?" The Scripture says he took the message from the hands of the messengers, he went up to the house of the Lord, and he spread it before God and began to pray. I suggest sometime that you read that prayer which was spoken by this man Hezekiah, but I say to you that at the end of his prayer, without any reservations whatever, without any knowledge of how to handle the situation, with a sense of abject poverty even though he was the King, in verse 19 of chapter 19, he says, "O Lord our God, I beseech thee, save thou us out of his hand, that all the kingdoms of the earth may know that thou art the Lord God, even thou only."

You know God sent the prophet and the prophet spoke a word for God, and the prophet said, "God has heard your prayer, and the power of God, because of your prayer, shall be released."

Now we cannot tell God *when* to answer prayer nor can we tell God *how* to answer prayer, but in the providence of God in verse 35 the Scripture says, "And it came to pass that night," — that very night that he had prayed — ". . . that the angel of the Lord went out, and smote in the camp of the Assyrians a hundred fourscore and five thousand: and when they arose early in the morning, behold, they were all dead corpses."

Here was God in response to prayer manifesting His great infinite power.

Go over to 2 Chronicles, chapter 20, and here was Jehoshaphat. He was faced with a military alliance, and there were the people of Moab and Ammon and Mount Seir. They had formed a military alliance against the people of God, and Jehoshaphat knew that his situation was desperate, and he had no resources on which to call, save the resources of God. He was a believer. The Scripture says that he was afraid of his existential plight, and in the midst of his circumstances he called or set himself to seek the Lord. He proclaimed a fast throughout all Judah, and all Judah gathered themselves together to ask the help of the Lord. The Scripture says, "one shall chase ten, and two shall chase a thousand." Then they began to pray.

Again at your convenience I recommend that you read the prayer of this King, Jehoshaphat, but I remind you that when he came to the close of his prayer, this is the word that he, the King of Judah, spoke. In verse 12 he says, ". . . we have no might against this great [enemy] that cometh against us; neither know we what to do: but our eyes are upon thee." And God sent His prophet, and then they went out to battle. They did, if you please, what was done during the Thirty Years' War when Gustavus Adolphus went out to fight and his army got on their knees and before they fought they sang, "A Mighty Fortress Is Our God, A Bulwark Never Failing."

The people of Judah went out to fight, and they went out singing the praises of God, for God had told them this one thing, "You shall not fight this battle; it shall be fought by God alone so that when the deliverance comes, no king and no man shall rise to say, 'We won the battle by our own strength.' " All glory remaineth unto Him who is the greatest power on the earth.

You know what happened. The enemy got to fighting among themselves, and they killed off each other. The people of Judah stood still and they saw the salvation of God. When the battle was ended it took them three days to collect the booty, the spoil, from the war which they never fought, and they called that place the valley of Berachah, for this was the place where God blessed them.

In this Congress so far we've talked a great deal about race, and I think that if we did more praying and less talking we might get some place faster. But, beloved, I am concerned about Vietnam, too. I am concerned about our being involved in an imbroglio from which we do not seem to escape. I wonder if perhaps the time has not come when our President, like Jehoshaphat, should call upon God and ask this nation to begin praying.

Some years ago the Congress of the United States voted a piece of legislation that the President of this country is to call for a day of prayer every year, and it's due sometime this fall. I hope that Mr. Nixon will make it known far and wide and have every church open on that day, and he himself go to church, and he himself offer this prayer, "O God, we know not what to do, but our eyes are upon Thee." We've tried arms, we've tried diplomacy, we've tried psychology — we have no solution. But God is bigger than all of our aims and our designs, and I say to you that we need God in this hour to deliver us.

Now let me turn from kings and powers and principalities — let's go over to the book of James. In this last chapter of the book of James the Scripture speaks about a man whose name was Elijah, and the word in verse 17 is this, ". . . he prayed earnestly." He prayed with agony. If you go into the Scripture in the Old Testament in 1 Kings, chapter 17, it doesn't tell you how it happened, but the apostle James gives us insight and light which the Old Testament Scripture doesn't give us. The Scripture tells us, ". . . he prayed earnestly that it might not rain; and it rained not on the earth by the space of three years and six months. And he prayed again, and the heaven gave rain, and the earth brought forth her fruit."

And, oh, listen, beloved, in the Scripture it tells us he took his mantle and he placed it over his head and he bowed his knees before Jehovah, his God, and he sent his servant out to look at the clouds in the sky. He sent him seven times, and on the seventh time the servant came back and he said, "I see a cloud in the sky the size of a man's hand," and that was enough for Elijah. He said, "Take the message to the King and tell him to get in his chariot and go lest he be stopped by the rain, for I hear the sound of the abundance of rain." And the Scripture says that the rains came because this man prayed.

You know there was a little girl in the New Testament. We don't know exactly how old she was. Her name was Mary, and God sent a messenger and God gave her a message. She offered a prayer, and the message that the angel brought to this little girl Mary, for she was a teen-ager, the message that the angel brought was this — "God is going to do a new thing, God is going to become manifested in the flesh. He shall become incarnate — the God of heaven is going to invade earth in the person of a man. You are my chosen vessel." This little maiden, Mary, replied and she said by way of prayer, "Be it unto me according to Thy Word." She became the human instrument in whose womb there was conceived by the power of the Holy Spirit, JESUS, the Son of the living God. What a prayer to pray!

Let me suggest one other incident. In Luke, chapter 24, when Jesus is ready to go away — He has tarried for forty days and He is speaking His last words to His disciples — He says, "I send the promise of My Father upon you: but tarry ye in the city of Jerusalem, until ye be endued with power from on high." And they tarried for ten days, and the Scripture in Acts 1, verse 14 says they "continued with one accord." Their hearts were knit together in the unity of the faith. They were not divided; their hearts were one, and they "continued with one accord in prayer and supplication."

The Scripture says in Acts 21, "When the day of Pentecost was fully come, they were all with one accord in one place," and the Spirit fell, the baptism came, the power was released. The greatest and the mightiest prayer meeting ever described in the Word of God is this ten-day prayer meeting which preceded Pentecost. So great were its effects that a man like Peter, who had denied the Lord Jesus Christ, who had refused to be identified with Him in His death, this man Peter could get the unction and go out and preach and 3,000 men could come to know Jesus Christ in his first sermon. And I can't even get 3,000 people to listen to me! This is the power.

You and I are called upon to communicate the Gospel, to evangelize the world, and all of the power that we need for this can be found in prayer, and in the Spirit, and in love. These are the instruments which are ours, for the weapons of our warfare are not carnal. If you look to education, you get what education can do. If you look to eloquence, you get what eloquence can do. If you look to organization, you get what organization can do. If you look to armies, you get what armies can do. If you look to diplomacy, you get what diplomacy can do. But if you look to prayer, you get what God can do.

Let me close with an illustration. A friend of mine is a missionary in Latin America. He has a brother who is a missionary to the Indians in Canada. His brother had labored for many years with no fruit. One day, receiving a letter from his brother, my friend communicated to the saints down where he was, to the nationals of his particular situation, and the response of the nationals was this, "We will pray for him." And they did, and when they prayed, everybody prayed at once. Everybody prayed out loud, and they kept praying. They told the missionary, "God has heard and God will answer." God broke up the situation in northern Canada and souls were converted. The Gospel prospered because these small, unknown, uneducated, unsophisticated believers in Jesus believed in the power of prayer, and you and I have got to get it.

I am going to suggest that we do something this morning. I want all of us to pray that the Holy Spirit will come upon us in this Congress this week in a new way. I am going to ask you to take the hands of the persons next to you, if you will, and I am going to ask you to bow your heads and close your eyes. You've listened to me, and now I want you to speak back to me and to God. In a moment I want you to pray and I want you to pray out loud — all of you. I want you to pray in your own tongue, English, Spanish, Portuguese — whatever it might be. I want you to pray whatever is on your heart, but above all, pray that God will make us people of prayer and that the Spirit of God may fall.

Pray now — pray in your own tongue.

STUDIES IN THE SCRIPTURES:
THE POWER OF LOVE

Dr. Harold Lindsell

From the Word of God this morning. 1 Corinthians, chapter 13:

"Though I speak with the tongues of men and of angels, and have not love, I am become as sounding brass, or a tinkling cymbal. And though I have the gift of prophecy, and understand all mysteries, and all knowledge; and though I have all faith, so that I could remove mountains, and have not love, I am nothing. And though I bestow all my goods to feed the poor, and though I give my body to be burned, and have not love, it profiteth me nothing. Love suffereth long, and is kind; love envieth not; love vaunteth not itself, is not puffed up, doth not behave itself unseemly, seeketh not her own, is not easily provoked, thinketh no evil; rejoiceth not in iniquity, but rejoiceth in the truth; beareth all things, believeth all things, hopeth all things, endureth all things. Love never faileth; but whether there be prophecies, they shall fail; whether there be tongues, they shall cease; whether there be knowledge, it shall vanish away. For we know in part, and we prophesy in part. But when that which is perfect is come, then that which is in part shall be done away. When I was a child, I spake as a child, I understood as a child, I thought as a child: but when I became a man, I put away childish things. For now we see through a glass, darkly; but then face to face: now I know in part; but then shall I know even as also I am known. And now abideth faith, hope, love, these three; but the greatest of these is love."

I said yesterday morning that we were concerned with the subject of power, and I had in mind for our three sessions together the power of prayer, the power of love, and the power of the Holy Spirit. I also quoted from Scripture that the weapons of our warfare are not carnal but spiritual. So the subjects that I discussed with you are weapons which the Christian has in his arsenal. We do not fight with atom bombs. We do not fight with hate. We do not fight with economic, and political, and social forces per se.

God has given to us strange implements for our warfare. In the museum of God you will find the slingshot and a few pebbles from David. You will find Aaron's rod, that branch which budded. God uses strange instruments, and one of the weapons of God for His people is the weapon of prayer.

The second weapon is the weapon of love. In a day, when, as never before, there is friction, there is hatred, there are wars and there are rumors of wars, God suggests that His people ought to be people of love.

DR. HAROLD LINDSELL, Editor of *Christianity Today*, Washington, D.C.

I would like to divide the Scripture which I read for you into three segments. The first segment is love contrasted. The second segment is love defined, and the third segment is love imperishable.

The apostle Paul, writing to this great church at Corinth, was aware of the fact that it was a singularly gifted church. It was a church which had manifested in its midst the gifts of the Spirit in abundance. They had tongues, they had prophecies, they had knowledge, and they had the gift of God. They could express what they had, but it was a defective church. It was a church that was marred, if you please, by certain kinds of sin. One of the greatest needs of this gifted church was love, and Paul, when he begins his great discourse on love, contrasts love with other gifts of the Spirit. He speaks about love as contrasted with the ecstatic gifts.

Now in our day there has been a recovery of the gift of speaking in tongues. Not all that goes by that name is genuine, but also we must recognize that some of it is not spurious but real, and we rejoice in the gift of tongues. I believe that it is a Biblical gift. Now Paul says, "Though I speak with the tongues of men and of angels" — that language which is spoken by those creatures who are spirits in the celestial world. Though I have all the gifts of tongues that men speak and that angels converse in, if it is not accompanied by the gift of love, then I am become a sounding brass or a tinkling cymbal. I am an echo. I am like the roaring of the sea. I am a hollow basin — not that he in any sense is diminishing the greatness of the gift of tongues, but he says, "unaccompanied by love it isn't worth too much."

He contrasts it, secondly, with the teaching gifts. Now I know and you know that the teaching gifts are absolutely necessary and indispensable to the church of Jesus Christ. There must be, if you please, the gift of prophecy. Indeed, if I myself would pray any prayer, I would not pray for the gift of healing, or for the gift of tongues, or for the gift of performing miracles. I myself would pray for the gift of teaching that I might be able to expound the Word of God. I think there is nothing greater than that.

Now Paul says, "If I have the gift of prophecy; if I am able to preach; if I am an expositor who can open up the Scriptures; if in addition I have the gift of knowledge which is part of the teaching gifts so that all of the Scriptures are opened up to me in a fashion that other men do not possess; if I am able to understand the deepest mysteries; if I am initiated into those things which are known only by the most elect company of God's believers; if I have all of these gifts and if I use them, and these gifts are not accompanied by the gift of love, I am a zero."

Then he contrasts love with the gift of faith. I must confess that across the years I have met some people who have been singularly gifted with the gift of faith. They have staggered me by their great confidence in God. I've watched them believe for impossible things, and I have wished that I could believe like them.

Now Paul says, "Though I have the gift of faith" — a mighty faith, a transforming faith, a transcendent faith, a faith that is able to move mountains (not bad faith, is it?) — if I've got it, but it isn't accompanied by love, then I am a flop-flunk. I haven't made it.

He speaks also about love in contrast to personal sacrifice, for if Christianity is anything, it is a religion of personal sacrifice. He says, "If I, in my own existential situation, take all of the goods that I possess and give them away, if I bestow them to feed the poor (I think this figure of speech might be rephrased something like this: If I take, as a mother take Pablum and spoon-feeds it to an infant a little at a time with sacrifice, if I spoon-feed people) and use all the possessions that I have; indeed, if I offer my body upon an altar as a sacrifice unto martyrdom and death, if I do this and I do not have love, it profiteth me nothing."

Now if I understand the apostle correctly, he seems to be saying to me that of all the gifts that you and I think about, and on which we place such a great premium, there is something that transcends them, that is greater, that is nobler, that is more like God than these, and it's love. So he turns to his discussion of what love is. He doesn't define it. I have a suspicion that love can't be defined. When a man loves a woman, how do you define that emotion, that feeling, that thing which wells up within him? Someone said that love of that kind is a ticklish sensation around the heart that can't be scratched. Paul does not define it, but he does something else. He says, "I can describe the characteristics which accompany love, and if you know what the characteristics of love are, you can ask yourself this question, 'Do I possess these characteristics?' and if I have the characteristics, I've got love." So he speaks, and he says, "I'll tell you what love looks like so that when you see these things you'll know the man has got it. First," he says, "Love suffers long." It has a long ardor, a long passion. Love puts up with what non-love would never accept.

Secondly, Paul says that love is kind. It is gracious. It is gentle in its behavior. Love is a lady; love is a gentleman.

I remember one time a well-known man in Christian work who now is dead visited in our offices in Pasadena, California. He was so uncouth, so ungentlemanly, so rude, and so brusque that I never wanted to hear him on the radio from that day on. He was not a gentleman.

Love doesn't envy. Oh, how Paul stabs my heart when he says that; how he stabs my heart when I look at people who can sing. I mention that specifically because I couldn't carry a tune in a bushel basket on my back, and when I hear these men sing, oh, how I'm tempted to envy the gift that God has given them and I don't have it. How I'm tempted to envy the man who can gather 50,000 people to hear him read the Gospel. How I envy a man who can stand up as Dr. Hoffmann does and read the Scriptures from the Greek, and I'm happy if I can even understand them in the English. Love is not jealous. "For envy they delivered Jesus Christ."

It was Satan who was envious and who was jealous of God. Paul says, "Love doesn't envy anybody the things that he has — material, spiritual, physical."

Dr. Fryhling said he stood next to Bill Glass, six feet — how many inches I don't know — 200 — how many pounds I don't know — bones big — and Dr. Fryhling's small. And he says, "Glass was so nice when he rose up to greet me. He only got up just a little bit so he was on the same level with me."

Paul says, "Love does not vaunt itself." It is not vainglorious, it does not play the braggart, it is not a boaster.

You know in the United States there are two states that are famous for their braggadocio — California and Texas. But I say to you, beloved, you ought to come to Washington and listen to the politicians.

Love is not vaunting itself. It is not vainglorious. It is not a bragger; it does not boast. Love is humble. It isn't puffed up. You know what a balloon is. It is a piece of rubber filled with hot air. I say to you, beloved, that the Scriptures make it painfully obvious that there are a great number of preachers who stand behind the sacred desk who have an awful lot of hot air. They need to have the balloon pricked, and when the balloon is pricked there is nothing left.

Paul says, "Love isn't puffed up. It doesn't behave itself unseemly." We live in an age in which the young people of our day are doing things which to me appear to be unseemly. Some of the things they do are positively indecent. But, mind you, they believe that some of the things that we, who are supposed to be respectable, are doing are indecent. They point the finger and they say, "Listen, racism is indecency," and you know they're right, because you can be indecent that way as you can be in your clothing. I'm not talking to you, I'm talking to myself today, beloved, because I've got needs in my own life and there are fingers that you can point at me.

Paul says that we are not to be indecent in our appearance. Yes. In our conduct. Yes. In our words. Yes. In the totality of life, so that we may stand unblemished before men, transparent so that they can look through us and see the beauty of Jesus and the holiness of God.

Yes, Paul says love doesn't seek its own. He wounded me. Each one of us has a great deal of egotism. Each one has known that sin of seeking to improve his own situation, to further his own interests. Paul says, "Love foregoes his own advantage. Love is willing to be hurt in favor of the other fellow. Love is willing to put God first, my fellowman second, and myself last. Love does not seek its own." He says, "It does not get provoked."

We had a confrontation last night with some Indians. The Executive Committee met with them. One of them had alcohol on his breath. They didn't speak the language of Zion, but they were men and they had needs. I could feel the heat of anger rising in me. Paul says, "Love doesn't permit paroxysms of anger to overtake. There will not be irritation of spirit. There will be a heart which is at leisure from self."

Oh, yes, how easy it is to get provoked and call it righteous indignation when God calls it sin.

He says, "Love thinketh no evil." It doesn't make a record of it, or take account of it. It does not put it on the ledger book and say, "I am going to pay you back later in your own kind." I find in my own life that when a man says something that stings me, I want to sting him back. If he says an unkind word I want to cut back with the same kind of unkind word. I want it to be eye for eye, tooth for tooth, strike for strike, wound for wound. Paul says that love does not take it into account, put it on the ledger, and wait for the opportunity to pull out the sword and to stab it back.

Love not only forgives, it also forgets. He says, "It doesn't rejoice in iniquity but it rejoices in truth." Listen, how many Christians have rejoiced in the fall of another Christian who had risen to great heights but fell into sin? And now they say, "Well, I knew it all the time, and it serves him right." And how happy they are to help in the process of pulling him down.

Paul says, "When a brother falls into sin, if we get satisfaction out of it, out of the misfortunes of others, then we don't have the beginning of an understanding of what love means." He says, "Love rejoiceth in truth." It rejoices in the positive, not in the negative, and whatever is truth, love is for it, and love entertains truth, and listens to it, and responds to it. When you've got truth, it rules out error.

Now Paul says, "Love bears all things." You know the Scriptures teach us that love covers a multitude of sins. I haven't got time to tell the story about the Anglican people who met and they were talking about this kind of thing, and one brother heard some gossip and he said, "My peculiar sin is gossip." After he had listened to all these confessions he said, "I can't wait until I get out and tell somebody."

Listen, my beloved, you and I should protect, and throw a veil over, and cover people. You and I should not go out and expose all the things that we hear, and pass out gossip. Many, many times that gossip is not even substantiated by fact. We ruin reputations and oh, how we love to pass on what we have heard which are rumors. Paul says, "Love bears all things; it believes all things." It isn't suspicious. It has a faith and a confidence in man. It isn't gullible and it's not taken in, but when I walk with you, talk with you, and pray with you, I take you at your face value until you prove yourself to be something else.

Love hopes all things. I need this word because I am not a man of great courage. I walk fearfully, and yet the Scripture says that the man who hopes does not give way to despair. I am a pessimist. I wear a belt and suspenders at the same time. But love sees the bright side. Love has hope. Love rises triumphantly to move forward. Paul says, "Love endures all things." It perseveres. It is stouthearted. Love hangs on when everybody else gives up.

Now Paul says, "If you've got these characteristics you've got love. If you haven't got them, you haven't got love, no matter what you think."

Then he comes back to his original theme for he has contrasted some of these things with love, and now Paul says, "I want you to understand there are some things which are temporal and there are some things which are eternal. The gift of prophecy some day shall not be needed. The gift of knowledge shall vanish away for we shall know all things. The gift of tongues some day will be superfluous when we get to the glory land." But Paul says, "I want you to know that when all these other gifts have disappeared, and the need for them has ceased, there are three gifts which shall remain — faith, hope and love. These are eternal." What he says is, "The greatest of all the imperishable gifts is the gift of LOVE."

You know in our day we look at the Communists, and sometimes they put us to shame. I would like to say this to you. The Communists out-think us; they out-talk us; they out-argue us; they out-work us; they may out-live us; they may out-die us; but they must not, they cannot, they will not, by the grace of God, out-love us. The perfection of love is expressed in the gift of Jesus Christ, God's Son. "For God so loved the world that He gave His only begotten Son; that whosoever believeth in Him should not perish, but have everlasting life."

And Jesus in the incarnation is the prototype of all our human love; for of Him the Scripture says that He so loved us that He died for us when we were ungodly. He so loved us that He died for us when we were sinners, and He so loved us that He died for us when we were enemies. Love cost Him His life, and love is going to cost you and me something.

Let me end with a poem from Amy Carmichael. She wrote this:

"Hast thou no scar?
No hidden scar on foot, or side, or hand?
I hear thee sung as mighty in the land,
I hear them hail the bright ascendant star,
Hast thou no scar?

Hast thou no wound?
Yet I was wounded by the archers, spent,
Leaned Me against a tree to die; and rent
By ravening beasts that compassed Me, I swooned:
Hast *thou* no wound?

No wound? no scar?
Yet, as the Master shall the servant be,
And pierced are the feet that follow Me;
But thine are whole: can he have followed far
Who has nor wound nor scar?"

Do you have love? It will scar you; it will wound you; it will break you; it may even crucify you.

Yesterday I asked us to pray out loud. Today I ask you to bow your heads in silence and in aloneness. Don't think about anybody else, and in the quietness of your aloneness with God, with your head bowed, and your eyes closed, for just a moment, let God speak to your heart and search it, and you answer this question, "Do I really have love?" If the answer is negative, then by the grace of God will you pray in your aloneness before God, "Oh, God, whatever the price, whatever the cost, make me a child of love"? Will you do it now?

STUDIES IN THE SCRIPTURES:
THE POWER OF THE HOLY SPIRIT

Dr. Harold Lindsell

I started by saying that the weapons of our warfare are not carnal but spiritual and I have suggested to you that there are certain powers which are available to the Christian in the arsenal, always available in Jesus Christ. On Thursday I made an effort to speak of the power of prayer which belongs to us as the people of God. Yesterday I spoke on the power of love, a love which when it is incarnate in the lives of each of us will do as much, even more perhaps, to commend the Gospel to unbelievers as the words that we speak.

Now today I would like to concentrate on the power of the Holy Spirit. When you pray, this is something that *you* do. When you love, this is something that *you* do. But when you are filled with the Holy Spirit, this is something that *God* does in you and in me.

Now it is true, of course, that there are prerequisites. There are conditions which must be met, but it is essentially the work of God who calls out His Spirit upon His people. You are familiar with the salvation process. I use that word "process" advisedly, because salvation is not something which simply occurs at one moment. It is something which involves in it a number of elements which are carried on throughout all the days of life.

We begin our spiritual pilgrimage by grace alone, through Christ alone, by faith alone, as Archbishop Loane suggested to us in his Bible studies. Now this journey is commenced when we have been justified by faith alone. At the time we are justified we are born again or regenerated; and when we have been justified and regenerated, then sanctification takes over and sanctification is a process which occurs all the days of life. It yields ultimately to glorification and there comes a time when everything that I ought to be I will be. But I shall not be all that I ought to be until I have been glorified, and glorification does not take place until after death. But during the period between the time that I was regenerated and the time that I shall be perfected and glorified, there is this great process of sanctification.

Now sanctification is a matter of holiness. It has to do with the quality of my life. It is supposed to be progressive in the sense that I should go from grace to grace and glory to glory. Every day I should be making advances in my Christian walk, but unfortunately sanctification can be retrogressive and recessive as well. It is possible for me to go backward. It

DR. HAROLD LINDSELL, Editor of *Christianity Today*, Washington, D.C.

is possible for me to become backslidden. It is possible for me to lose the dynamic and the holiness which ought to be mine.

In this Congress we have heard a great deal about what the Christian ought to be doing. I am deeply concerned, not only with what we ought to be doing, but with what we are in our inner man. Before ever you *do* something you must *be* something, and I suggest to you that being is more important than doing. For what you do tells me what you really are, and I think that all action should spring from being. And for the Christian to be what he ought to be has to do with the fullness of the Holy Spirit of God.

The Scriptures tell us that Christians can be either carnal or spiritual. Let me suggest what are the marks of a carnal Christian. A carnal Christian is a worldling. He is characterized by spiritual adultery. He has a life of fruitlessness. He does not bear fruit in relationship to the vine as he ought to bear. He has a life of infancy, he is a babe in Christ who has not grown up. There is hypocrisy connected with his life. He experiences spiritual defeat. He has inner tension and inner conflict.

Now I'm not speaking about the kind of inner tension that we ought always to have, for the Christian life is persistently a life of tension, and that's good. But I'm speaking of tension in the sense in which it takes over and becomes a defect and a fault. I'm thinking of conflict which divides us and makes us schizophrenic.

This kind of Christian is living in Romans 7, of whom the apostle Paul wrote when he said, "Those things which I would not, those I do, and those things which I ought to do, I do not." But the Scriptures say that we do not need to live this kind of life. There is a life on a higher plane, there is a life of victory, there is a spiritual kind of life the quality of which is marked by fruitfulness, by spiritual maturity, by a life of victory over sin as we are overcomers, as an inner peace and radiance come which transcend all that we have ever known, and we live a blameless life which is not perfect, but nevertheless the whole tendency and direction of the life is toward the will of God.

It is a life of transparency in which men can see through us, and see that we are what we ought to be.

The question that I've always asked myself is this: "Is it really possible that we can live this kind of life? Can we get from Romans 7 to Romans 8? Can we have a vitality, a dynamic, and is it promised in Scripture? How do we get it?" Now notice that in this Congress over and over again reference has been made to the Holy Spirit and to His power. I am concerned this morning, not only that we should recognize the work of the Holy Spirit, but that we should know how we can obtain His fullness and go on to a life of victory.

Jesus, in the 10th chapter of John's Gospel, verse 10, made this statement, "I am come that they might have life." And then He said, "And that they might have it more abundantly." Jesus came to bring us abundant life. He came to make us partakers of His divine nature. He came to reproduce within us, when we have been regenerated, that quality and kind of life which was his kind of life.

The apostle Paul, in Colossians, chapter 2, verses 9 and 10, says this, "In Him dwelleth all the fullness of the Godhead bodily. And ye are complete in Him, which is the head of all principality and power." Ye are complete in Him. Whatever it is that I need for completion, for fulfillment, for being what I ought to be, to be a wholistic person, to have integration, to have the dynamic — whatever it is — Paul says that in Him dwelleth all the fullness. And in His fullness you and I find our completeness, for we are complete in Him.

In John, chapter 4 and verse 14, Jesus said, "Whosoever drinketh of the water that I shall give him shall never thirst; but the water that I shall give him shall be in him a well of water springing up into everlasting life."

A little later in John 7, Jesus said, "If any man thirst, let him come unto me and drink. He that believeth on me, as the Scripture hath said, [from within him] shall flow rivers of living water. (But this spake He of the Spirit, which they that believe on Him should receive: for the Holy Ghost was not yet given; because that Jesus was not yet glorified.)"

The rivers of living water, of which Jesus speaks, have to do with the gift of the Holy Spirit. I think we need to distinquish carefully between the sealing of the Holy Spirit and the filling of the Holy Spirit. The apostle Paul in Ephesians, chapter 1 and verse 13, says this, "In whom ye also trusted, after that ye heard the word of truth, the Gospel of your salvation: in whom also, after that ye believed, ye were sealed with that Holy Spirit of promise."

Every Christian who has been regenerated, who has been justified, has been sealed. The Spirit of God has marked us off as the people of God. We have the seal of God upon us. Now notice this, that every Christian has this, but not every Christian is filled with the Spirit. We need not only to be sealed, which we must be if we are to be the people of God, but we must also be filled.

Paul in the epistle to the Ephesians (5:18) wrote these words, "Be not drunk with wine, wherein is excess; but be filled with the Spirit." Now notice that the apostle Paul would never have said this if all Christians were filled with the Spirit. He could not have said it if it was not a possibility, so Paul establishes the truth that being filled with the Holy Spirit is a part of the Christian's birthright. It belongs to me through redemption. It is part of that which God gives me when I become His child.

The Scripture, from what Paul says, also makes it evident that I need this. It is something which belongs to the essentials of the Christian faith and it is something which I need desperately, that I ought to possess.

There is something else I would add to it, that if it is what God wants me to have, and if it is possible for me to get it, then it becomes my responsibility to attain it. If I need it, I ought to have it. If I can get it, I should meet whatever conditions are required of me in order to have it.

Now I know that there are differences of opinion as to whether being filled with the Spirit is a second work of grace. I do not choose to go into that today. I think there can be differences of opinion and different ways in which you can define it. But my chief concern is not whether you can define it, but whether you can possess it, whether you have it; and when you've got it, I don't care how you write about it as long as you've got it. And maybe if you have it you'll be less concerned about writing about it than you will be about manifesting it before man.

When we have the fullness of the Holy Spirit, we have the sense of the presence of Jesus Christ — that He's not someone off here, but He is Christ in me, the hope of glory — and there is an intimate, abiding fellowship which I have with Him, in His presence in my heart.

I know that there is bad theology in the chorus that we used to sing, "You ask me how I know He lives. He lives within my heart." Now however bad the theology that is connected with some of our choruses may be, it still is true that Scripture teaches that Christ is in me, the hope of glory. And when I'm filled with the Spirit, the Spirit has come to reflect Jesus Christ, to manifest the beauty of Jesus Christ, and to create that sense of Christ's immediate and abiding presence in my life. He walks beside me day by day.

Secondly, the Holy Spirit intends to reproduce in me the life of the Lord Jesus of whom the Scripture says He lived without sin, that He knew no sin. Here was the life of perfection. Here was the life that the Spirit comes to reproduce in me. He has come to reproduce the life of the Lord Jesus in me.

But there is something else that He intends to do. When I am filled with the Spirit, I have not only the abiding presence of Jesus, and I reflect the life of Jesus, but I get His supernatural power. There is something that comes to me, a dynamic, which when I am filled with the Spirit will make my witness, my preaching, and everything else an effective tool for Almighty God. That's why I say *being* is more important than *doing*. And Jesus, when He gave His last commandments to His disciples in the 24th chapter of Luke's Gospel, knew that. The world was waiting for the Gospel and men everywhere needed to be converted to the message of salvation, but He still said to His disciples, "Tarry . . . until ye be endued with power."

I think your preaching and mine, your witnessing and mine, would be a lot more effective if we waited first to get the dynamic, and then went out to do the witnessing. Now I'm not speaking to you, I'm speaking to myself. I'm speaking from the knowledge of the pressures that come upon us. I speak from the knowledge that the demands of the world are such that we're always tempted to do what we have to do, without recognizing that there are some things that we don't have to do. But one of the things that God calls us to do is to tarry until we have the power.

Now let me suggest this morning how it's possible to get it. Before we can have the power we must be cleansed. Our hearts must be empty before they can be filled. The Scriptures speak about the Holy Spirit, and they give Him different titles. He is called the Spirit of Truth, and when gossip and criticism occupy my heart, the Spirit of Truth is ruled out.

He's called the Spirit of Faith, and when I have doubt and distrust, the power of the Spirit cannot operate.

He's called the Spirit of Holiness, and when I do not come with clean hands and a pure heart, the Spirit's power cannot be with me.

He's called the Spirit of Wisdom, and when ignorance and conceit and arrogance overtake me, when egotism becomes central in my life, the Holy Spirit and His power cannot operate.

He's called the Spirit of Power, the Spirit of Love, the Spirit of Life, the Spirit of Discipline, so that our weakness, our fruitlessness, our lack of control grieve Him. Our indifference and our lukewarmness, our worldliness, our earthly, fleshly living keep Him from filling us with His power. And before He comes in to fill the vessel, the vessel must be cleansed.

In 1 John 1:9, the apostle gives us our words of hope, our words of cleansing. "If we confess our sins, He is faithful and just to forgive us our sins, and to cleanse us from all unrighteousness." He tells us that the means of cleansing is the blood of Jesus Christ and that blood which cleansed us from our sins and gave us redemption is the blood which cleanses us day by day and moment by moment with respect to sanctification. That blood we need to claim repeatedly all the days of life. But when He operates He cleanses the vessel, He opens it up to the possibilities and potentialities of the Holy Spirit.

I believe, my friends, that the problem with most of us is that we like to hang on to our sins. We don't want to give up those things in our lives which are displeasing to Him. I would be willing to say without fear of equivocation, that within the sound of my voice this morning, there are people who are living immoral lives. There are people here this morning who do not hesitate to tell lies. There are people here whose eyes are eager to look upon things which no sanctified eye would ever look upon. I'm absolutely certain that there are people here who through the course of this week have told dirty stories one way or another, either overtly or by innuendo. I think there are people here who have been insidious. I won't tell you what my pet sins are, but I'm no less guilty except perhaps in some different way. And the Scripture says if you want the abundant life that Jesus has come to give you, if you want those wells of water which spring up, first get clean, confess, repent, make whatever restitution is necessary.

You know we've had a lot to say this week about social action. Would I be doing less than the honest thing if I told you that there were residual elements of racism in me? I know the doctrine, I know as an evangelical that all men come from Adam, we all stem from the same father, we are a common humanity. But I discover elements of racism in me that I've never yet extricated. Now that may not be your problem. Yours may be something else. But listen, beloved, are we ready to confess?

Now thirdly, if you want the fullness of God's Holy Spirit you first must give yourself to Him. I remember many years ago I graduated from college, I was in graduate school, and I went to visit my uncle who lived in Seattle, Washington. The woman who now is the wife of Billy Graham gave me a book for my birthday, many years ago. My birthday happens to come on December 22nd, and it was during the Christmas vacation that I was up in Seattle, Washington with my uncle. And this book came to me and it was Oswald Chambers' "My Utmost For His Highest."

I'd gone all through college, I was a Christian, I loved God, but up to that point in my life I never had laid my life on the altar for Jesus Christ. I'd been raised in a Presbyterian church, I was a child of God but I never had laid everything upon the altar, and God did not have me in my totality.

I began to read Oswald Chambers' little book, a daily devotional reading, one for each day, and within about three days' time I read through the whole book. For the first time in my life I got on my knees and I said, "I am yours, all of me. Take me, use me, make me what you want. Send me where you want me to go. I'm yours forever." My commitment has not changed from that day to this.

There have been moments of tension. There have been times when perhaps I strayed a little bit from the pathway, but always and ever the Holy Spirit has brought me back to that first commitment, for it was a definite act. It was a final and complete act. It was an act which shall be through all the days of my life. I never shall repeat that act. I only have to come back, if I stray from it, to the realization that I did it once before and to bring myself back into conformity with that which I did that day so many years ago. And I'm saying to you today that if you want the fullness of the Holy Spirit of God, He's got to have you. Your will, your intelligence, your life of affection, your heart, your all.

Now in Scripture, in 2 Corinthians, chapter 8 and verse 5, the Scripture says they first gave their own selves to the will of God. In Romans, chapter 6, verse 13, Paul says, "Yield yourselves unto God, as those that are alive from the dead." That is your person. And then he gets specific and he says, "Your members," that means your eyes, your ears, your tongue, your fingers, your feet, your sex life, your heart life, your heart, and "yield your members as instruments of righteousness unto God." Yield everything, everything.

Jesus is waiting for that kind of commitment. The Holy Spirit hovers over my life waiting for me to do that which is required so that He will fill me.

One other thing. We were saved by faith, we walk by faith, indeed we must die by faith, and I say to you if we're going to have the fullness of the Holy Spirit of God, we must claim it by faith. As I read the Scriptures I understand clearly that God's promises to all of His people everywhere must be claimed by His people by faith. There are 5,000 promises in Scripture, and they belong to you and to me if by faith we'll claim the promises. One of the great promises of God is this, that we shall have abundant life if we want it. We shall have abundant life, and from within us shall flow rivers of living waters if we meet the conditions. We are not to be drunk with wine, but we ought to be filled with the Holy Spirit. If we meet the conditions we can claim the promise and God by His Spirit will fill us, if we claim the promise by faith.

You know there are cases in the Scriptures where we are told that Jesus had the Spirit without measure. We are told that John the Baptist was filled with the Spirit of God from his mother's womb. And God says that you and I need to be filled. We ought to be filled. We *can* be filled but whether we *are* filled is our responsibility.

I want to leave this Congress to go out and to do something for Jesus Christ, but I'm keenly aware that before I *do* anything I must *be* something. I must not only be filled with the Spirit, but I must continue to be filled with the Spirit day by day, and moment by moment. I need to grow so that He can fill me even more, so as I grow He will continue to make me more and more what I ought to be, until that day when at last I am glorified.

So I leave this parting question with you this morning, "Are you filled with the Spirit?" If not, why not? Dr. Hoffmann started this Congress by saying "Get with Christ and go with Christ." And I'm saying to you that the only way you can get with Christ as a Christian is to be filled with the Holy Spirit. He will fill you if you meet the conditions and claim the promise. Shall we bow our heads?

While our heads are bowed, our eyes are closed, and our hearts are tender, let's ask ourselves the question, "Am I filled?" If not, ask yourself the question, "Will I confess my sins and make myself a prepared vessel?"

Ask yourself the question, "Does God have all of me? Have I given Him the control of my life and all that I am?" And then ask yourself the question, "Will I claim the promise of His fullness by faith?"

THE CHURCH AND EVANGELISM
IN A DAY OF REVOLUTION

Dr. Leighton Ford

In London's Highgate Cemetery a huge granite pillar stands atop the grave of Karl Marx. On it is a bust of Marx, his cheeks puffed out like Kris Kringle, his eyes set deep and resolute. Chiseled on the granite is this dictum of the father of Communism: "The philosophers have only interpreted the world. The point is to change it."

I agree with Karl Marx! The world needs to be changed! But how? That *is* the point.

Today I have been asked to speak on "The Church and Evangelism in a Day of Revolution." But what has evangelism to do with revolution? Just this — that Christ's work never goes on in a vacuum, and today the Christian church is being called to evangelize people caught up in cataclysmic change.

This truth was smashed into my heart nearly a decade ago, as a friend and I were flying in Africa. Africa was throbbing with the great drive for freedom; the thunder of change was in the air. My friend handed his Bible to me, pointing to this passage from Jeremiah: "The Word of the Lord came to me . . . saying, 'What do you see?' And (Jeremiah) said, 'I see a boiling pot, a seething cauldron . . .' "

"A seething cauldron." That was a perfect image to describe our world — an age shaken and convulsed by the most fantastic revolutions of all time. When the mobs stormed the Bastille in 1789 to start the French Revolution, King Louis is said to have remarked, "This is a revolt." Someone replied, "No sir, this is a revolution." Indeed, this is the mark of our age — not an isolated revolt, but total revolution.

Revolution is change — total, constant, irresistible, rapid, pervasive change — which affects every part of our lives. In America there is a demographic revolution as great groups of humanity move about in gigantic population shifts. By 1980 the Christian church will find its evangelistic mission focused on the 90 percent of all Americans who will live in great strip cities, already dubbed with such revolting (!) names as Boswash, Chipitt, and Sansan. We live, too, in a blindingly fast technological revolution. From the time telegraph was discovered until it was commercially applied took 112 years; for transistors that application gap shrank to 5 years! Our exploding technology is like all the rockets at Cape Kennedy going off at once in some Fourth of July spectacular!

DR. LEIGHTON FORD, Associate Evangelist, The Billy Graham Evangelistic Association.

The strange plight of modern man is that while his knowledge is exploding, the whole idea of "true truth," truth which is the opposite of falsehood,
is disappearing. In art, philosophy, theology and the total pattern of his
thinking, 20th century man seeks to escape from reason. Everything is
relative. This has led inevitably to a moral revolution, the shift from an
absolute ethic to a situation ethic, from a morality based on God's eternal
law to one based on man's personal "likes."

Neither pot nor pornography forms the moral crisis of our time. That
crisis lies in the widely-held assumption that no moral standard is really important. There have always been those who have violated society's moral
codes, but has there ever been a generation which repudiated the very idea
of *any* binding standard?

All these changes are compounded by the communications revolution
which has shrunk this planet into one world and extended our eyes to the
moon. The immediacy of the media, especially TV, has placed us all in what
Marshall McLuhan calls a "global village." Today's news today is not just
what's happened; it's what's happening!

The children of the electronic age are the first generation ever to know
more than their parents! When young people say that those over 30 don't
understand, they may be arrogant, but they are also partly right. Most of the
changes we've mentioned have taken place in the last 30 years. Those of us
born before 1939 are like immigrants, feeling our way around a new land.
Only the young know this world as natives know their own country. Change
is the natural habitat of today's youth.

To those of you at this Congress under 30 I say: we need to hear you. In
2 years the average age in America will be 24. The task of confronting this
changing age with a changeless Christ belongs largely to you. Yours is the
vocal generation, so don't be silent here! Listen and learn. But speak. Tell it
like it is. Plead. Provoke. Make us mad if you have to. Do it with love and
humility. But do it!

Revolution also means radical political change. A few years ago that
prospect seemed very remote on this continent. Did you ever think you
would live to see a revolution in America? Yet today the radical extremist
groups in our society call for just that. What the radicals have in mind is
not akin to the American Revolution, with its limited goals. Their vision is
much closer to the French and Communist revolutions, which totally re-
jected the old regimes. Radicals in contemporary America have made their
goal clear: they are convinced that American society is so corrupt and so
unworkable that the system cannot be changed; it must be destroyed. When
asked what they have to replace it, many of them answer that this is not their
concern. It should be ours, for they are out to create a vacuum which would
quickly be filled by totalitarianism of the left or the right.

Yet we dare not be blind to the lesson all modern revolutions have
taught: when men of privilege abuse their power, and refuse justice, sooner

or later upheaval will come. President Kennedy put it memorably: "He who makes peaceful revolution impossible makes violent revolution inevitable."

Today revolution is fueled by the freedom drive which is surging up through the entire world of men — the struggle for identity, dignity, security, and equality. In America the flash points of the freedom revolution are poverty and racism.

The poor we have always had with us, but the gap yawns wider every year. The new factor is that poor people are learning that not every one is poor and that change is possible. Put a TV in a ghetto, let a slum mother see ads for low-calorie dog foods and electric toothbrushes when her baby has had his ears chewed off by a rat, and you've got a revolution!

Racism is not just a problem of the South, or of America, or of the white man. It is a worldwide symptom of sin. But God has told us to confess our own sins, not those of the rest of the world. I hold no brief for James Forman's Black Manifesto. Yet if our reaction is simply to lash back at Forman, and if we do not seek to heal the gaping, aching, rubbed-raw wounds of racial strife, then we shall deserve "the fire next time."

It is to the shame of the Christian church that we have been so slow to face the demands of the Gospel in the racial revolution of our time. With some notable exceptions, we have moved only when we have been run over from behind. We have enjoyed, many of us, our privileged position at the "white hand of God."

What, you may ask, does this have to do with evangelism? Well, let me ask what kind of Gospel we are preaching when a church sends missionaries to convert Africans, but suggests to the black American that he go to his own church with his own kind? Why should the black man listen to us talk about a home in heaven, when we refuse to make him at home in our neighborhood and our schools? What, I ask you, does this *not* have to do with evangelism?

The right of men to freedom, dignity, and respect comes directly from the Bible, from the story that God made man, that God loves man, and that the Son of God laid down His life for man. This is the ultimate source of human worth. The whole idea that the course of history can be altered, that man is not the slave of fate, arises from the Christian view that history moves toward a climax in the return of Christ.

What then should be the stance of the Christian church in an age of revolution?

Some call for the blind rejection of all revolution; others demand a naïve acceptance of all revolution. Some would like to ignore change; others would like to baptize change as the new messiah. As responsible Christians we must reject both extremes.

We cannot be worthy of our high calling if we try to keep God in some private, undisturbed corner of our lives, and ignore the strong driving winds of change. While revolution was raging in Petrograd in 1917, the Russian

Orthodox Church was in session a few blocks away having a hot debate — about what color of vestments their priests should wear! God help us if we strain at gnats while the camels of revolution are marching!

Some change should be opposed. We Christians have a stake in preserving the historic truth of the Gospel and the worthy values of the past. Like Jeremiah we say, "Ask for the ancient paths, where the good way is." But we also know that sin infects every man and every human institution. So we need a holy discontent with the status quo. The Gospel calls for constant change. Conversion is a change of direction. Repentance is a change of mind. The Christian life is a continual change from glory to glory.

We cannot identify our Gospel with the past and oppose all change. God is not tied to 17th century English, 18th century hymns, 19th century architecture, and 20th century clichés. God is constantly prodding us as He did the people of Israel and saying, "Strike your tents and move on!"

The naïve approval of revolution is an equally foolish mistake. There are those who would recast Jesus into the patron saint of guerrilla fighters, and see the Church's task as being "the hand-maiden or water-boy of world revolution." One theologian lists the various changes going on in the world and concludes, "God is in all these revolutions." I think it's fair to reply: how do you know? How does one know whether it is God or the devil at work in revolution? Jesus told of a house where one demon was cast out and seven more came in. A revolution that takes place in a spiritual vacuum will open the door wide for the invasion of the demons!

Communism is a prime example. We should repudiate the efforts to couple evangelism with a crude, sword-rattling anti-Communism. Yet we cannot blind ourselves to the brutalities that have marked the Communist movement. This ruthlessness is more than the excess of a young revolution. It is the direct outgrowth of an atheistic doctrine which deifies the system and dehumanizes the man.

A close link has been forged between sexual rebellion and political subversion. There is something demonic about the obsession with the obscene. The sex of the sixties is sick. It's a symptom of spiritual rebellion, of man's attempt to tear down his relationship with his Maker. TIME recently noted that four-letter words have become a tool of protest against the Establishment. The "Playboy" philosophy of sex as recreation is almost outdated; it is now sex as revolution. If we ignore this connection between sexual and political anarchy, and go around patting all the radical revolutionaries on the head as God's secret agents, then we are spiritually blind, theologically naïve, and politically stupid.

The abuse of drugs is another part of the anarchist rebellion. Herbert Marcuse, the oracle of the New Left, has called for a fight to legalize marijuana as "a means of total opposition."

Faced with these realities the Christian cannot blindly approve all revolution. There is really only one course open to us: neither to be total resisters nor total rebels, but to be revolutionaries — Christian style!

Charles Malik, the distinguished Christian statesman from Lebanon, has said that the "West is afraid of being revolutionary." Is he right? If so, then we are traitors to our Christian heritage. History's greatest revolution began not under a red star in Petrograd in 1917, but under the star of Bethlehem two thousand years ago in the cradle where God invaded history. In Jesus Christ, God began the great reversal. Human categories were turned upside down and the proud and the humble, the mighty and the weak, the rich and the poor switched places.

The early Christians were a band of revolutionaries, Christian style. The book of Acts gives us a series of glimpses of them scattered in the cities of the Roman Empire.

At Jerusalem you see an economic revolution! "All who believed were together and had all things in common" (Acts 2:44, RSV).

In Antioch you see a social revolution! "In the church at Antioch there were prophets and teachers, Barnabas, Symeon who was called Niger, Lucius of Cyrene, Manaen a member of the court of Herod the tetrarch, and Saul" (Acts 13:1, RSV). They were two Jews, two Africans, and a Roman aristocrat! All races and classes had become beautiful in Christ!

In Corinth you see a moral revolution! Corinth was a cesspool of evil and perversion. Yet Paul, writing to the Christians in that city, catalogues the vices of Corinth and then exclaims: "And such were some of you. But you were washed, you were sanctified, you were justified in the name of the Lord Jesus Christ and in the Spirit of our God" (1 Corinthians 6:11, RSV). At the end of the book of Acts you see Paul in Rome — a spiritual revolutionary at work! "And he lived there two whole years at his own expense, and welcomed all who came to him, preaching the kingdom of God and teaching about the Lord Jesus Christ" (Acts 28:30, 31, RSV). When these Christians showed up in Thessalonica their enemies paid them a backhanded compliment and said, "These men who have turned the world upside down have come here also."

One of our main failures in evangelism has been "undersell." We have made the Gospel seem cheap, tame and dull. We ought to be saying to the students and the people of the world, "We too are revolutionaries! We too want to see things changed. But we believe only one revolution is big enough, and deep enough, and powerful enough to change the world. It will take everything you've got — but come join Christ's revolution!"

Ponder those pictures of the early Christians. What impression do you get? Here was a *revolutionary God*, releasing *revolutionary power* through a *revolutionary community*, in *revolutionary action*. These are still the essential ingredients in the Christian recipe for revolution.

"I believe in God the Father Almighty, maker of heaven and earth." We gladly confess that faith. But do we also believe in God the Father

Almighty, the *shaker* of heaven and earth? Or have we lost our poise because somehow we feel that our world has gotten beyond God's control?

When those early Christians were arrested for disturbing the peace, they lifted their voices in prayer and quoting their Bibles said, "Sovereign Lord, who didst make the heaven and the earth, and the sea and everything in them, who by the mouth of David . . . didst say by the Holy Spirit, 'Why do the Gentiles rage?' " According to the Psalm from which they quoted, when men rebel against God's authority,

> "He who sits in the heaven laughs;
> the Lord has them in derision."

These early Christian revolutionaries had implicit confidence that their God was at the master controls of history. Rebellion against His rule was bound to fail. He laughed from heaven at the empty posturings and vain plans of those who set themselves to topple Him from His throne. The rushes and changes of history were under His supervision. When Jeremiah saw the vision of the seething cauldron, the Lord said, "Look. *I* am calling . . . the kingdoms of the north . . . and they *shall come*." Heathen nations and kings were His personnel. If the Jews would not carry out God's plans then He would use the heathen. He calls Assyria "The rod of my anger, the staff of my fury" (Isaiah 10:5, RSV). He describes Cyrus, the heathen king of Persia, as "my anointed" (Isaiah 45).

Assyrians, Chaldeans, Persians! Violence, tumult, upheaval! All of this permitted by the God of the Bible! He is not dead. He is not sick. He is not asleep. He is the Lord of history, who is working out His purposes as year succeeds to year. He who made Cyrus His unconscious tool is not dismayed by Mao Tse-tung! This God will take the wild rage of the ghettos, the apathy of the suburbs, the unrest on the campus, the nightmare of Vietnam, and weave these tangled threads into the fabric of His plan.

When the first Christians prayed to this God, the place in which they were gathered together was shaken (Acts 4:29-31). Shaken by the Lord of hosts who said through Haggai, "Once again, in a little while, I will shake the heavens and the earth and the sea and the dry land; and I will shake all nations, so that the treasures of all nations shall come in, and I will fill this house with splendor" (Haggai 2:6, RSV).

When we see our world shaken as never before, it is not a time to despair. It is a time to watch God opening doors that have never before been open! A black Ph.D. who is working in the New York ghettos told me of the upheaval which is coming in the inner city. Then he made this significant comment: "The present revolutionary ferment in the city, when people have come to the end of their resources, is a perfect opportunity for preaching the Gospel."

In a day of revolution, evangelism must begin with a new vision of the revolutionary God who is shaking all nations so that their treasures may come in — so that from every people, and tongue, and tribe, and nation may come the parade of precious lives, human treasures, redeemed by the blood of the Lamb, and giving glory to God!

At this point let's ask ourselves some questions and answer as honestly as we can. Have we lost faith in the power of God to change men? Paul went to the power centers of his day saying, "I am not ashamed of the Gospel of Christ, for it is the power of God" (Romans 1:16). Do *we* think that *man's* power is all we have?

The Church stands with all mankind at a common crossroad, sharing a common concern: which way do we go to make a new world? There are some who say, *"Learn"* — education is the way. Some say, *"Earn"* — economic development will solve our problems. Some voices are crying, *"Burn"* — society is so corrupt we must destroy it. There is truth in all of this. But Jesus Christ says, *"Turn.* Be converted. Put your trust in God. Seek first His will. Then you can be part of the new world God is making."

Most revolutions fail because they are not revolutionary enough. They fail to grasp the heart of the problem, which is the problem of the human heart. So these revolutions are aptly named: they revolve! They throw out one set of sinners and put in another set of sinners.

I believe it was Churchill who once said that the root error of Communism and all utopianism was an over-optimistic view of human nature. Every revolutionary movement must come to grips with the fact of sin. What we need is a more radical, more revolutionary revolution which understands that before there can be real revolution there must be genuine repentance.

Christians are often accused of undue pessimism in always harping on sin. Yet, paradoxically, only when sin is faced as a moral reality is there hope! If the human dilemma rises from a wrong combination of chemicals, or from psychological factors beyond man's control, then man is just programmed wrong and we should abandon ourselves to evil. But if the cause of our dilemma is rebellion against God — then there can be an answer from God's side.

Our Gospel claims that Almighty God came into human history to liberate human nature. He came to do for us what we could never do for ourselves. By the supernatural birth of Jesus Christ, God has begun a new humanity into which we may enter by a new birth. By the death of Jesus Christ for our sins God has made it possible to wipe the slate clean, and to free those who believe from the crippling paralysis of guilt. By the risen life of Jesus Christ, shared with us through the Holy Spirit, God enables us to shake off our moral failure. And in the community of forgiven and redeemed men God gives us a place where we can foretaste the new wine of God's new world.

This Christian conversion is so revolutionary because it is so complete. When a man meets Jesus Christ, God begins to heal all his broken relationships, to put him right with God, and with himself and with his fellowman.

Today, when our churches are being torn apart between the so-called "soul savers" at one pole and the so-called "social reformers" at the other, it's absolutely imperative that we keep in view the completeness of the Gospel and resist the temptation of both extremes.

When Abraham Vereide, founder of International Christian Leadership, died last May someone described his vision in terms that should be true of the entire church: "For him, a scheme to reconstruct society which ignored the redemption of the individual was unthinkable; but a doctrine to save sinning men with no aim to transform them into crusaders against social sin was equally unthinkable."

Our evangelism must insist that conversion is a beginning, not an end. Too often converts keep looking back to what happened when they were converted, instead of what happened next. We have sometimes said too blithely, "The best way to change the world is to get men converted." That statement has an important kernel of truth, but it can be misleading. The new birth gives the potential for personality change, but the change does not take place automatically. Conversion must lead to Christian growth.

At this point we must be realistic in the expectations we have for social change that results from personal conversion. Let's be very wary of saying that the preaching of the Gospel will solve all of society's ills. In the first place there is no Biblical warrant for believing that will happen. And in the second place we know that there are "Bible belts" where the Gospel is preached and people are converted, but where there are built-in structures and attitudes of prejudice that change very slowly. That does not mean people are not converted, but it does mean that the Holy Spirit has a great deal of work to do in all of our hearts and minds *after* conversion.

Meanwhile, we can give ourselves in joyful abandonment to the task of making Christ known, because the Gospel of Christ is God's revolutionary power! What a revolution is taking place in our world today as Christ invades human personalities! Is there any other system in the world that can match transformed lives against those that Christ has touched? Think of a gang leader like Tom Skinner who will tell us how Christ changed him into an apostle of love. Think of a wiretapper like Jim Vaus, who has followed Christ into youth work in ghettos. Think of addicts whom Christ has redeemed from the roller coaster of the drug scene to a spiritual trip which never ends!

Bob Dylan had a song called "Blowin' in the Wind." Its theme was a sad lament for man's inhumanity to man. How many years must a mountain exist before it's washed to the sea? And how many years must some people exist before they're allowed to be free? To these questions he can only reply cryptically that the answer is "blowin' in the wind."

A Christian university student has written another version of this ballad:
> "How many miles will a people tread
> Before they lift up their eyes?

How many tears will they shed as they go
Before they turn to their Christ?
How many deaths will they die alone,
Before they find new life?
The Spirit of God is blowin' in the wind,
The answer *is* blowin' in the wind!"

On the day of Pentecost that "strong driving wind" of God came upon the first Christians and "they were all filled with the Holy Spirit and began to speak in other tongues, as the (Holy) Spirit gave them (power of) utterance" (Acts 2:4, RSV). God communicated revolutionary power through a revolutionary community.

Here, I must confess, I come to my biggest question mark, and perhaps yours. How does the Church — especially the local church and its evangelistic program — fit into God's revolution? If we take the New Testament seriously, evangelism apart from the church is a contradiction. The Lord added to the church daily such as were being saved, says Acts 2:47. Yet we all realize that the church, as we know it, is often our biggest hang-up in evangelism. There is a widespread disillusionment, almost disgust, with the church. The brightest and most sensitive of our youth too often turn from the church, accusing us of having as our theme song, "I Believe in Yesterday," and of being irrelevant to the realities of the 20th century. The radical activists would scuttle the church and say, "Get into the world where the action is." Evangelicals have often taken the same route. Feeling bottle-necked by the apathy of certain churches they simply by-pass them and channel their evangelistic concern through a host of specialized organizations. God has blessed these efforts, but sadly there has been an unhealthy sense of rivalry, on occasion, between these movements and pastors and churches.

It is no adequate response to this age of revolution to turn the Church's evangelistic responsibility completely over to specialists. Too often we have talked of missions and evangelism as if they were adjuncts of the Church's life, optional activities to be supported by those who are interested in that sort of thing. In truth, mission and evangelism are the heartbeat of the Church, for the Church lives by the Spirit of her Lord who said, "As my Father sent me into the world, so send I you" (see John 20:21). When the Church ceases to evangelize, she ceases to live. We need to wrestle with the question of what sudden and radical change is needed so the churches themselves can be the agents of revolutionary evangelism. The issue is not primarily one of numbers. We can expect that the Christian church will always be a minority movement, as Jesus predicted. So we must measure evangelistic success by the quality as well as the number of the converts. Could anyone have predicted that the tiny handful of disciples at Pentecost would eventually conquer the mighty Roman Empire? There were only 120 of them, among an estimated 4 million Jews in Palestine alone. That's a ratio of 1 to 33,000. It's as if we here at this Congress were all the believers in the United States! So-called "minority movements have always turned out to be the most crucial . . . for they cast the shadow of the future" (Sydney Harris). Really, the crucial issue is not "How big is the church?" but "What is the church?"

In the Bible, the basic idea of the church is not buildings, or programs, or budgets, but "people" — God's redeemed people. At the very beginning of Jesus' ministry His strategy was to gather a group of men who would continue, deepen, and spread His work. Out of all His followers He chose twelve into whom He could pour His life. What distinguished these men? First, they had a personal commitment *to* Christ. Mark 3 tells us that Jesus "called . . . those whom he desired; and they *came to him*." Second, they had a unique fellowship *in* Christ. They included men of different temperaments like impetuous Peter and quiet John, and of varied political persuasions, like Simon the Zealot, a member of the resistance, and Matthew who worked for the Roman forces of occupation. Before they met Jesus, Simon would gladly have slit Matthew's throat! But when Christ accepted them they accepted each other. Third, they had a clear mission *for* Christ. Jesus called them to "be with Him" in personal fellowship, so Mark says, but also to "be sent out to preach and . . . cast out demons," to make Christ known by word and deed (Mark 3:13–15).

If the church today is to be the agent of revolutionary evangelism, we must be clear that by the church we mean those who have made a personal commitment to Christ. You can train people to be evangelists who have a motivation to share Christ. But if people lack this motivation no amount of training will help. What such people need is an encounter with Christ. At this Congress we ought to be considering seriously the question of what it means to have "conversion within the church." Why do so many students seem to abandon their faith when they go to college? Why do so many couples stop attending church when they move to a new city? And how do we help people with a second-hand faith really to come alive in Christ?

It's also essential that the Church be able to give a convincing demonstration of fellowship in Christ. Four hundred thousand young people went in mid-August to a music fair at Bethel, New York. Psychoanalyst Rollo May says that event "showed the tremendous hunger, need and yearning for community on the part of youth." Can these people find in your church and mine the thing that drove them to Max Yasgur's farm, the real belonging they were seeking? Are our churches "Bethels" where people are accepted and known as persons, whatever their bank account, or the color of their skin, or the length of their hair? One night at the New York Crusade I looked down the row where I was sitting on the platform. On one side of me was a black friend and an Italian. On the other side was a Jewish Christian. And I thought: this is what the church should be— the place where black is beautiful, and brown is beautiful, and even white is beautiful — in Christ!

Then we also must understand that the whole church has a mission for Christ. By loving fellowship, compassionate service, patient suffering, and by sharing the good news of the Gospel, every Christian has a responsibility to make Christ known. Will we take in our churches whatever radical changes are necessary to mobilize the entire membership for continuous evangelism?

Let me make two specific suggestions at this point. If our churches are to become committed, caring, witnessing fellowships then it will take at least:

1. A revolution in our patterns of ministry. All of us, pastors, teachers, evangelists, and laymen are going to have to understand that the church cannot afford to be made up of many spectators who pay and watch a few specialists do the work of evangelism. We pastors and evangelists must see that we are not to do all the work. We are coaches. Our job is to build an evangelistic team, starting with the leadership.

What I am saying here is a commonplace. But the thing that concerns me is how few churches are doing anything about it! How many churches have a specific training program to teach their people how to give away their faith? Does yours? Why not? When are you going to start? How many of us pastors and evangelists are choosing twelve men as Jesus did, or even one or two, and equipping them for the work? How many of you laymen are actually *insisting* that your pastor turn over some of his tasks to others in order that he may give you this kind of training?

2. It will take a revolution in the structures of our church life. Jesus preached to the great crowds; He also poured His life into twelve men. In a mass society I believe there will be an increasing place for mass evangelism. The 400,000 youth at Bethel showed that it takes mass gatherings to make people understand. But our emphasis will also have to be on small, intimate fellowships, or else people will get lost in the crowd. Inter-Varsity Christian Fellowship recently made a depth study of the effect size had on its college chapters. They found that once a campus group passed 30, there was actually a decrease in its evangelistic outreach. In a smaller group everyone had a chance to participate. But as the groups grew in size the sense of involvement was lost.

I wonder if this doesn't point up a real lesson for the churches? Small groups aren't cure-alls. In fact, without adequate spiritual leadership they can encounter serious problems. But I suggest that the church of the future may well be made up of many such small groups. They will pray, and study, and share their problems, and encourage each other in witness and service. One group might be made up of young couples; another of social workers; a third of Apollo astronauts; a fourth of converted hippies and motorbikers; a fifth of retired folk. All would come together on the Lord's day to break bread together, to sing joyous songs of celebration together, to listen together to God's Word, to share testimony of God at work through their lives, and then to scatter for another week of witness.

God's revolutionary power was released through the church in *revolutionary action*. Luke opens the book of Acts by saying, "In the first book . . . I have dealt with all that Jesus began to do and teach" (Acts 1:1, RSV). He implies that Jesus continued "to do and teach" through those He left behind. This dynamic combination of deed and word characterized the apostles. Their words acted and their actions spoke! Acts is full of action verbs: they prayed, they spoke, they healed, they gave their testimony, they sold their goods, they went about preaching. So we need to match our words with our deeds, and our deeds with our words. God will judge us and this Congress by whether we let our convictions be translated into revolutionary action.

This must begin with witnessing where we are ("in Jerusalem") and doing what we already know. Perhaps the first test of whether we are willing to be God's men will be right here in Minneapolis this week! If God is speaking to us then we ought to be speaking to men — to cab drivers, and waiters and maids in the hotels, and friends we eat with, and people we meet on the street. Will Minneapolis know by Friday that God's revolution is going on?

Revolutionary action in evangelism will mean breaking some new ground. It will mean acting with other Christians from other churches. Our task is to confront everyone with the Gospel, and no one church can accomplish that job. Think what it would mean in your neighborhood if the Baptist, and the Presbyterian, and the Lutheran, and the Bible church sent out teams of visitors to say, "We've come from all these churches to ask you to receive our Lord into your life and follow Him in whichever of our churches He leads you!"

Revolutionary action in evangelism will mean taking the message to people *where they are*. According to an old saying, the church should be "in the world but not of it." Well, I believe that evangelism should always be *of* the church but not always *in* it! Jesus preached on farms, by the roadside, in boats, at dinner parties in the homes of sinners. Those who are really touching people for Christ today are largely following His pattern. I think of Billy Graham going on the Mike Douglas and Johnny Carson shows to make "sinner contact." I think of the inner city "block parties" put on by the Cross-Counter work in Newark. A street is blocked off. Fried chicken is served. People eat and sing together. Then a man, chained to a wall, is dramatically released by a key labeled "love power," and tells the crowd how Christ has set him free.

The local church can take the Gospel "where the people are." Why don't you consider buying spots on the football game on Sunday afternoon? or having your choir put on its next Christmas program in the shopping mall? or renting a theater for your next series of evangelistic meetings?

Revolutionary evangelism will mean taking the Gospel to revolutionary people. Most of our evangelism involves reaching the family and friends of those who are already Christians. Usually these are middle-class, respectable citizens. They need Christ! But meanwhile, we have to think about the "sub-cultures." Is anybody reaching out to the hippies in your town? the student radicals? the ghettos? the intellectuals? the motorcycle crowd? the rock crowd? the swingers in the apartments? Relating to these people will mean praying that God will call some Christians to be missionaries to these "sub-cultures" just as we send missionaries to Brazil or Thailand.

Revolutionary evangelism will mean earning the right to speak to lives bruised and battered by social upheaval. Can the Gospel win a hearing, for example, in the urban ghettos, where militants wear buttons saying, "I hate Jesus," and where the Black Muslims say that Christianity is "whitey's" religion?

I asked this question this summer of several men who are giving their lives to the Gospel in New York's ghettos. Each of them agreed, *love is the key*. One said, "It's not until love is felt that the message is heard."

Evangelism must be love with flesh on, what Bill Milliken calls "tough love." We must echo Amos as well as Paul, Micah as well as Peter. Our message has got to combine the prophets, who called for repentance and justice, with the apostles, who called for repentance and faith in Jesus Christ.

What I'm saying boils down to this: As Christians we have to be concerned both for love and justice. Love goes beyond justice, and only the saving power of Jesus Christ can produce real love. But love is not a substitute for justice, and since not all men are or will be converted to Christ, and since even we Christians have imperfect love, we have a responsibility to seek justice in society. A Christian politician who seeks to pass laws that create guidelines for justice is doing God's work just as truly as a Christian pastor who seeks to win the lost to Christ.

William Wilberforce was converted to Christ as a young man in England. Then God put within his heart a burning passion to abolish the slave trade, and Wilberforce went on a campaign to wipe out the evil not only by preaching the Gospel but also by fierce debate and political action. Such action should not be confused with evangelism. Neither should it be separated from it.

Please note carefully: I am not saying that we can build a perfect world by our efforts. We can make some things better, but the new world will not come until Christ returns. Nor am I saying that the Church should stop giving priority to evangelism and become a political lobby. What I am saying is that God wants to give through our lives as Christians a kind of preview, an advance demonstration, of the love and peace and justice which will mark His eternal kingdom. Then, when from a platform of love in action we ask men to be reconciled to God, the Church's message will sound with the ring of truth.

Now let's stop and think what we have seen today: the revolutionary God who is shaking all things, and releasing His revolutionary power through

His revolutionary people, in revolutionary action. The sweep of God's work takes my very breath away. It makes me ask, how can I be a revolutionary for Christ when God's plan is so big and my strength is so small? I am much more like Snoopy, daydreaming on top of the dog house about fighting the Red Baron, than I am a daring revolutionary. I bow my head in shame when I contrast the tame Christian I am with the bold Christian I should be.

Is what we have been talking about "mission impossible"? Remember that Israel's slogan is, "A nation of unlimited impossibilities." Should that be less true of Christ's people in a day of such great challenge?

Are the demands too great? A leader of Students for a Democratic Society recently said, "For S.D.S. people there is no summer vacation. We see ourselves working 18 hours a day forever. We're in this for a lifetime." Dare we have less of a reckless, joyful abandonment to the revolution of our God?

When our lives and our churches fail to meet God's revolutionary expectations, what has gone wrong? Is it not that we have failed to let the Holy Spirit, the master agent of God's strategy, have control?

God's revolution is going to go on, with or without you and me. But I don't want to get left behind. So this is my prayer:

LORD, START A REVOLUTION, AND START IT IN ME!

Is it your prayer, too?

And this, from Ezekiel 21:27, is God sovereign answer:

"I WILL OVERTURN, OVERTURN, OVERTURN . . . UNTIL HE COME WHOSE RIGHT IT IS; AND I WILL GIVE IT HIM!"

EVANGELISM AND THE DAY OF REVOLUTION

Rev. Nelson W. Trout

I trust that the theme of evangelism and the day of revolution does not suggest that revolutions are categorically evil. Another way of saying the same thing is to suggest that evangelism and our day of revolution are antithetical. It is unfortunate if we assume that evangelism has to be on the opposite side of every revolution.

In the picture "The Road Sign of a Merry-go-round" there's a poignant line. That line goes like this, "What is important, God, is how you dwell on the earth." Dr. Bruce Boston in his article in the July issue of "Theology Today," says, "There is an intricate relationship between revelation and revolution." He suggests in support of this thesis that revelation must be seen as a function of revolution and he uses as a basis of support here Isaiah 43:18–19, "Remember not the former things, nor consider the things of old. Behold, I am doing a new thing; now it springs forth; do you not perceive it?"

Now this last question is the critical question. Do you see what God is doing on the earth? Do you see in the revolutions of our day that God is doing His thing? If we do not see it, then we have nothing to say.

Evangelism does not have its own message. It merely proclaims what God has done and is still doing.

Dr. Boston asserts, and I agree with him, "In historical events the presence of God infringes upon man's experience of himself, moves him beyond that experience, and pushes him toward the future." Such movement necessarily implies change, and we will argue revolution. Yahweh is the one who brings things to pass, the creator, the performer of His promises. It is Yahweh who stands over against tyranny.

There is a form of piety which is more at home with the status quo than it is with the experience of change.

The World Council of Churches suggested that for the immediate future it would be addressing itself to the consideration of man in nature and in history. The Commission felt that to deal with man in nature and in history, it would be imperative to talk about the way man experiences change. The Commission asserted that modern man is not necessarily like his predecessor, Biblical man. The two differ essentially in the way they understand their environment and in the way they understand themselves in their relationship to that environment.

THE REV. NELSON W. TROUT, Commission on Evangelism, Urban Evangelism, American Lutheran Church, Minneapolis, Minnesota.

For centuries men have experienced the world of nature as static, holy orders created and guaranteed by God. And in this kind of system God is in trouble too if He does anything new. So it seems that God in this kind of system becomes one who maintains law and order. I just threw that in.

God becomes the keeper of a status quo. He keeps things the way they are. But modern man knows full well that he is capable and responsible for mastering and ordering his world in the interest of human progress.

I assert here that the church, as a human institution, is not bound by its Lord to sanctify forms or structures — for every sanctified structure is still under the judgment of God.

Now we, the church, are in trouble today, because our proprieties are threatened with the advent of the new. The person who has difficulty with the new is not only uncomfortable with it, but he is preoccupied with that which is old just because it is old. Therefore he is suffering with what we call an addiction to the way things are. Because of this attitude in the church there is an increasing discontent, on the part of the less addicted, with the efforts of some to confine the new wine of the Gospel in the old skins of tradition and religious experience. The cry has gone across the church, "See what God is doing, and for God's sake give God credit for what He is doing."

I would have liked, with all due respect to the message that we heard today — and I certainly heard the Gospel and I thank God for it — to have had that message in a capsule. I would have liked to have taken it with me three days ago in this city which I have made my home, when I picked up a telephone and called a real estate lady and asked her about the availability of a certain home. The lady told me that home was available. Then I said to her, "Look, lady, this morning I didn't feel like being insulted, and tomorrow morning when I look at that house I don't want to be either, and I don't want you to be insulted either. I'm a black man. Am I going to have any trouble looking at that house?" The lady said, "What do you mean? I don't operate like that." I said, "What about the lady who's going to sell the house?" She said, "Oh, yes, there are some problems like that." She said, "I will call you back." In 15 minutes she called me back and this is what she had to say, "I have to be very frank with you, Reverend Trout. Are you going to move into our neighborhood and bring some more with you?"

I would have liked to have had that message that we heard because you see, when I got there the lady who owned the house said, "I am a good Lutheran and Dr. So and So lives down the street. He's our pastor." It's in this kind of world that the Gospel is not happening. We can keep saying it, and saying it, and saying it, but until Christ indwells us, we're in sad trouble.

We don't impress the black militants or anybody else with the accuracy of our theology. The only thing they understand is the person who is willing to stand where they stand, to sit where they sit, and ultimately to die where they have to die.

I realize that the church is a human institution, and as a human institution is subject to all the foibles and the limitations that are indigenous to life. But, for God's sake, let us be honest with the world and say that we are human beings, that we struggle to do the right thing, but that we have not yet reached perfection.

At no place can the church be adequately defined in terms of its excellent performance in evangelism, or stewardship, or charity, or the involvement of its youth or young people. At no place is the church adequately defined in terms of these. Somehow or another, above all of these, as commendable as they may be, God's mission imposes upon us a greater risk. It demands exposure to hurt, to the new demands that the world places upon the church, it faces us in the direction of impossible odds. It demands of us what God demanded of Abraham, to get out of our country, for God Himself will show us a country that He will give us.

Oh, I have traveled the length and the breadth of this country and I have been in the basements of many churches where I have been face to face with the lack of the indwelling of Christ in people in our churches. And I would say to you, my brethren, for God's sake, give the black ministers a place to stand today. We're still talking about the same Jesus Christ but we have lost our people and everybody else, because we cannot find integrity in the church. Give us a place to stand.

Never have I been so torn up in my mind as I am today, because I read the same Bible, and I preach the same Gospel, but my people aren't interested any more, because the church has failed to do what it says so well it is called to do. Here in America the greatest need for revival and renewal in the life of the church faces the leaders of the church with a great challenge to see that the indwelling takes place in people's life. It is certainly dramatized in the presence of racism in the church. And I have a friend in Chicago who says, "There is no doubt about it. Very few churches have ever sat in judgment on racism, not really for real."

I stood right here at this platform several months ago and addressed a congregation of women, 8,000 people, on the theme "Light in Dark Places." There were six black people here and I brought them. They were my family and I said to myself, "The theme should have been 'Black in White Places.' " It would have been more relevant.

Dr. Lueke has summarized, I think very well, what is wrong with evangelism in the church today in his Lenten booklet entitled *Violent Sleep*. Dr. Lueke says, "Like Jonah we have gone down into the bottom of the ship, and we haven't just fallen asleep, we have *gone* to sleep. Not against our brother but against God."

If these things that I am saying are true, can it account for the fact that most of our people are willing to sacrifice the new wine of the Gospel for the old skins of tradition and custom? And why is it that we insist on confining the explosive dynamics of the Gospel within the narrow confines of our prejudices?

What is happening, I think, in too many confirmation classes, in too many sermons, is what Bruce Cronbeck talks about, when he says that we have in an appalling sense succeeded in making Christianity a propositional matter and in doing so we have made it linear. And because of this linear nature of our Christian practice, we manage to escape so many of the tensions and the concerns that are part and parcel of life.

It may so happen that in the pursuit of the specific spiritual goals that we set for ourselves, namely personal holiness, we may ignore the call of Christ to participate with Him in His suffering in the world. We may not hear His call to wait with Him in Gethsemane.

Have we done everything we can do to make the Gospel appealing, to make it relevant? It seems to me that the greatest source of renewal will come to the church as it finds new power in a proper understanding of the indwelling of Christ. And at this time in our life we must say that the indwelling is being systematically aborted. People won't let Jesus Christ happen. People want to keep Christ impaled against the Cross so that they'll have some object of worship. Jesus Christ wants to get down off the Cross. He's got work to do in the market place and He wants to get on with His revolution.

The question that we must be asking today, the kind of question that we must put before people today, isn't, "Who was Joshua?" or, "Do you love Jesus?" but, "Are you ready to be offered upon the altar of the world's needs?" This is the question.

Brethren, finally we are committed to a ministry of renewal. It should be a source of encouragement to note what God says in His Word, "Behold, *I* make all things new." It is God who will turn our brokenness into indivisible unity. It is God who will turn our sacrifices of death into the celebrations of life. It is God who will change the nature of the lamb and the lion so that they can lie down together. It is God who turns our swords into plowshares and our spears into pruning hooks. It is God who causes justice to flow down like water and righteousness like an ever-flowing stream.

As you and I face the future, let us vow that we will cross the cataracts of time and learn to live with discontinuity, being committed to Jesus Christ, who though He leads us into green pastures and beside still waters, will also lead us into the valley of the shadow. But even here we need not be afraid, for God, in a revolutionary way, promises to make all things new.

THE CHURCH AND THE JOURNEY INWARD

Dr. Paul S. Rees

The world of the West has made whirl its king, technology its trust, and externals its impassioned preoccupation. If there is a certain rhetorical overkill in that assertion, it nevertheless has enough going for it to be startlingly contemporary. When Professor Pitirim Sorokin was active at Harvard, he saw it coming, and branded ours a "sensate culture."

To anyone wishing to have that phrase spelled out in a fashion suited to plebeians, Professor Sorokin might have called to his aid a zingy sort of rhyme that appeared in the lately-deceased *Saturday Evening Post*:

> "This is the age
> Of the half-read page
> And the quick hash
> And the mad dash
> The bright night
> With the nerves tight
> The plane hop
> With the brief stop
> The lamp tan
> In a short span
> The Big Shot
> In a good spot
> And the brain strain
> And the heart pain
> And the catnaps
> Till the spring snaps
> And the fun's done."

Thus, speaking culturally and not Christianly, the journey outward, spaceward, and every-where-ward has become so obsessively popular that the journey inward has been turned into a mode of travel as antiquated as trolley cars or, if not quite that, as much on the decline as passenger trains in the age of jets. One is reminded of the swift exchange between two prominent, well-respected Englishmen years ago. One said, "How is it with your soul?" To which his friend replied, "I have been so busy I have forgotten that I had a soul."

"But that is society writ large," we say. (The "we" here is the beloved pronoun for pious, or semi-pious, or pseudo-pious churchmen who

DR. PAUL S. REES, Vice-President, World Vision International, Inc.

have the eyes of a lynx when it comes to looking around and finding a whipping boy on whom to pour the indignant energies of their own refused guilt.)

For example, think of the advocates of the voguish phrase "worldly holiness." (The phrase, incidentally, is capable of being interpreted in such a way that it is neither contradictory nor unbiblical.) Most of its employers, however, are radicals of the theological Left for whom the disciplines of private prayer and the stated forms of public worship are alike anathema. Douglas Steere, in his *On Beginning From Within*, says that they remind him of the gobbledegook he was once handed by a man who was a drop-out from the school of prayer. Said he, "The more I pray, the less I pray; and the less I pray, the more I pray." "This," says Steere, "was meant to indicate an advanced state of spirituality where all life now took the place of specific prayers." "Such persons," he goes on to observe, "point to works, generous philanthropy, social reforms, or selfless devotion to scientific research, and insist that these are the devotional exercises of the modern Christian, and that they are infinitely more acceptable to God than the fat-ram sacrifices of private and public prayer." [1]

Add to this confusion the tendency of the Barthians to over-objectify the Christian faith, and the proneness of conservative evangelicals to pay nothing more than lip-service to the disciplines that deepen and enrich "the life of God in the soul of man," and you have a state of affairs that bodes anything but good for the health of evangelism. The evangelistic impact upon those who are "without," as St. Paul puts it, is blunted by the non-evangelical impoverishment of those who are within. If candor is to rule us, we must say that the road of the inward journey is crying out for more travelers.

Let's do a reverse spin on the wheel of time. We shall call up twin pictures — one from the New Testament, one from the Old. They are differently focused, differently framed. Yet each has a bearing on the matter with which we are here engaged. The central figure in each instance is called, interestingly enough, "Son of man."

First, the New Testament picture. The frame is double. One is night; one is day. One is public; one is private. One is open; one is hidden.

Picture Jesus before Pilate: the irritated, anxiety-ridden, resentful judge . . . the cool, callous soldiers . . . the crafty, determined accusers . . . the howling, embittered crowd. Picture Jesus, condemned and forsaken, bearing His cross on the lonely trek to the edge of the city for execution. Picture Him hanging from the pitiless nails, dying in an agony that masks His victory, rising again in a predicted triumph that forever unveiled that victory, and, through the Holy Spirit in His elect people, moving

[1] Douglas Steere, *On Beginning From Within*, p. 88 (Harper & Row, New York, 1964).

redemptively through history. That, surely and incomparably, is the journey *outward*.

Now picture a scene that preceded all of this. The locale: Gethsemane. The engagement: between two wills — the Father's and the Son's. The issue: the final sorting out of alternatives and costs in the divine act of man's redemption ("If it be possible, let this cup pass"). The outcome: the unambiguous blending of the two wills, the intensity of the resolution ("Shall I not drink the cup which the Father has given me?") met and matched by the increase of the power ("And there appeared to Him an angel from heaven, strengthening Him.") to go through with it.

What we have here, surely, is the journey *inward*.

The outward and the inward! They belong together, like the alternating beats of the heart. They belong together not because they are identical but because they are inseparably complemental.

So we learn from the life and death of the "Son of man" who is called Jesus.

Turn now and look at another "son of man" — called Ezekiel. Ezekiel is possibly the most underrated of Israel's prophets. To some, he appears weirdly incomprehensible. To others, he appears more legalistic than Isaiah, more rigid than Jeremiah. To most readers he seems difficult and remote. And certainly it is highly doubtful if the prestige to which Ezekiel is entitled has been helped in the least by the highly fanciful and amusing Negro spiritual in which the intriguing rhythm has "The toe-bone connected to the foot-bone, and the foot-bone connected to the heel-bone," etc., etc.

Yet in the multitude of his detractors and his neglecters Ezekiel is not without his advocates. Dr. Andrew Blackwood, Jr., is one of them. He has written a substantial and worthy volume called *Ezekiel: Prophecy of Hope*, in which he says: "Ezekiel is an existentialist. He lives his truth. He knows God, not in abstraction from the tensions and heartaches of existence, but in the midst of the struggle." [2]

How then, we may ask, does Ezekiel's career as a servant of God and of the people stand related to our theme?

For this man, the journey outward was that of a man who had to go among the exiled people of Judah with word and spectacle that spoke of God's judgment and mercy. It included, moreover, an exercise in prophetic confrontation with Gentile nations and the heads of nations. It covered more than twenty years of burden, courage, and capacity for identification with others.

But what of the journey inward? It is precisely on this that we wish to dwell. Consider the situation: thousands of Judeans transported to Babylon following Nebuchadnezzar's successful siege against Jerusa-

[2] Andrew Blackwood, Jr., *Ezekiel: Prophecy of Hope*, p. 24 (Baker Book House, Grand Rapids, 1965).

lem . . . some of the captives better off than others . . . Ezekiel, perhaps 25 years of age, living in comparative comfort . . . Jerusalem conquered but not destroyed . . . the anxieties and queries of these exiles
over the fate of their beloved city . . . and the "elders" beginning to ply
Ezekiel with questions as to the future — their own and that of the country-
men they have left behind.

For this young seer, important public business lies just ahead. But,
before it commences, the living God will have some very personal business with the prophet. The first three chapters of his book provide us
with the data we need. First comes a vision — shot through with strange
forms and mystic symbols — in which the majesty, sovereignty, mystery,
and glory of God are powerfully impressed upon him. That is given in
chapter 1. In chapter 2 we have the combination of divine *directive* and
divine *dynamic* by which Ezekiel is put on his feet and set toward the
task that lies before him: "Son of man, stand upon your feet, and I will
speak with you" (v. 1) — the *directive*; and "when he spoke to me, the
Spirit entered into me and set me upon my feet" (v. 2) — the *dynamic*.

But the journey inward carries him further. The report of it sounds at
first as if it were descriptive of the journey outward, which it is in part —
but only in part. Listen to the prophet's witness: "The Spirit lifted me up
and took me away, and I went in bitterness in the heat of my spirit, the
hand of the Lord being strong upon me; and I came to the exiles at Tela-
bib, who dwelt by the river Chebar. And I sat there overwhelmed among
them seven days" (3:14, 15, RSV). The King James version is more
terse and trenchant: "I sat where they sat, and remained there astonished
among them seven days."

No counseling here. Not yet. No preaching. No prophesying. No con-
demning. No comforting. No mounting of the public platform. Instead, the
cracking open of one man's interior capacity for identification with others
and their needs and concerns.

For years I have traveled in and out of the Hawaiian Islands —
nearly always swiftly in and swiftly out. I have set foot on only three of
the islands; never, for example on the island of Molokai. Yet never, I
think, has the captain of an airliner told us where we passengers might
look to see this smaller island without my suddenly associating another
name with Molokai: Molokai/Damien . . . Molokai/Damien. Many of
you will instantly guess the reason for that mental association. Father Damien
working in Christ's name among the lepers quartered there — respected,
appreciated, even loved. Then came the discovery that he himself had
contracted leprosy. And the arrival of that day when, in his sermons, he
began saying, "We lepers"! And, with that, a new note of reality, a
new invisible bond between him and those he was wooing to Christ, with
Christ's own love and empathy.

Henry Drummond, the scholar evangelist, was once called the "prince of buttonholers," since he was forever engaging people personally about the meaning of life in Christ. Yet he was never a nagger, never a purveyor of evangelical clichés, never a slave of those evangelistic techniques by means of which you become a soul-winner "in four easy lessons," never the statistically-minded huntsman avidly waiting to notch another "victim" on the handle of his evangelistic pistol. What then? Sir George Adam Smith said that trying to describe his presence, his spirit, and his manner would be like trying to describe a perfume. Drummond's own remarks about effective personal evangelism are an enlightening, albeit unconscious, commentary on his way of relating to people:

> To fascinate the unit . . . by a mysterious
> sympathy . . . To draw souls one by one . . . and
> steal from them the secret of their lives. . .
> To get a man to appreciate God's ideal for
> him, and to introduce him to himself — this
> is the spiritual science which is most difficult
> to acquire and so hard to practice.[3]

I wish to underline the claim that this ability, this developing capacity to identify with others, however *outer* may be the circumstances of its exercise, is part of the *inner* furnishing that makes us convincing transmitters of the Gospel. "I sat where they sat."

Let me try now to gather up some of the values that accrue to us as we reflect upon our theme in the light of the example set before us by Ezekiel, whom Dr. Blackwood has called "the other son of man."

For one thing, the phrase "journey inward" is *symbolically felicitous*. The noun speaks of mobility, advance, pilgrimage; the adjective speaks of invisibility, hiddenness, depth. All greatness of person is *iceberg* greatness — for every measure of it that appears in the open, there are five measures beneath the surface.

Look across our land today. Wherever you find individuals, or groups, or congregations undergoing one of God's springtimes, you will find, of course, a variety of effects. No two cases are exactly alike. Yet I think it is right, even as I think it is significant, to say that they have one thing in common: the changes that are taking place — the rusty traditions that are being either broken or brightened, the new vitalities and sensitivities that are surfacing, the old attitudes that are being replaced, the ruptured relationships that are being healed — are all being undergirded through exercises and disciplines that belong to the interior life. Is it the East Harlem Protestant Parish in New York; or the Church of our Savior in Washington; or, also in Washington, Fourth Presbyterian Church; or First Methodist Church, Germantown, Pennsylvania; or the "Knoxville Ex-

---

[3] Cuthbert Lennox, *Henry Drummond*, p. 22 (Andrew Melrose, London, 1901).

periment" in Tennessee; or St. Stephen's Episcopal Church in Houston; or the First Church of the Nazarene in Pasadena, California, to name only some out of many? Whatever new ground is being visibly broken has beneath it a subsoil of rediscovered prayer vitality, new dimensions of relevance and power in the Bible, new applications of forgotten or neglected ways to sanctity and integrity of living.

Frederick W. Faber, a 19th century saint — so saintly that not even the Pope could possibly *un*canonize him — once wrote these stabbing staccato lines:

> Look out to God,
> Love His glory,
> Hate yourself,
> And be simple,
> And you will shine,
> Fortunately without knowing it
> Or thinking of it,
> With a Christlike splendour,
> Wherever you go
> And whatever you do. [4]

If life — personal or corporate — has no inner growing edge, it will have no outer cutting edge. Ezekiel found it so. So shall we.

Our second observation is less exhilarating. If the "journey inward" is symbolically felicitous, it is at the same time *understandably hazardous*. Was this not one of the lessons that Ezekiel had to be taught — the lesson that private vision, however authentic, is usually less costly than practical action? At the end of chapter 1 we find the young prophetic hopeful prostrated by the splendor of the divine mystery and glory to which he has been exposed. How different is the opening of chapter 2: "Son of man, stand upon thy feet" (v. 1)!

If the journey inward has the effect of laying us low, shattering us, silencing our easy glibness, decontaminating us where pride has poisoned us and self-sufficiency has infected us, all the better. Some of us who are called leaders may have thought we were growing when we were only swelling! Ezekiel's testimony, "I fell upon my face" (1:28), may well be ours. It's a good place to *land*, but it's no place to *lie*. "Son of man, stand upon your feet." There's a job to be done. There's a mission to be carried out. There's a burden to be carried.

It will be costly, sweaty business. Let's get on with it!

Come with me to England and, if you who are free churchmen, like myself, will overcome your reluctance, I should like to take you to the Church of England. We are in the diocese of Coventry. The year is 1959.

---

[4] Ralph Turnbull, *A Minister's Obstacles*, p. 169 (Fleming H. Revell Company, Westwood, New Jersey, 1964).

The Cathedral of Coventry, which one morning in World War II lay in ruins from German bombs, was rising again, bit by bit. Three years hence, from 1959, it would be ready for dedication. Cuthbert Bardsley, chief shepherd and ecclesiastical officer of the diocese, was, and is, a man of prayer. If you say that such a comment is pointless, since all Anglican bishops are men of prayer, I must remind you that there are bishops who live in the depths of prayer. If you doubt that, I must conclude that you have never read Bishop John Robinson's *Honest to God*.[5]

Bishop Bardsley, in his waiting on God, became convinced that to have a physically-rebuilt cathedral without a spiritually-renewed diocese would simply be to substitute "pomp and circumstance" for Christian reality. So he gave to a young clergyman by the name of Stephen Verney the title and task of "Diocesan Missioner," or what most of us, in our free church circles, would call "Conference Evangelist." He began by visiting all the "chapters," or districts, of the diocese, gathering the clergy in small groups. "We very soon came to see," says Verney, "that what God wanted was not just a consecrated Cathedral, but a consecrated people living round it."

"And," he adds, "there followed quickly the second uncomfortable discovery, that if there was to be a consecrated people, it would have to begin with ourselves." So they decided to spend a long day together, raising questions (with God and themselves) and seeking answers. The day began with Holy Communion. After breakfast came Bible study, prayers, and silence. In the afternoon, out in the open, in a garden, came discussion. The agreed topic was: "What has God said to us? What does He want us to do — the clergy of 'Monks Kirby Chapter' of Coventry Diocese?" Nothing emerged with any clarity until an elderly member of the group said he believed they ought to meet like this "every week."

The others laughed. "How ludicrous," they thought, "busy parish leaders like ourselves getting together every week!" And for prayers, of all things! And reading the Bible together! And being silent together! And being open together — to God and to one another! Impossible!"

Yet when laughter subsided and reality was faced, those men sensed that God had spoken. His answer was "simple, obvious, yet revolutionary and costly: 'Meet weekly.'" Regarding that important moment Stephen Verney remarks, "They must do what they were told, for there is nothing more dangerous that to hear the word of God and not to do it."[6]

Shades of Ezekiel! The vision breaks upon us. We are down on our faces. Then comes the order: "Son of man, stand upon your feet!" And that is always a hazardous moment — where the journey inward begins

[5] John A. T. Robinson, *Honest to God*, Cf. pp. 19, 20 (SCM Press, London, 1963).
[6] Stephen Verney, *Fire in Coventry*, pp. 13, 14 (Fleming H. Revell Co., Westwood, New Jersey, 1964).

to face its alternating effect in the journey outward, where initial impressions, seriously sifted, meet their first test in even the smallest obediences.

If you have not read Stephen Verney's book *Fire in Coventry*, I shall momentarily leave you dangling in curiosity's mid-air while another facet of hazard claims our attention.

If one danger attending the inward journey is *unfulfilled impulse* and/or *emotion*, a second is that of *unhealthy self-containment*. This risk belongs to both forms of the journey — the private and the collective. On the private side, the contemplative outpourings of some of the more extreme mystics were horrifying to a man like John Wesley. Jakob Boehme for example, built an incredible structure of theology — Mr. Wesley would have called it theosophy — not out of the words and their meanings but out of the *syllables* of the Lord's Prayer in his German Bible. This exercise in futility is not the less nonsensical for being so eminently pious and self-assured. Unchecked subjectivism is the handmaiden of unwarranted presumption.

On the corporate side, too, despite the safeguard found in numbers, there are perils. A member of the National Committee for this Congress, a man who has had extensive experience with "small groups" seeking inner renewal and outer effectiveness, is Rev. Bruce Larson. In his recently published book *Living on the Growing Edge* he frankly states; "There is no magic in small groups. They can be as ingrown or lopsided as any local church, emphasizing only Bible study, *or* prayer, *or* sensitivity training in mental health, *or* action on social concerns." [7] Mention might be made of "charismatic groups" which, while proving salutary and liberating to some, have had the effect of making others distressingly judgmental and damagingly pharisaical.

By this time it should not be news to any of us that the journey inward, for us as for Ezekiel, is not free from risks or hazards. Yet the risks must be taken; and the hazards, thank God, can be surmounted.

We learn another thing from the case of Ezekiel: the inward journey, if it is to achieve its purpose, must be *honestly audacious*. The words, "Son of man, stand upon your feet," imply something more than a summons to action. They suggest the inward exercise that may be described as *tackling oneself before tackling others*. As Verney puts it in previously quoted phrasing, "We have to begin with ourselves."

Tackling ourselves is never easy. It is hardest of all when we carry about with us an image of ourselves as public figures. If there's a task to be performed, a problem to be solved, a mess to be cleaned up, we usually begin by trying to pin the responsibility on someone else. Or, if not that, by plunging headlong into the business at hand, with little concern for the question of whether *we* are fit to do anything or go anywhere. Pertinent

[7] Bruce Larson, *Living on the Growing Edge*, p. 23 (Zondervan Publishing House, Grand Rapids, 1968).

Biblical insights at this point find expression in such random passages as, "They made me keeper of the vineyards; but, my own vineyard I have not kept" (Song of Solomon 1:6 RSV), or "Restore to me the joy of thy salvation, and uphold me with a willing spirit. *Then* will I teach transgressors thy ways, and sinners will return to thee" (Psalm 51:12, 13, RSV), or "Take head unto *thyself*, and unto the doctrine" (1 Timothy 4:16).

When a man is in his own way, it is easy for him to think that everybody else is. That piece of remembrance should come repeatedly to all of us. It is a therapeutic exercise.

Involved in this brave tackling of ourselves is the honesty of *listening*. God said to Ezekiel, "I will speak with you" (2:1, RSV). But even a speaking God is grieved and thwarted unless He can find a listening man. Sometimes God is obliged to say, "I have called and you refused to listen" (Proverbs 1:24, RSV).

There is, however, another form of listening for which the inward journey should condition us. It is the listening that we find it hard to do *with one another*. This is notoriously true of persons or groups that have no natural bond of congeniality or identity. So we have all manner of pesky annoyances that fall under the head of the *generation gap*, or the *race gap*, or the *capital-labor gap*, or the *rich nations-poor nations gap*. And the plague of it all is that for every sensitive, teachable soul who wants to listen there are ten who want to talk.

Again we are reminded of that blessed audacity that Ezekiel exhibited when he went down among the most wretched of the Judean exiles and sat in listening silence for seven days. He was learning what some of us have never learned: that good communications do not as a rule begin with *our* speeches to others but with our receptivity to what *they* have to say to us. We work our oratorical powers until we are hoarse; we neglect our auditory powers until they atrophy.

Most people listen *selectively*. Some listen *negatively*. Too few listen *attentively*. We listen selectively when we tune in the stuff that confirms our prejudices, and we tune out the material that challenges or rebukes them. We listen negatively when our general predisposition is to find something wrong with almost everything that anyone else tries to tell us. We listen attentively when we try to put ourselves in the other person's (or the other group's) place, not necessarily committed to agree but committed to be open, and prepared if need be to make new decisions in response.

In 1950 the Chicago *Daily News* ran a social documentary series on teen-age youth and their parents. It was based on the results of a confidential survey made among 1,400 young people in five representative high schools. A quarter of the girls and a third of the boys thought their parents were "mostly swell." On the negative side there was a variety of gripes. One of the six or seven complaints ran like this: "They don't care or give you a chance to explain anything" . . . . "They are always right and don't respect you, but they want your respect" . . . . . "We can't give them our opinions, but they constantly criticize us."

When the parents of twenty years ago have had their day in court and unloaded all of their rebuttals, the stark fact remains that too many of us were not listening. Oh, we *heard* them all right — their jazzy music, their beer-lively parties, their version of laugh-ins as they competed in goldfish-swallowing, their roaring on the drag-strips. We *heard* them, but were we *listening*? Hearing may be little more than a physiological reaction; listening is a spiritual art.

And what of today — two decades later? Are we doing any better? Still we hear, and what we hear we don't like. We hear the marching, and the screaming, and the protesting, and the burning, and the four-lettering. We hear the bitter attacks on the "old crowd" that runs the country, runs the schools, runs the economy, runs the social caste system, runs the labor unions, runs the wars. And we match their screaming with ours. Theirs is frantic, often irrational, repeatedly destructive, sometimes cruel, and then again — in a negative sort of way — stunningly lucid, for they have at least gone mad about terribly real and vital issues, not about panty raids, goldfish-swallowing, and flag-pole sitting as did their predecessors a generation back. Our screaming is of course less a shriek and more an angry shout. "Law and order," we cry with an unctuousness that declaims the obvious, since law and order we must have, but with an unimaginative desperation that too often appears to have no real *listening* behind it.

And with *that* I have the joy of returning you to Coventry Diocese in England. Those ten clergymen of "Monks Kirby" district met every Monday on the understanding that at the end of three months they would take the measure of their situation and review their decision. Let Stephen Verney report:

> "But when three months were over, the position
> was so changed as to be hardly recognizable. The
> Chapter consisted no longer of a number of iso-
> lated parish priests, each battling on heroically
> alone. It had become a team of men who knew one
> another, cared about one another, belonged to one
> another, and, most important of all, had begun to
> admit to one another their weaknesses" (p.14).

So there was no turning back! Verney goes on:

> "About a year later, they had reached a
> point of brother love" (the inward journey,
> you see!) "where each man was allowing a
> sermon to be tape-recorded, and then played
> back to the others for their criticism" (p. 15)!

But even this was not the end of that audacious listening to which they gave themselves. The journey inward (as well as outward) was to carry them to a more advanced stage of courageous openness. Bishop Bardsley called a meeting of all the clergy of the diocese. He asked the Diocesan Missioner to make a report on what had been taking place in the clergy groups, and then to suggest further steps. Under the latter head, Verney proposed that from October to Easter there should be meetings of clergy and laity in small groups, a group for every three parishes and three laymen present for every clergyman. Looking at the notes he urged in presenting this proposal, Verney said that they read like this:

> "Get laity to tell us how they see the Church,
> and what needs doing. Listen before we talk.
> How can clergy and laity help one another?
> Get off our pedestals. Admit we are only on
> the threshold of understanding. Painful
> meeting necessary. Radical and revolutionary
> questions asked. Listen to criticism, accept
> and absorb it. Let lay perspective be re-
> vealed. Let the groups be open to the Spirit
> to make adventures (if led) in prayer and
> obedience" (p. 19).

The proposal was adopted, with only one dissenter vociferously objecting. He was a person who said that he was thoroughly annoyed by all this talk about clergymen "getting down off pedestals." Yet even he, before midnight, came to see that his objections sprang from his sense of insecurity — as do a lot of our objections on both sides of the clergy-laity line.

You will want to know what happened in this second stage of Coventry's inward journey, in which the experience of being honestly audacious was broadened to include the laymen (who in some instances were lay-ladies). Stephen Verney says that the three most appropriate descriptive words were "humility" . . . "love" . . . "prayer." He observed that where these three elements came dynamically together "the groups began exploding." The "humility" factor was often a shattering thing. One vicar was "physically in tears after a group meeting, because he had come to see how shallow had been his whole ministry up to that moment."

The first group to catch fire was in a "remote country district" where two of the vicars were elderly and the third, to use Verney's phrase, had "a groggy heart." "This was the last place in the world where you might have expected a religious revival." But even in so unpromising a situation the combination of brokenness, openness, and prayerfulness released God's miracle of renewal. "The lay people in this group," says Verney, "were so excited by what was happening that they summoned a public meeting. They hired a hall, and a band. The Anglican Dean of the district, hearing about it, got nervous, telephoned the office of the Diocesan Missioner, and said he feared things were "getting out of hand." To which Verney replied, "Out of whose hand?" "When the meeting took place," he goes on to say, "these laymen and women spoke simply about their rediscovery of the Christian faith, and those who had come to listen were moved by their words" (pp. 26, 27).

The journey inward, we must see, was beginning to find fulfillment in the journey outward. The audacity of listening was being followed, as it was with Ezekiel, by the audacity of speaking. Note the juxtaposition in chapters 2 and 3: "Son of man . . . I will speak with you" (2:1). "Son of man . . . speak with my words to them" (3:4).

Consider, finally, how this inward journey becomes *creatively momentous*. As it turns out, neither journey — the inward or the outward — can be worthily and workably made "on our own." We 20th century churchmen are not less likely to find it so than Ezekiel did. His witness at this point is more than suggestive. It is normative. Listen to him: "And he said to me, 'Son of man, stand upon your feet' . . . And when he spoke to me, the Spirit entered into me and set me upon my feet" (2:1, 2, RSV). (The word "spirit," you will have noticed, which is spelled with a small "s" in the King James Version, is, rightly in the view of many scholars, spelled with a capital "S" in the Revised Standard.)

It should be noted, moreover, that when Ezekiel refers to the Holy Spirit of God in the passage just quoted, he is not sharing with us some isolated and incidental insight. The reference is repeated, underscored, flung up into instructive prominence. Twice in the following chapter (vs. 12 and 14) he testifies, "The Spirit lifted me up." Or move on to chapter 11 and hear him say it again, "The Spirit lifted me up" (v. 1) . . . "The Spirit of the Lord fell upon me" (v. 5).

At the beginning of the 1930s the Christian Church celebrated the nineteen hundredth anniversary of Pentecost. Sadly, the observance was more of a celebration than a realization. I recall that at that time one of our leaders spoke of "the teaching on the Holy Spirit" as "the vaguest thing in the life of the Church." Our dilemma is fairly sharp: we can have dogmatic clarity that belies the mystery of the Holy Spirit, or we can have such complacency with the mystery that we are unconcerned about confessional clarity.

Professor Albert Outler has recently suggested that if we are wondering why a systematized doctrine of the Holy Spirit is a "low priority topic in classical theology," we shall find an answer in the fact that "it is the most easily abused of all the great Christian doctrines — by one or another of our human passions *to domesticate the divine or to become divine ourselves.*" [8] Pretensions to a new identity, in which the human becomes divine, go as far back as the second century, to an enthusiast like Montanus who, claiming to be the Paraclete, exclaimed: "I am the Father, the Word, and the Paraclete." [9]

Maximila, a female devotee of his, cried, "I am the word, and spirit, and power." [10]

As for Professor Outler's suggestion that the doctrine of the Spirit is abused when we try, in ways however subtle, to manipulate, or "domesticate," the divine, we should not forget how easy it has been for Christian groups, large and small, to build fences around the Holy Spirit. It has been too easy for some of them to pre-determine and pre-announce *how* He will work: whether with signs or without, whether with tongues or without, whether in certain ecclesiastical rites or independently of them, whether with the laying on of hands or without, whether by bishop's consecration or without, whether in *crises* or *processes* of personal experience. Confusion abounds and desire languishes. Controversy soars and hunger subsides.

And all the while the Church's living Head is saying: "You shall receive power when the Holy Spirit has come upon you; and you shall be my witnesses . . . to the end of the earth: (Acts 1:8, RSV).

With no attempt to "tell anybody off" or set anyone right, save as my poor words may be authenticated to you by the Scriptures of God and the Spirit of God, let me venture the claim that the three following observations are valid insights and highly relevant to this discussion:

1. The Holy Spirit is power *where* it counts for most — within. Remember David Reisman's distinction between people who are "other directed" and those who are "inner directed"? This inner-directedness reaches its deepest dimension when it becomes the work of the Holy Spirit in motivation and mastery. A disgusted citizen was protesting to his Congressman over a vote he had cast in which this constituent of his felt that he had traded principle for expediency. "But," said the Congressman in self-defense, "you don't understand what outside pressures I was under." "Outside pressures," retorted the angry citizen, "where were your *inside braces*?" Let that phrase be seized on behalf of the Holy Spirit: *He* is the Christian's "inside braces."

2. The Holy Spirit is power *for* what counts for most — Christlikeness. Remember St. Paul's prayer for the Ephesian Christians: that "he may grant you to be strengthened with might through his Spirit in the inner man." Note what immediately follows: "that Christ may dwell in your hearts through faith" (Ephesians 3:16,17, RSV). In Bishop Stephen

[8] Albert C. Outler, *New Theology No. 4*, p. 197 (Edited by Marty and Peerman, Macmillan, New York, 1967).

[9] Didymus, *De Trinitate III*, p. 41.

[10] Eusebius, *Ecclesiastical History, V*, p. 16.

Neill's *The Unfinished Task* there is a moving passage in which he tells us that in the part of India he knew best hundreds of foreign missionaries have worked through the years. Of these only two have an eminent and secure place in the memory of the Indian Church. Neither one was brilliant. Both rendered faithful service. Yet each is remembered for one quality in particular: "he was a saint." The Bishop follows with a sentence for the missionary that searches like an X-ray: "Unless he stands out, amidst the low level of devotion which is all too common in the Church, by a conspicuous and recognizable likeness to Christ, perhaps he would have done better to stay at home." [11] Whether this Christlikeness comes as sudden gift or slow growth (or a combination of both), what is certain is that it will never come apart from the sanctifying energies of the Holy Spirit.

3. The Holy Spirit is power *through* what counts for most — a self-surrendering trust. The language of the New Testament varies at this point. It may say, "Deny" yourself, and "follow me." It may say, "Yield yourselves." It may say, "Yield your members." It may say, "Present your bodies." However it speaks, the principle is the same: total self-surrender to the total ministry and mastery of the Holy Spirit. And let's not get hung up on that word "total." Not total *quantitatively* but *qualitatively.* The total *mutual* self-giving of a man and a woman at the marriage altar is never quantitative. It has to be worked out. There must be room within its terms for growth and discovery and testing. But it is qualitatively total there and then — "for better, for worse, until death do us part."

I like the words of the late Paul Scherer: "To take all that we are and have, and hand it over to God, may not be easy; but it can be done, and when it is done, the world has in it one less candidate for misery."

And I am turned inside out by the surgically piercing language of Meister Eckhart: "There are plenty to follow our Lord half-way, but not the other half. They will give up possessions, friends and honors, but it touches them too closely to disown themselves." [12]

After all, it is precisely at this point of surrender that the Holy Spirit's power begins coming through at high voltage.

Ye shall receive . . . power! Not ours, but His! Philosophy can explore, psychology can examine, morality can entreat, liturgy can enamor, theology can explain, but it takes the Holy Spirit to *empower*.

Ezekiel's experience has its counterpart in the Acts of the Apostles. "The Spirit entered into me." That is part of the journey inward. "Son of man . . . get you to the house of Israel, and speak with my words to them." That is the beginning of the journey outward.

[11] Stephen Neill, *The Unfinished Task*, p. 141 (Lutterworth Press, London, 1958).
[12] Thomas R. Kelly, *A Testament of Devotion*, p. 52 (Harper & Brothers, New York, 1941).

"Ye shall receive power." The journey inward! "And ye shall be witnesses unto me." The journey outward!

Somewhere along the trail God will grant us to discover our slight kinship with that amazing little man called Paul who, in the superb portrayal of F. W. H. Myers, is heard to say:

> "Oft when the Word is on me to deliver
> Lifts the illusion and the truth lies bare;
> Desert or throng, the city or the river,
> Melts in a lucid paradise of air, —
>
> "Only like souls I see the folk thereunder,
> Bound who should conquer, slaves who should be kings, —
> Hearing their one hope with an empty wonder,
> Sadly contented in a show of things: —
>
> "Then with a rush the intolerable craving
> Shivers through me like a trumpet-call, —
> Oh, to save these! to perish for their saving,
> Die for their life, be offered for them all!"

OUR NEED FOR THE POWER OF CHRIST

Dr. Kenneth L. Chafin

I very personally respond to Dr. Paul S. Rees, whom I met for the first time today but whom I have known in his writing for a long time. Only last week I read his book *Don't Sleep Through the Revolution*, which I notice is out on the bookstand and which I would recommend to you as one of the most readable and inciting books dealing with the whole area of missions in evangelism that I've read in a long, long time.

I would like to take in these 17 minutes a tack — I was tempted, as I watched him edit out three and a half pages from his manuscript, to get up and read the uncut version of his paper — but I had read the manuscript through several times yesterday and prepared a response. I would like to take a theme which runs through the paper — that the two go together, the outward journey and the inward journey — make a suggestion about it, make one application, and illustrate it in one way.

My homiletics professor was asked one time, "How many points does a message have?" He said, "At least one." I hope to have one.

Now this is my point and I will simply go round and round this point in an effort to jab it home. These two journeys go together, and we must not separate them by the way in which we relate them. It's entirely possible for us to gather here and affirm the necessity of both the inward journey and the outward journey, but — by the way in which we relate them to each other — to accomplish the same thing as if we had separated them. For instance, spatially. If we think of the inward journey as being in one place and the outward journey as being another place, we will divide them because really there cannot be this spatial division. Or in time, in sequence, if we think that *first* we must have the inward journey, *then* we must have the outward journey, there is a terrible danger that we will never in the closet of our life realize what is out there in the road. Consequently we will not come with desperateness to realize how much power we need, how desperately we need His presence. These do go together.

Now in the arena of obedience, I think this is where we learn our need for the power of the living Christ, in our lives and in the world. Often we do not pray fervently or study with a desperate urgency, because we have not been exposed to the task and its difficulties. I have a feeling that most of us have made a studied effort to stay where we can run the operation in our own resources.

Now by way of parenthesis from the scribbled notes. My conviction is that we don't need any more power than we have, to do what we are doing

DR. KENNETH L. CHAFIN, Director, Division of Evangelism, Southern Baptist Convention, Atlanta, Georgia.

right now. We're like a team that's practicing but doesn't have a rough schedule. Are you following what I'm saying? We do not know that the power has gone, because we have not gone out to wrestle with the Philistines. I'm suggesting that it's entirely possible that while the inner road becomes the source of power for the doing of the task, sometimes to walk out on that road and take a good look at the task drives us, with a desperateness we ordinarily would not have, into our closet.

Now let me, just for practice here, suggest a small Philistine for you to wrestle with during lunch. He is so small that you will — I started to say "swear" but I could not think of a religious equivalent — claim that you have whipped him already. All right, now listen. To be obedient to Christ, the church needs to enlarge its target area for evangelism. This enlarged target will require spiritual resources that we do not presently have, relationships and barriers to be crossed, costs that we are not now willing to pay, and it could drive us in desperation to God for power.

Now you will say, "How can you enlarge the Great Commission?" You can't, but that's not what you and I go by, for you and I have learned in our ecclesiastical way to domesticate the Great Commission.

You recall when Jesus, as recorded in Acts 1:8 said to the disciples, "But ye shall receive power, after that the Holy Ghost is come upon you; and ye shall be witnesses unto me both in Jerusalem, . . . in Judaea, and in Samaria, and unto the uttermost part of the earth." What do you think they heard Him say? Those words? No. One very perceptive commentary said, "Though these are the words which Jesus spoke, *this* is what they heard, 'Ye shall receive power after the Holy Ghost is come upon you, and ye shall be my witnesses to the Jews who are in Jerusalem, to the Jews who are in Judaea, to the Jews who are in Samaria, and to the Jews who are in the uttermost part of the earth.' "

Isn't that fantastic? Here is this group of people called from their vocations by Jesus Christ, washed of their sins, filled with the meaning of His presence; they have witnessed His crucifixion and have now tasted the power of His resurrection. He's sending them out with a universal Gospel and He's promising His power, but they are hearing a very provincial Gospel. And this commentator went on to say, "The whole book of Acts is nothing but the record of how the Holy Spirit of God worked on His church to get it to preach an unhindered Gospel to the whole world."

Now if the men who walked with Him in the days of His flesh, and witnessed the crucifixion, and tasted the power of His resurrection could hear that Commission and yet not catch the broader implications of it, isn't it entirely possible that you and I could domesticate it too?

For instance, I'll give two areas in which we do it, just to illustrate how unequipped we are for these tasks. I don't see any way in which we can go away from this meeting claiming to be obedient to Jesus Christ and His command to win all men to Him, unless we are willing to lead our churches to seek to win to faith in Jesus Christ young people and adults who were not reared in the church.

Now you and I should face it that most of what we call evangelism is merely the winning and the baptizing of the children of the church members. It is such an occasion when someone not reared in the church becomes a follower of Jesus Christ, that he becomes almost a freak, he becomes almost such a different person that about all we can think about doing with him is to take up an offering and mail him to seminary. Which, incidentally, we'll be glad to take.

Now hear me. The church that is nothing but the sociological extension of the families will never come to feel the relevance of its Gospel and it will never need the power of the resurrection. For you remember that it was Eli — that prophet of God who had such fellowship with God that he could give spiritual guidance to other people's children — who reared his children in the Temple and they did not know God; and when Phinehas died and his son was born on that fateful day, they named him Ichabod, meaning "the glory of the Lord hath departed." Not only does the church need in every generation to seek a veritable confrontation with each generation for its people, but it needs to reach out.

Now I am a part of a group and whatever your group is the problem is the same, that feeling that if you do not get them when they are little, you will not get them. Now let me remind you very kindly that the church was not begun by building an elementary education building on the slopes of Jerusalem. The church was begun with an adult Gospel, preached in an adult world, with power to convert adults. I cannot forget taking a group of 125 of my students to Pittsburgh, most of them reared in the church, many of them struggling with whether or not the Gospel was relevant, whether or not the Gospel had power. We sat, night after night, in that stadium and watched young people and adults. The No. 1 group responding were adults ages 30 through 49, and the No. 2 group responding were young people 16 through 19.

Now I'll tell you this. When we move outside of this hothouse in which we have grown our own converts, and we move into this world that Christ died for, and we begin to learn how to share the Gospel of Jesus Christ with young people and adults in this world, we will discover how desperately we need the inner resources, how desperately we need His power.

Quickly let me mention one other which is really an amplification of the same point. If the church will make an effort to break out of evangelism as a class process, if the church will break out of the straight jacket of class evangelism, it will suddenly discover how desperately it needs the power of God and how unequipped, as far as spiritual resources go, it really is.

Now I don't think you need the power of God to continue to get people into your church that are like you. There's sort of a sociological gathering of the clan that does not really take religious power. What I mean by class evangelism is seeking to win to faith in Christ only that segment of the world that is already like us.

Now this is very easy to understand intellectually. When I was a young professor I got a copy of Gibson Winter's *Suburban Captivity of the Churches* to review. I read it and although he had written it in Chicago, I could label the churches in Fort Worth, Texas, that it identified. It suddenly dawned upon me that the church had become sort of a little homogeneous society — one group of people, one class of people — and that we had made evangelism the collecting of other people like us. So I began to go up and down the length and breadth of the land at conventions "beating on" people about this, tearing them up, and pouring salt in their wounds. Some of my brethren are here and they will testify to the almost contemptuousness which I showed them about this.

But I discovered an interesting thing. It is one thing to discover with your *head* that your responsibility is trapped in a social class and it's unwilling to preach the unsearchable riches of Christ to every person, but it's another thing to discover it with your *heart*.

I remember when I visited the London Crusade at Earls Court and sat with a group of Anglican ministers as they discussed problems which had been created by the success of the crusade. Most of my problems have never been created by success. They said, "Billy, many of these people who are accepting Christ in Earls Court are getting a Bible, and coming to church, and they are upsetting our people because they are not the church type."

Be careful, be careful. I sat there fuming with all of my American indignation, quoting Gibson Winter — although I'd not been asked to be on the program — to myself at least. Let me tell you something. In this year of our Lord, I discovered how emotionally attached I am to evangelism that seeks to work within a class.

In connection with a crusade our denomination was planning, a youth meeting was planned. They got a young man from the West Coast to come and I thought it would be like most youth meetings, a lot of kids, a little singing you know, a little off-beat music, and a testimony or two, a zippy sort of sermon, then cookies and Kool-Aid in the basement and then, you know, just forget about the whole thing. Well, this boy walked in and he said, "You folks don't know the lost people in Louisville, and if you did, you wouldn't like them."

Well, you do not say to a Southern Baptist who is part of a crusade that we'd been planning for two years, "You wouldn't like them." We said, "Try us." So he got the young people, and he got the adults, and they began to visit. They went to the hippie community and they began to invite them to the meeting. They went to the bars down on Fourth Street, they went in, they invited all the customers, they invited the owner, they invited the bartender, they invited the "go-go" girls. Some of them came. I know what your question is and I'm not going to tell you. They went to the Negro section of town, they invited these young Negroes. They went to some of these dropout kids. They invited them. They simply invited everyone, and they came.

So as Professor of Evangelism I thought I'd go down and see what happened and it was almost a scary thing. We met in the Walnut Street Baptist Church in Louisville. I went in, and it was a different group of people than I'd seen. They dressed differently, they responded differently, but something was going on. As I felt uneasy I looked up and there were the stained glass windows, there were the pipes on the organ, there were the pews, there was the pastor, and there was a certain sense of comfort I got from that. But when the invitation was given, about 70 people responded and I began to see a miracle. I saw two Negro brothers who I learned later had been in trouble with the law and were some of the roughest boys in the West End, both come confessing Christ. I saw a Baptist deacon who four years before had felt called of God to ride shotgun on the front door to make sure none of them came in. I saw that same man standing there with his arm around that boy, with a Bible in his hand, counseling him concerning his faith in Jesus Christ. It was an amazing thing.

Then a terrible thing happened. So many people came we couldn't get them into the sanctuary, so we rented a Municipal Auditorium. That's where we made the mistake, because you see, we had to do it overnight and those stained glass windows are very hard to move, and the organ, and the pews. So there we were in an atmosphere very much like this, and when I went in I knew I was in trouble emotionally. Because you see, all those people who'd been wanting to come but wouldn't come to a church house, came to this. Nobody told them how to dress so some of them came in mini skirts, some of them wearing bell-bottom trousers, some of them wearing leather Indian uniforms, the band and the feather, dressed every conceivable way. No one told them how people acted at 11 o'clock on Sunday morning in an evangelical church. So they just stopped by that popcorn machine and the coke machine out in the front, got them a coke and some popcorn, and they came in and sat down to enjoy the service. No one had told them that usually we pass out a bulletin and the service proceeds without announcement. The truth is you can on Sunday morning almost look at your watch and tell whether the Baptists or the Lutherans are standing, or sitting, or bowing, or whatever they're doing.

An interesting thing happened. As the young man began to preach on the Prodigal Son, a young hippie who was a part of the group who had come, came up and began to talk to him on stage. Now the hippie was under the influence of drugs, it was obvious, and the man who was preaching knew this and so he dealt very kindly and very carefully with him. But this bothered me. So I called one of the ushers over and I said, "Get a policeman and get that creep out of here." And suddenly it dawned upon me what had taken place. Here was a young minister preaching on the Prodigal Son, here was one of the prodigals and many others out there, and here was Kenneth Chafin, Professor of Evangelism at Southern Baptist Seminary, sitting out there with the usher playing the role of the elder brother. Now let me tell you something. You can laugh, but it suddenly dawned upon me that what I had been willing to deal with with my head, I had not yet faced with my heart, that I have a fantastic emotional attachment to an approach to evangelism that only brings in a certain kind of person. It suddenly dawned on me what is so wonderful about Sunday morning. You can be reasonably sure nothing will happen. That's right.

Oh, we meet to worship, yes, but you can usually be sure that these people will not come and bother us in our worship. Now let me tell you something. There is no way for you and me to closet ourselves and ask God for His power, if we do not intend to use this power to obey His commandment and that is to win the world to Jesus Christ.

I'm fairly convinced that we already have the power to do what we're trying. We are simply not trying enough, but if we're to be God's revolutionary agents of redemption, if we're to become the instruments of His reconciliation, if we are to preach Christ's Word and win men to Him, we must have a power that we do not have.

What is the exceeding greatness of the power to us who believe? It is according to that power which works, it is according to the working of that strength that He wrought in Christ when He raised Him from the dead. Amen.

EVANGELISM AND THE RENEWAL OF THE CHURCH

Dr. Richard C. Halverson

I would like to make a few remarks which will not be in the paper that you will receive. The paper was prepared months ago and sent in, and this has been such a rich experience that I feel that I should say this first.

Early Tuesday morning we were in a prayer meeting in the hotel. One of the young men who was praying in that prayer meeting, in the process of praying, was deeply moved with the thought that gathered in this auditorium would be 4,000 or 5,000 people all following the same leader, Jesus Christ. That's a thrilling thought. We talked about it and it occurred to me as we talked before coming here for the first hour that with few if any exceptions, it is assumed that each of us holds a right relationship with Jesus Christ as we're gathered in this room. But the question is, what about our relationship to each other?

We evangelicals have been so preoccupied with the defense of the deity of Jesus Christ for so long that we have almost, if not entirely, forgotten His humanity. And we have grown into the image of a dogma so often, instead of into the image of a person. Hence, the inhumanity among us evangelicals with ourselves, and with those outside the body, and with those with whom we disagree. We tolerate tragic inhumanity in our midst. We proclaim a message of reconciliation which we do not practice, and the world no longer takes us seriously.

Why preach God's love to the world when we don't have it in our congregation? That's what this paper is about.

I'd like to take some quotes, and read them as a kind of backdrop to the remarks.

From *The Unexpected Universe* by Loren Eiseley, Benjamin Franklin Professor of Anthropology and the History of Science, University of Pennsylvania. To be published by Harcourt, Brace & World in October, 1969. Taken from *Science*, 11 July 1969, Vol. 165, No. 3889, a publication of the American Association for the Advancement of Science:

"We are a society bemused in its purposes and secretly homesick for a lost world of inward tranquillity. The thirst for illimitable knowledge now conflicts directly with the search for serenity obtainable nowhere on earth. Knowledge, or at least what the twentieth century acclaims as knowledge, has not led to happiness. . . . . We appear to exist . . . amidst a meaningless mosaic of fragments."

DR. RICHARD C. HALVERSON, Pastor, Fourth Presbyterian Church, Washington, D.C.

From a letter by an Indian evangelist to me:

"It is interesting to note that the intellectuals of these days do draw a difference between Christ Himself and the tradition of the Church. While they are willing to listen to and even accept Christ, they reject the idea of the church as more a tradition charged with human 'opinion' than the pure transmission of Christ Himself who is the gospel."

From a letter by a college student to me:

"I look around me on Sunday morning at people who are once again leaving the worship as lonely as when they came."

". . . and let us consider how to stir up one another to love and good works, not neglecting to meet together, as is the habit of some, but encouraging one another. . . ." (Hebrews 10:24–25, RSV).

One of the signs carried by those who demonstrated when Billy Graham spoke at the University of California at Berkeley bore the inscription, "Jesus Yes — Christianity No!" Those sentiments, expressed in a multitude of ways, reflect a general and alarmingly deep disenchantment with the Christian establishment by a large segment of American society of all ages and classes.

The church of course is under no mandate to develop public relations techniques which will enhance her image and certainly she is not interested in, nor does she expect to win, a popularity contest, nor to gain acceptance by large majorities. Nevertheless one stubbornly persistent view of the Church today, held by insiders as well as outsiders, is not only not supporting her outreach, it is sabotaging it. It can hardly be said of the Twentieth Century Church what Dr. Luke reported of the primitive Christians, "And day by day, attending the temple together and breaking bread in their homes, they partook of food with glad and generous hearts, praising God and having favor with all the people" (Acts 2:46–47, RSV).

For the purpose of this paper may we refocus our thinking about evangelism and concentrate on a basic aspect of the Church, that is Community, which we tend to "assume" at best, or to relegate to an inconsequential position if considered at all, but which is fundamental to renewal and mission.

Inevitably, when evangelism is discussed today, the population explosion is a major consideration which generates either an atmosphere of pessimism and frustration, or urgency bordering on hysteria, or both. As attempts are made to resolve this imponderable, discussion invariably gravitates to solutions on a massive scale: 1) traditional mass evangelism; 2) ways and means of employing the mass media; or 3) some program for "beefing up" personal evangelism classes and courses in order to involve as many individuals as possible in a massive attack upon the alienated world. The enormity of the task seems to demand dramatic, spectacular, gigantic effort.

Obviously such a focus is important. Such massive means must be considered, lest the Church be guilty of neglecting the tools available in this incredibly knowledgeable, technological age. However, preoccupation with massive response overlooks the condition of the Church, although isolated pockets of individuals here and there are renewed under the compulsion. Furthermore, such an overwhelming challenge tempts the Church to ignore or despise the quiet, invisible, but basic and powerful forces about which Jesus spoke: the inexorable penetration of salt and seed, and the infusive power of love.

The focus of this paper is the dormant potential of the local congregation when it is in fact an authentic New Testament community; when its corporate life vitally demonstrates the redemption and reconciliation professed and proclaimed; when it reveals through the quality of its internal relations the nature of the Kingdom of God; when its members deploy and dissolve into all the social structures surrounding them with benevolent and contagious love. Imagine the potential of the thousands of congregations represented in this Congress, if each were a warm, loving, sacrificial community of faith with members concerned for one another, fulfilling their priestly responsibilities one to another, and sensitive to the sick and alienated world around them. Suppose each were a "company of those who believed (and) were of one heart and soul, and no one said that any of the things which he possessed was his own, but they had everything in common" (Acts 4:32, RSV).

Is this an impossible dream? It is Biblical! It is realistic! This is renewal! From such will flow the broadest possible outreach to a world conditioned to demonstration. The fact is, we have been so busy with individualism that we have developed a people oblivious to Community as the essence of New Testament life. They neither aspire to it, nor are they convicted by its absence. We simply have not envisioned the potential of the local congregation when it conforms to the instruction and example of the New Testament. The great burden of New Testament exhortation is not to mission or evangelism as conventionally understood, but rather to each believer's role in the body — his responsibility to his brothers in the Lord, and their mutual interdependence.

Community is the matrix of mission. A congregation without Community cannot fulfill its evangelistic mission, whatever is done to exhort or train.

Conversely, when a congregation is spiritually healthy — that is, committed to Jesus Christ and to each other and constrained by a selfless concern for all men — evangelism will occur spontaneously, effortlessly, continuously, effectively. Not only will the life of the community attract the alienated and lonely to its accepting, reconciling warmth, but in dispersion its members will radiate that redemptive love infectiously to the world.

Everything the Church does is not evangelism, but everything the Church does should be evangelistic. That is to say, in conventional terms, no member of the Church is telling the Gospel all the time (not even the professional evangelist); nor will all the members of the church engage in telling the Gospel some of the time (many simply do not have the gift of verbalizing, for many different reasons). But the total Church, individually and collectively, ought to be witnessing to the redemptive love of God in Christ in all that they do all the time. Witness, by presence and performance as well as proclamation, is the product of the Spirit-filled life.

"Truly, truly, I say to you, he who believes in me will also do the works that I do; and greater works than these will he do, because I go to the Father" (John 14:12, RSV). "But you shall receive power when the Holy Spirit has come upon you; and you shall be my witnesses in Jerusalem and in all Judea and Samaria and to the end of the earth" (Acts 1:8, RSV).

In other words, evangelism is happening all the time in and by a congregation rightly related to Jesus Christ, to each other and to the world around them.

"And day by day, attending the temple together and breaking bread in their homes, they partook of food with glad and generous hearts, praising God and having favor with all the people. And the Lord added to their number day by day those who were being saved" (Acts 2:46–47, RSV). "And the word of God increased; and the number of the disciples multiplied greatly in Jerusalem, and a great many of the priests were obedient to the faith" (Acts 6:7, RSV). "So the church throughout all Judea and Galilee and Samaria had peace and was built up; and walking in the fear of the Lord and in the comfort of the Holy Spirit it was multiplied" (Acts 9:31, RSV).

Even failure and sin witness to Christ. Not the failure and sin themselves, obviously, but the way the Christian — and the Christian community — handle failure and sin. If they are covered and hid, if we pretend failure and sin are not, if we make excuses rather than acknowledge and confess, we not only deprive ourselves of forgiving, renewing grace ("the blood of Christ cannot cleanse excuses, only sin"), we suspend fellowship with God.

"If we say we have fellowship with him while we walk in darkness, we lie and do not live according to the truth" (1 John 1:6, RSV).

And we fail to demonstrate to the world the practical remedy for human inadequacy available in the Gospel. Admission of sin, and confession open the door to forgiveness, renewal and fellowship with God, and witness to the absolutely unique and life-changing dynamic of the atonement.

This is borne out by the very pragmatic James who admonished, "Therefore, confess your sins to one another and pray for one another, that you may be healed" (James 5:16, RSV). Significantly this appears in the context of a most remarkable prayer promise which has been largely ignored by the Church. It is not unreasonable to assume that for want of such confession among brethren, such openness, such honesty — such "walking in the light" — the promise of healing is neglected and unbelieved, fellowship fails, and the community degenerates. Confessing to one another in the fellowship is dangerous because it makes one vulnerable, and we have invented very sophisticated rationalizations to justify our failure to practice it. So we hide behind masks, remain strangers to one another, and disrupt authentic fellowship which Dr. Luke indicates was as much a part of primitive Christianity as doctrine, sacraments and prayer.

"And they devoted themselves to the apostles' teaching and fellowship, to the breaking of bread and the prayers" (Acts 2:42, RSV).

John, the beloved, certainly took fellowship seriously. It is a major theme in his first epistle.

Confession to God and to one another is essential to Community. The opposite is walking in darkness, which obviates Community.

"If we say we have fellowship with him while we walk in darkness, we lie and do not live according to the truth; but if we walk in the light, as he is in the light, we have fellowship with one another, and the blood of Jesus His Son cleanses us from all sin" (1 John 1:6–7, RSV).

The peril of being closed to one another in Christ is that one is closed as well to grace. Freedom is gone, formalism is substituted, and the Church presents a graceless, loveless, inhumane, non-accepting image to the world. Is it not tragedy in the first magnitude that one ecclesiastical tradition has institutionalized and depersonalized the confessional with faceless confessors, while another has ignored or abandoned it altogether? In either case the healing therapy of confession has been surrendered by default to the professional therapist, Alcholics Anonymous, and other such groups.

To be perfectly frank, we ought to rethink critically our traditional attitudes toward evangelism. If we should lay aside momentarily our conventional views for the purpose of rediscovering what the New Testament says about evangelism, we would probably be surprised at the few references to the subject as such. We would find it treated, not as a task to be done, a department of church life (which we have made it) — not even as the primary role of the Church. Rather evangelism is something that is happening all the time when the Church is truly Community, truly in fellowship, truly renewed and renewing.

"So the churches were strengthened in the faith, and they increased in numbers daily" (Acts 16:5, RSV).

And, incidentally, such a reappraisal might help to dissolve the destructive polarization between evangelism and social responsibility which is rending the Church.

Why, for example, do we isolate and emphasize evangelism as being more important than the two great commandments which comprehend all the law and the prophets, to love God and neighbor? Why do so many who are zealously committed to evangelism, so often seem to disregard the explicit admonitions to: "Do nothing from selfishness or conceit, but in humility count others better than yourselves. Let each of you look not only to his own interests, but also to the interests of others" (Philippians 2:3–4, RSV).

"Owe no one anything, except to love one another; for he who loves his neighbor has fulfilled the law" (Romans 13:8, RSV). "Be subject to one another out of reverence for Christ" (Ephesians 5:21, RSV). "And be kind to one another, tenderhearted, forgiving one another, as God in Christ forgave you" (Ephesians 4:32, RSV). ("Love is kind.") "Put on then, as God's chosen ones, holy and beloved, compassion, kindness, lowliness, meekness, and patience, forbearing one another and, if one has a complaint against another, forgiving each other; as the Lord has forgiven you, so you also must forgive. And above all these put on love, which binds everything together in perfect harmony. And let the peace of Christ rule in your hearts, to which indeed you were called in the one body. And be thankful. Let the word of Christ dwell in you richly, as you teach and admonish one another in all wisdom, and as you sing psalms and hymns and spiritual songs with thankfulness in your hearts to God" (Colossians 3:12-16, RSV). "So, whether you eat or drink, or whatever you do, do all to the glory of God" (1 Corinthians 10:31, RSV).

How do you separate the Great Commission with its mandate: ". . . teaching them to observe all things whatsoever I have commanded you" — from the Beatitudes and the Sermon on the Mount with its terrifying conclusion — "Not every one who says to me, 'Lord, Lord,' shall enter the kingdom of heaven, but he who does the will of my Father who is in heaven. On that day many will say to me, 'Lord, Lord, did we not prophesy in your name, and cast out demons in your name, and do many mighty works in your name?' And then will I declare to them, 'I never knew you; depart from me, you evildoers.' Every one then who hears these words of mine and does them will be like a wise man who built his house upon the rock; and the rain fell, and the floods came, and the winds blew and beat upon that house, but it did not fall, because it had been founded on the rock. And every one who hears these words of mine and does not do them will be like a foolish man who built his house upon the sand; and the rain fell, and the floods came, and the winds blew and beat against that house, and it fell; and great was the fall of it" (Matthew 7:21–27, RSV). In these crucial days, how seriously ought we to take our Lord's last parable (Matthew 25:31–46) spoken as it was in the context of readiness for His second advent? Are these instructions not to be included in "the whole counsel of God"?

One often hears intimated in one way or another the idea that if circumstances were just more favorable, the Church could be more effective in its outreach. Yet our times are generous and friendly by contrast with those into which the New Testament Church was thrust. It faced a violent, hostile, corrupt, anti-Christ culture, degraded and demoralized.

What is the explanation for the incredible impact of that tiny, faithful minority upon its sick, alienated world?

Mark records that Jesus "appointed twelve, to be with him, and to be sent out to preach. . ." (Mark 3:14, RSV). With a whole world to reach,

Jesus separated twelve men to Himself and devoted much of His brief three-year ministry to them. This was their "seminary," their preparation for the work He was to begin and they were to continue. In what did their education consist? What were they learning which would equip them to preach? Did they have homiletics and speech courses? Philosophy of Religion? Systematic Theology? Anthropology? Sociology? In a sense, yes, for all of these themes were undoubtedly in some way implicit in their training. They learned much about Jesus, about the God Who had entered history to serve, about man and about themselves. Most of all they were learning how to live together, how to support one another, how to submit to one another, how to serve one another, how to defer to each other, encourage each other, pray for each other, love each other. They were learning Community, practising it daily, around the clock, under the delicate direction of the gentlest of teachers, the humblest of men, the servant of servants, whose life was to be a "ransom for many." What they learned was to be infused into the life of the Church following Pentecost.

At Pentecost, Christ gave to His Church a three-phased strategy by which to continue His work and fulfill its mission. 1) Dr. Luke reports that: "When the day of Pentecost had come, they were all together in one place. And suddenly a sound came from heaven like the rush of a mighty wind, and it filled all the house where they were sitting. And there appeared to them tongues as of fire, distributed and resting on each one of them. And they were all filled with the Holy Spirit and began to speak in other tongues, as the Spirit gave them utterance" (Acts 2:1–4, RSV). It was the intention of Christ that every disciple be equipped for mission, that being filled with the Holy Spirit was for every believer, and witness was the normal effect of such infilling. Every believer was to communicate the Gospel, each in his own way "as the Spirit gave them utterance." In the course of time a professional class emerged who devoted themselves "full time" to the various tasks of ministry, which was as Paul promised (Ephesians 4:8, 11). But an aberration gradually developed as various structures and forms for mission grew, and the time came when the work of mission was relegated to the professional class. This idea persists in large measure to this very day (with some glorious exceptions), and large segments of the laity assume that evangelism is the work of the professional who is to be "subsidized" by the man in the pews. Nevertheless the original pattern stands as integral to mission, and the Great Commission requires the witness of every believer.

2) The negative reaction of the multitude who gathered at the "sound from heaven like the rush of a mighty wind" to the many-language witness of the individual disciples demanded an explanation. It was given by Peter and the second phase of the strategy was indicated — the sermon-proclamation. This, too, eventually was submerged in the traditions and forms which accumulated through the years, until the altar became central and liturgy replaced the sermon. The Reformation put the pulpit back into worship,

restored the sermon to its essential role and opened the Scriptures to the people. Significantly we are seeing a "liturgical renewal" in our day accompanied by increasing criticism of the sermon as irrelevant to be replaced by various forms of "dialogue" and "confrontation." Interestingly, this discrediting of the sermon seems to come mostly from sources where "popular" preaching rather than Biblical exposition has been the practice. But proclamation has never been abrogated. It remains fundamental to mission and it still "pleases God by the foolishness of preaching to save them that believe." No self-respecting evangelical today would deny the imperative of preaching, especially expository preaching; nor would most deny (in principle at least) the essential of individual, Spirit-filled witness.

Yet strangely, there remains among us a decided indifference, if not outright opposition, toward the third phase of the strategy given at Pentecost.

3) The third thing that occurred at Pentecost and which clearly was central to everything else about primitive faith, was Community. That day a new, absolutely unique social entity was born. Those individual disciples were magnetized into a supernatural unity by the baptism of the Holy Spirit. They became one indivisible, inseparable organism, the body of Christ, the Church.

"For by one Spirit we were all baptized into one body — Jews or Greeks, slaves or free — and all were made to drink of one Spirit" (1 Corinthians 12:13, RSV).

Suddenly they were "members one of another," interdependent, indispensable to each other, "arranged . . . in the body . . . as [God] chose" (1 Corinthians 12:18, RSV), God-adjusted so that there would be no discord in the body. So delicate, so complete was this adjustment that the members "(had) the same care for one another. If one member suffered, all suffered together; if one member were honored, all rejoiced together" (see 1 Corinthians 12:26, RSV). One simply cannot read descriptions of the New Testament Church without feelings of nostalgia. And the fact is inescapable that this incredible Community was the strength of the Apostolic Church, the matrix of mission.

"While they were worshiping the Lord and fasting, the Holy Spirit said, 'Set apart for me Barnabas and Saul for the work to which I have called them.'" Then after fasting and praying they laid their hands on them and sent them off" (Acts 13:2–3, RSV).

At the heart of that Community were the eleven who had learned so well the art of a common life during their days of intimate contact with Jesus, and who wrote their epistles to nurture the new society.

Gradually in the early centuries the professional priesthood developed, and with it the discontinuance of the practice of the priesthood of all believers. Until today, it is assumed that the professional has full priestly-pastoral responsibilities for the congregation. It is he who must call on the sick, visit those in prison, counsel the needy, exhort, instruct, encourage, etc. So institutionalized has the caricature become that failure to spend his time in these tasks, which rightfully belong to all the members, earns him their displeasure or worse.

We would not think of abandoning the witness of the individual. Indeed, this emphasis on individualism is one explanation for our neglect of Community. We hold to proclamation as indispensable to mission. By what rationale therefore do we not see absence of Community as intolerable? The fact is that the burden of instruction in the New Testament weighs upon this aspect.

If there is one thing worse than the pressure for institutional union without regard for doctrinal purity which is being asserted today, it is the sad indifference to unity so characteristic of many evangelicals. The plain truth is that espousal of a creed is not necessarily evidence of one's fellowship with Jesus Christ ("the devils believe and tremble"). Love is!

"But whoever keeps his word, in him truly love for God is perfected. By this we may be sure that we are in him." "He who says he is in the light and hates his brother is in the darkness still. He who loves his brother abides in the light, and in it there is no cause for stumbling." (1 John 2:5, 9–10, RSV); ". . . whoever does not do right is not of God, nor he who does not love his brother" (1 John 3:10b, RSV); "We know that we have passed out of death into life, because we love the brethren. He who does not love remains in death." (1 John 3:14, RSV); "Beloved, let us love one another; for love is of God, and he who loves is born of God and knows God. He who does not love does not know God; for God is love" (1 John 4:7–8, RSV); "If any one says, 'I love God,' and hates his brother, he is a liar" (1 John 4:20a, RSV).

In our Lord's sermon (Matthew 5–7) great emphasis is placed upon a reconciled body of believers.

"So if you are offering your gift at the altar, and there remember that your brother has something against you, leave your gift there before the altar and go; first be reconciled to your brother, and then come and offer your gift" (Matthew 5:23–24, RSV). "For if you forgive men their trespasses, your heavenly Father also will forgive you; but if you do not forgive men their trespasses, neither will your Father forgive your trespasses" (Matthew 6:14–15, RSV).

Who can measure the incalculable, invisible fragmentation in the average congregation, despite its regular use of the Lord's prayer, because of the unforgiveness and alienation tolerated between members. If we do not forgive men their trespasses, our Father does not forgive us. No gifts to God — no service — are a substitute for the constant practice of reconciliation among believers. Not to forgive is to remain unforgiven by God — hence fellowship is broken between the unforgiving member and his brother, and God.

The Christians of Uganda, Africa have been enjoying continuous renewal for many years. Their formula is simple. In the words of Dwight L. Moody, they "keep short accounts" with God and with one another. It is not difficult to imagine the impact of such honesty and love upon the unbeliever, and the effectiveness of proclamation and individual witness in such an environment. Reconciliation is continual — renewal is sustained!

When renewal is sustained through Community, the Church disperses in strength. She gathers that she may be equipped to go into the world with the healing love of Christ. Jesus described this process in the parable of the sower and the seed in Matthew 13:24–30, 36–43. Every believer is "good seed" planted by Christ in the world. "The field is the world." The work of the Church is in the world and it takes every disciple to do it. As they gather in Community, believers must be made to realize their togetherness is in order to be scattered between Sundays. Each has a role — a mission — a ministry which begins where he is, in what he is doing in the normal course of his life. His witness involves doing all that he does, wherever he is, all the time. He is drawn to fellowship whenever possible that he may be nurtured and instructed and prepared for the ministry beyond the Community. He must believe he is engaged in full-time service for Jesus Christ, doing "everything to the glory of God."

The trouble is we pastors are on the backs of the people so much of the time, we exhort them to witness and scold them for failing instead of feeding them so they will be healthy — rightly related to Christ and the community. Rebuke has its place, but the deepest need is for the nourishment which the "whole counsel of God" provides in authentic fellowship.

Permit a personal word. Fourteen years ago I was called to Washington, D.C. as an associate in a lay movement. The "modus operandi" was fellowship in small groups (though not exclusively) by which to develop and encourage responsible Christian leadership. For nine years I had been on the staff of the Hollywood First Presbyterian Church in a "small group" ministry, with no obligation to "get members" for the church, but simply to reach men for Christ and bring them to spiritual maturity.

Eleven years ago a call to Fourth Presbyterian Church seemed to my associates and me to be of God. It was understood by the church that I would continue in a subordinate way with the lay movement. Having been out of a conventional pastorate for twelve years, I began my ministry without any predisposition as to program. I assumed however, that small groups would be developed rather rapidly, an expectation which did not materialize. Out of disappointment came the conviction that God would do with an entire congregation what He had done in small groups.

The vision of a whole congregation demonstrating New Testament Community gripped me, and I began to order my ministry accordingly. The vision was shared with official boards and the people. Associates joined the team with the understanding that our ministry conform to this vision. Acts 2:42 became the pattern for program, 1 Corinthians 12 the norm for church life. By preaching, teaching, counseling, and especially in personal relationships we endeavored to emulate 1 John 1:3. We dedicated ourselves to a people-oriented ministry with all ages.

The result has exceeded our expectations. The vision is becoming a reality. Outsiders are drawn by the quality of Community life. Warm love and caring flow among us. Members disperse between Sundays with a sense of vocation in Christ. Not that the vision is complete; we have a long way to go of course. But we are growing together and it is literally true that "day by day the Lord is adding to the numbers those that are being saved."

In preparing this paper I asked an associate, Bob Strain, to assess our ministry in a brief statement. He wrote as follows: "Our preaching and pastoral work emphasize good relationships with members and visitors as the way to healthy social units (church, family, community, nation). Since the Body of Christ is an organism, we expect continuous renewal when people are priority rather than program. In our congregation there is little if any formalized/organized evangelism, but it is the continuous experience of the Community's accent on fellowship." God has done that. He gave the vision, He is fulfilling it. My associates and I are a product of it. It can happen to any congregation who desires it, expects it, and works for it.

Multiply that by ten thousand and you have a small picture of the potential for evangelism when congregations are renewed through fellowship. At a time when men are searching for meaning in a dehumanizing, depersonalizing technological culture; when humanity suffers so destructively from alienation, languishes so desperately for Community, the Church alone, when she is the Church, offers hope. This is our unique, unprecedented opportunity — the pastor's golden hour.

THE EMERGING CHURCH

Rev. Bruce Larson

This past summer we had a fantastic vacation. We took a houseboat from the Jersey shore, up the Hudson River, through the Erie Canal to Lake Ontario, up into the St. Lawrence River and back through the Champlain area. I'd never driven a boat in my life, and this is faith at work. We had some marvelous times on the boat, unforgettable days of fishing and swimming and being a family. Along the way my two older children had to leave for summer jobs, and my wife and our 12-year-old son took the boat back, but along the way we had some harrowing experiences. We almost got run over by a submarine in the St. Lawrence River, almost sank in a storm on Lake Champlain, and things like this, and it was frightening. The last day in New York my wife got off and said, "This is enough for me. You and Mark can take the boat under the bridge and home." So we did and it was terrifying that last day. A tug almost ran over us, Queen Elizabeth almost sank us with her wake, but we got there. My 12-year-old is a game little guy, and he never let on once, but I knew he was scared silly. We finally came to our home port, and he said, "Dad, I'm so grateful for this trip this summer." I said, "You are, Mark? Why?" He said, "It sure has taught me to trust the Lord."

Well, God launched not a houseboat but an ark, I think, here on Monday. I don't think anybody knew where this ark or this Congress was going, but something's happened to us here that nobody predicted and nobody planned. *There* has been, I think, the mark of the authenticity of this Congress in that there's been something here to offend everybody. There is no safe group here. I think when God is really here, and is let loose, and the windows are open, and His Spirit can blow through all kinds of people and unplanned circumstances — and you know some of them that I mean — when these things happen I think everybody feels uncomfortable (maybe for different reasons), and God is disturbing us in our complacency.

I want to say that we've heard men like Leighton Ford say things that were exciting, and Tom Skinner, and Ken Chafin, and Keith Miller, and this morning Dick Halverson, and more. I don't believe that we will ever be the same again, or that things in the church will ever be the same again. I believe something has been let loose here that nobody planned.

The REV. BRUCE LARSON, Executive Director, Faith at Work, New York, New York.

And let me just suggest something that I'm hearing. Tom Skinner spoke about black people still having a slave mentality, though being free a hundred years. Let me suggest that I've come into the Christian life and the church through evangelicals and I'm glad of it, but you know there's been a "last days" mentality. "We're living in the last days," and they've been living in the last days for 2,000 years. Now suppose you businesssmen here were in a business and they said, "Now you've got to retire at 65." You have no children, you're 63, you're president. How do you run that business? Well, you've got to hold things together, keep it honest; and keep the thing afloat until you can get yours, get out, and go to Florida, you know.

But suppose you're starting a business that you want to leave to children, and grandchildren, and the unborn generations. The way you come to your office in the morning, the way you conduct your staff meetings, the long-range integrity and vision is very different. I think there's something wrong about a "last days" mentality. Now it's true, Jesus Christ may come again and close the curtains on this life today, tonight, tomorrow, next week, next year. This is true. But I believe we've missed a point.

I believe that maybe we are *not* in the last days or at the end of the Christian era. I believe with all my heart we are at the *beginning* of the Christian era. I believe that God in His graciousness has allowed the early and first believers maybe 2,000 years to wrestle with the implications of the incarnation, the resurrection of Jesus Christ, and the presence of the Holy Spirit. For 2,000 years we've had a laboratory in the world, and different groups have tried to experiment with obedience, community, worship, and service, etc. We've had a few models that have worked a bit and some blueprints. And I think this doesn't change a bit what happened historically on the Cross, resurrection morning, and Pentecost. But what's happened is that we have not begun to see what the new being in Christ is to look like en masse or what the new Jerusalem and the new community is to be like. And whether Christ comes tomorrow or in a hundred thousand years, let's begin to believe that we are in the beginning of something new that began 2,000 years ago and God is saying, "Now, I've given you time. Can you begin to live out, and see, and be, and do the implications of the most fantastic act in the history of the cosmos?" God invading a little pea-sized world and becoming one of us! And now we're beginning to see something of what this can mean in community, responsible action, love, and worship.

I believe that we are not experiencing a new reformation but coming into a new era, the Christian era. This is what I've heard these days here together. And I'm excited.

I want to respond to Dick Halverson's paper simply by saying that I've sat at the feet of my friend Dick for years, read his books, heard him whenever I could. I've never heard him say, or read anything he said, that I didn't say "Amen" to, and wished I'd said it. I want to muster all of the loudest emphasis I can from all of my spotty career, to say the loudest "Amen" I can to what Dick said this morning among us.

He dropped a plumb line, as many before have done in different ways, about being the authentic people of God, and being a demonstration to the world, about what it means to belong to one another because Jesus Christ belongs to us.

We're talking about an emerging church, a church which we hear; we see some of the designs coming about here. An emerging church that is about to be born, but there's nothing new about the concept of an emerging church. Three thousand years ago God said to His faithful people, "Behold, I am doing a new thing. Do you not perceive it? The old has passed away. I am doing a new thing."

Here we find the fact that though the Cross and the resurrection are historical facts, the Christ of the Cross and the resurrection is not back there. He is in the present and the future, saying as He said to the first disciples who wanted to relive something in Jerusalem, "I go before you. I go *before* you."

Recently I was with some 1,200 Methodists at a great meeting they had, most of them laymen, and I saw some marvelous authentic examples there of the lay apostolate. The tragic thing was that all the hymns we sang were about a hundred or more years old, many of them Charles Wesley's hymns, and I thought to myself, "They've missed something here." Something is happening in spite of what we clergy and others have done. The Wesleys, as we heard this morning, took contemporary tunes and put contemporary words to them, to worship and praise God. They found contemporary means of reaching people; so camp meetings, and colliery pit meetings, and impromptu things came about. Now the followers of Christ who are Wesleyans have baptized those old forms and still sing the hymns the Wesleys sang. If Charles Wesley came back today I'm sure he would say, "Don't sing those hymns. Let's write our own today."

You see, we can do this. If we would take a tune, that everybody knows — for example, "Do Re Mi" from "Sound of Music" as I've heard done — and somebody would write words worshiping the living Christ, and put the words to that tune, then you could sing on Sunday morning a hymn that one member of your church had written the Monday before, and the words would be on mimeographed sheets. There's something wrong about having hymn books, because it takes years to compile one and many more years to wear them out. In the meantime, the living Christ is doing new things, expressing Himself through His people in new ways, and yet these never find expression in music until decades down the pike.

So worship this contemporary and future Christ who expresses Himself through His people in new architecture and new songs, because the one who was born at Bethlehem and died and rose again is not there. He's here, and before us, and we've got to express this in our worship and preaching on evangelism.

Now this emerging church. My closing point is: what is the mark of this emerging church? I think Dick Halverson's paper spells it out. I think the primary thing he says, and the primary thing I'd say "Amen" to, is that in this new church, this emerging church — as the church is always the emerging church — laymen are the center. The layman is God's primary means of accomplishing His will in the world. We clergy at best are coaches, or chalk-talk experts, or first-aid men, or something like this; but you laymen are the ones who are to be the prophets, the evangelists, and the healers of our time. God depends primarily on laymen. They are the royal priesthood that we heard about.

Now last night we heard an Episcopal layman talk to us. Keith Miller is a part of a new breed of laymen God is raising up and the exciting thing before us is that in every church represented here, in every church across our land, across the world, there are hundreds of Keith Millers, housewives, stenographers, businessmen, lawyers, janitors, teachers. Just people. He was an oil man waiting to be called by God into community, equipped for ministry, commissioned to be sent out to a marketplace to break open his life, to live vulnerably, to identify, to praise God. This is the new breed of evangelist and prophet. And as we clergymen go back, as we emphasize the Golden Age of the church, let us see there is a latent force in the church — this new priesthood — who will confront America with the claims of Christ in new language, new forms, and by themselves. I'm getting the message. But I think that it's an exciting thing, that these laymen are specially equipped to do this.

Do you know why? We clergy are conceptually hung up, laymen-relationally. My 16-year-old son went out to a ranch, a Christian ranch last summer, and when he came back he said, "Dad, I didn't learn a thing out there I didn't know before about Christ, but I met Him." You see the power of God is transmitted relationally, not conceptually. We clergy are overtrained conceptually, the layman is not, usually. So he can begin to relate his life, and lay his life down beside people, and Jesus Christ can move out, and we will find millions of evangelists emerging.

So I just thank God for being a part of you, and of this Congress where God has done a new thing and we are moving into a new era.

EVANGELISM AND COMING
WORLD PEACE

Senator Mark O. Hatfield

Last December I had the privilege of visiting India. There are grave problems facing that land, which holds one-fifth of humanity. One particular area of the country is plagued by a minor, yet serious, revolutionary movement. This is in the northeastern frontier region, where members of the Naga tribes have been in rebellion against the central government. When I went on to visit Thailand, I then became more thoroughly informed about the insurgency that threatens the northeastern section of that country.

I was fascinated to learn that both of these areas had experienced the extensive influence of Christian missionaries. In my judgment, this is perhaps more than coincidental.

The Christian message of salvation includes the truth that all men are equal and valuable in God's eyes. Old customs, social mores and class distinction are dispelled. The gods that freeze men in cycles of superstition, fear, and resignation to fate are destroyed. Man is offered the possibility of new life — with social and spiritual dimensions. So when social patterns of oppression and inequity continue, isn't it plausible that revolutionary pressures claiming allegiance to human dignity and equality may be related to the influence of the Good News?

As I began thinking about my topic for this Congress — "Evangelism and Coming World Peace" — I remembered these reflections from my visit to Asia. The relation between evangelism and peace in the world, I concluded, is far more complex and stimulating than many of us would like to believe.

Recently I was told of another incident that also prompted reflection about the impact of Christ's message and the problems of world peace. A young official in our government told me of his experiences dealing with the Nigerian-Biafran conflict. He was participating in negotiations to break the deadlock between these adversaries over arranging for relief supplies to reach starving elements of the Biafran population. Recently, he returned from the area after speaking with key officials from both sides as well as those trying to administer the meager air-relief effort that is being conducted. The primary obstacle to achieving greater relief efforts, in his judgment, went beyond the tangled political and diplomatic complexities. Fundamentally, he said, the problem rested with the stubborn, unreasonable intransigence and prideful resistance that personally characterized key individual leaders on each side of these warring factions. Shortly before

SENATOR MARK O. HATFIELD, Senator from the State of Oregon.

leaving, my friend, who is a Christian, was discussing the relief problem with an African Bishop who had major responsibility for co-ordinating the effort. After exploring at great length possible solutions, all of which were pronounced futile, and unable to break the political deadlock, my friend finally mentioned that there were some people in America who were working for another approach to the situation. They were praying that the pride and selfish resistance of the key leaders might be overcome; that they might have a change of heart, and reach some reconciliation on at least arrangements to feed innocent starving people.

The Bishop at first was somewhat taken back. Having been working for months with the political complexities of this matter, it seemed utterly naïve that prayer might actually be beneficial in a concrete way. But after some thought, he admitted that he wouldn't be a Bishop if he didn't believe people could be changed. Faced with such a complete diplomatic impasse, prayer (as well as action) aimed at changing the personal attitudes of those involved seemed just as feasible as any other solution.

In different ways, these incidents raise provocative thoughts about evangelism and world peace; they also prompt questions about the true meaning of peace. What do we mean — and what does our Faith teach — about this issue?

I. *The Dimensions of Peace*

Some academic strategists and national security advisers avoid even speaking about terms as vague and idyllic as "world peace." Rather, they would like to increase the probability of a world "that minimizes the incentives for armed, violent solutions to conflict situations." In other words, this means that if there is anything one can call peace, it means the absence of war or violent conflict. This, I suspect, is the notion many of us share about the meaning of peace. We also hear of how the "balance of power" is the guarantee of peace. The United States and the Soviet Union together possess explosive power equivalent to 15 tons of TNT for every person on the earth. Yet, many postulate that such a "balance of power" — or "balance of terror," to be more precise — is the only trustworthy condition of peace.

But there is not true peace when the threat of instant annihilation hangs over the head of the majority of mankind. There is no peace when fear of destruction, rather than hope for reconciliation, is the only force restraining the use of our arsenals of nuclear devastation. I reject the simplistic notion that peace is the absence of conflict. Peace is fulfillment, harmony, satisfaction, understanding, and well-being.

As long as there is deprivation, suffering, alienation, self-seeking, exploitation . . . there is no real peace.

Peace can come only when needs — physical and spiritual — are fulfilled; for us, peace means far more than simply avoiding conflict.

In the Old Testament, the Hebrew word for peace is "Shalom." The full meaning is actually "wholeness, soundness, completeness."

Peace is a "wholistic" concept. It entails the fulfillment of needs, whether this be within a nation or within an individual. It has both a political and spiritual dimension, and an inner and outer component. A true understanding of peace includes harmony between nations, reconciliation between people, and the well-being of individuals.

Too often we speak of world peace as though it were completely unrelated to peace within nations, within communities, within families, and within individuals.

It is inconsistent, for example, for a citizen to urge warring nations to make peace if he lives in hostility toward his neighbors. It seems unreasonable to protest against violence in Vietnam by employing violent tactics here at home. And it is hypocritical for a Christian to claim he has the peace of God in his heart, if he remains oblivious to the violence and destruction in the world.

For a nation or an individual, peace becomes a form of relationship; it is a continuing attitude and activity, not a static condition. Fundamentally, peace is achieved by creative love — love that senses needs and possibilities in another that are not realized, and seeks their fulfillment in order to create "wholeness, soundness, and completeness."

II. *The Obstacles to Peace*

When I discuss these matters with some of my fellow Christians, they will often claim that the reason we have no peace in the world is because of man's sin. As long as sin abounds, there will be "wars and rumors of wars," they say. I, of course, do not dispute the reality of man's selfish and sinful nature. But I do take issue with those who reject any responsibility for overcoming the obstacles to peace simply because sin is a reality. That was not the way of Christ. He has not told us evil will ultimately triumph, and that we should resign ourselves to such a fate. Rather, He asks that we follow Him into the midst of man's turbulent world with His reconciling and redeeming love. Recognizing the existence of sin does not eliminate our mandate to act as peacemakers.

Deprivation, suffering, hunger, alienation from God and man, lack of dignity, oppression — these beguile the world's hope for true peace. These are the obstacles to peace. True, they are perpetrated by sin — the sin of those who, absorbed by their wealth, power, privilege, and supposed self-righteousness are blind to the responsibility of meeting these needs. Such sin is too often our own.

Christ calls us to witness to His love through our lives. That witness involves ministering to man whenever and wherever he is in need.

Christ's description of the Good Samaritan provides us with valuable insights into our responsibilities as Christians. After telling of the necessity to love one's neighbor, Christ was asked, "Who is my neighbor?" The story of the Good Samaritan follows, in which the victim of this incident was a complete stranger to those who passed by without stopping to help, as well as to the Good Samaritan. Notice that the persons in this story are not individually identified; there is no indication of who it was that was robbed and injured. The point is that one's neighbor is *anyone* in need. We cannot choose our charities. When confronted with simple human need, we are called to act — and to love. As we heal wounds, we nurture peace.

We all know of those who suffer from deep personal needs — meaninglessness, emptiness, futility, estrangement, alienation, and lack of love. These needs, when unfulfilled, will frustrate peace. They will create envy, bitterness and discord in families and between friends; they will sustain anxiety, turmoil, and despair at the core of one's life. Here is where the obstacles to peace have their beginning — in the individual life that lacks fulfillment.

Helmut Thielicke has written:

"It is possible to have Christian ideas without actually believing, and to be taken up with the social teachings of Christianity without becoming engaged personally. Then these ideas lose their connection with the Lord of Christendom and degenerate into ideologies, namely into instrumentalities of power and world mastery. Thus, it is possible for Christianity to become merely a pervasive atmosphere, a climate of social order, while faith dwindles away and the matter of *salvation* is forgotten."

The love of Christ brings inner, personal peace. The gift of His Spirit is the true resource for wholeness of personality. Then the task of peacemaking includes the call to evangelism.

Peace, however, is also frustrated by unjust social conditions. In the communities where we live, there are those who suffer from impoverishment, through no fault of their own, despite the prosperity of our land. Twenty-nine million Americans live in the conditions of poverty. And although those who are non-white comprise only 11% of our population, they comprise over 30% of the poor in our land. Million of blacks and minorities have been the victims of racism, have been denied dignity and justice, and are overwhelmed with hopelessness and despair. These deprivations are the power adversaries of peace. We may attempt to enforce stability — or "law and order" — through the use of force, but we will never have peace in our land until we repent from this sin, correct such injustice, and fulfill these needs.

Communications have transformed our world into one neighborhood. Today more than ever before in history, our neighbor includes anyone who lives with us on this globe. Consider the condition of our world; but rather than looking at ourselves from a limited terrestrial perspective, let us remove ourselves from the confines of our earthly environment. Picture our planet from outside of ourselves — from outer space. Look back on this blue, beautiful sphere floating through space. And then consider that the inhabitants of that planet spend 15 times more money on creating weapons to destroy each other than on efforts to cooperate together for social and economic improvement. Yet, 10,000 of its citizens die each day because they do not have enough to eat. Two out of every three children suffer from malnutrition. Nevertheless, the average diet in one portion of that globe contains about 5 times more protein than the average diet of the remaining portion. Eighty percent of that planet's wealth is controlled by only 20% of its inhabitants. The total wealth of those "developed" parts of this world is broken down to an average of $2,107 for each inhabitant; yet, the total wealth of the remainder of the world equals only $182 for each person.

That is how we look from outside ourselves. And our Creator views His world from this perspective.

As long as such an unjust distribution of the world's resources persists and continues to grow, as it is at present, we can never expect to be granted true peace on earth.

A fundamental obstacle to peace, then, is the deprivation of mankind, both individually and corporately. There can be no peace within man, peace in his family, peace within our communities, and peace in the world until we seek to fulfill the total needs of mankind. The call to evangelize is a call to proclaim and to love; it is a call to respond to these needs, and it involves us totally in the mandate of peacemaking.

Peace remains illusive as long as man continues to suffer; but peace is also destroyed when one man seeks to dominate another — when men and nations seek selfish, lustful goals.

We must not overlook the reality that peace is frustrated by self-assertiveness, pride, paternalism, and brutality. These are also the obstacles to peace.

Living in a country that we somehow feel bears God's seal of approval, many of us as evangelicals tend to discover these foes of peace only in other people and nations. But Christ warns us about criticizing the speck in our brother's eye when we ignore the plank in our own.

In all candor, it is my conviction that this is precisely the case with our involvement in the Vietnam war.

Let us face this matter honestly. Any discussion of peace today cannot ignore the gravest, most destructive event that presently keeps our world seething in violence and our nations seething in unrest. It is my conviction that peace will not come to Vietnam as long as we persist in applying military solutions to fundamentally social, political, and cultural problems.

We intervened in what was esentially a civil war, in my judgment, having its origins in the desire of the Vietnamese people to rid their country of foreign domination and bring themselves independence and dignity. This cause has been constantly frustrated, in ancient history by the Chinese, and in modern history by the French, the Japanese, the French again, and now by our own involvement. But such a nationalistic determination can never be quelled by bombs and bullets. By interpreting the war as an ideological struggle, we have lost sight of the human dimensions of the conflict — of the passion, will, and suffering of individuals which lies at the roots of this war.

We have failed to understand the Vietnamese people and to sense their true needs. And once having imposed military measures which have only escalated the violence, we have resisted any change in our action, and any admission of our misunderstanding.

The war will cost us about $30 billion this year, one out of every five tax dollars. Currently, we spend this at the rate of about $950 per second. Most tragic, as of two weeks ago this war has claimed the lives of 38,313 Americans, 95,961 South Vietnamese, and 541,847 "enemy" Vietnamese. Through our effort, then, more than half a million Vietnamese have died because, somehow, we believe that they individually are our enemy, and a threat to our nation. We continue to measure our success in these efforts by the brutalizing nomenclature of "kill-ratios" — by comparing how many of the enemy are killed for every American that dies. Christian compassion, I believe, cannot remain quiet when the basic value and dignity of human life is depreciated in such a manner. This war has been brought into each one of our homes. Living in our comfort-laden sanctuaries, we are spectators to this hatred, slaughter, and death. Gradually, we become insensitized to it all; the nerves of compassion that once caused us such anguish so easily become numb.

For almost a year and a half now we have been involved in talks at Paris; yet we seek to "save face" and speak of "negotiating from strength." We have sought in vain so far for some position or formula that would avoid any admission of our misjudgment or blame for the extent and duration of the war. And during that time, more than 15,000 American lives have been lost.

We are told, though, that one must fight fire with fire. We can never take risks for peace, it is said, because the enemy might be preparing for another offensive, or be taking advantage of our lack of resolve. So there is never any respite from the bombing (we have changed the location but not the intensity), and the fighting and the killing.

Yet, we believe our nation embodies great ideals; that our vision is grand and our historic purposes noble. I agree. Much has been given to us. But therefore, in the words of the Scripture, much is required.

Why should we — a nation founded by those seeking a New World blessed by God — now be bound by "an eye for an eye, a tooth for a tooth"? Do the fruits of the Spirit — love, joy, peace, patience, kindness, generosity . . . and self-control — do these have any relevance to the concrete realities we face?

Pride, self-righteousness, and brutality often do prohibit peace. For individuals as well as nations, needs cannot be fulfilled, and peace cannot be experienced, until man and nations repent, receive forgiveness and become reconciled.

As the Lord said to Solomon, "If my people who are called by my name shall humble themselves, and pray, and seek my face, and turn from their wicked ways; then I will hear from heaven, and will forgive their sin, and heal their land." (2 Chronicles 7:14).

III. *God's Strategy of Peace*

We must always remember that regardless of the circumstances the world is in, history remains under God's sovereignty. In Ephesians, Paul writes that God "purposes in his sovereign will that all human history shall be consummated in Christ, that everything that exists in Heaven or earth shall find its perfection and fulfillment in him." (Ephesians 1:9, 10, Phillips)

God's entrance into history through Christ has revolutionary implications for our attitudes toward our fellowman. Again in Ephesians, "He has made a unity of the conflicting elements of Jew and Gentile by breaking down the barrier which lay between us. He . . . made in himself out of the two, Jew and Gentile, one new man, thus producing peace. For he reconciled both to God by the sacrifice of one body on the cross, and by this act made utterly irrelevant the antagonism between them. Then he came and told both you who were far from God and us who were near that the war was over." (Ephesians 2:14–17, Phillips).

In God's eyes, then, every individual is of the most infinite value. God does not judge people as Americans or Russians or Chinese; He does not categorize them according to nationalistic, political, or ideological labels. Christ has broken through those barriers. God views each person as His creation — as unique and as infinitely valuable to Him, so valuable that He gave His Son for each of them.

God's purpose is to bring all creation into unity through Christ.

In the Old Testament, the vision of God's final peace is clear. In Isaiah, for instance, as well as in Micah, we are told of the day when nations "shall beat their swords into plowshares, and their spears into pruning hooks; nation shall not lift up sword against nation, neither shall they learn war any more" (Isaiah 2:4; Micah 4:3). God's strategy is to bring this to pass; we do not know the time, but we know that He controls history and is moving it toward this end. It is true that formidable adversaries face the realization of God's peace and purpose in the world. ("For we wrestle not against flesh and blood, but against principalities, powers and rulers of darkness" see Ephesians 6:12.) Yet we know that God's power, which raised Christ from the dead, has put Him at "a place that is infinitely superior to any conceivable command, authority, power or control, and which carries with it a name far beyond any name that could ever be used in this world or the world to come. God has placed everything under the power of Christ . . ." (Ephesians 1:21, 22, Phillips). Although we will find trouble and turmoil in the world, yet we know that Christ has overcome the world.

I make no claim to be a theologian. But there is one example used in theological circles that clarifies this point with me. It is a comparison of present history with the time between D-Day and V-Day during the war. We know that God has entered into history and accomplished His work of redemption. And we know that God's ultimate control and victory over history is assured. We have His promise to establish a new heaven and a new earth. He has won the final victory, but it is not yet accomplished. It is as though we are between D-Day and V-Day. Although our final victory at the end of history is certain, we must be involved in the skirmishes and battles that are yet necessary before God's triumph is fully manifested. Thus, we do not simply sit on the beach, knowing that we will ultimately win, but we move forth into battle. God is constantly at work in our world to accomplish His ultimate will. We must be obedient to His call.

IV *Our Mission of Peace*

Our evangelical responsibility is to bear witness to the love of God through Christ. This is a mission of peace, and we are under the call of God to fulfill it. In this task, we must not be bound by rigid categories of what is a spiritual message and what is a social action. We cannot build a complete barrier between theological issues and social questions. We must not make the mistake of believing that the Good News we proclaim has no relevance to our attitudes and actions toward political as well as personal problems in our homes, our nation, and our world. For too long the artificial polarization between those who preach the truth of individual conversion and the activists who proclaim some form of a "social gospel" has prohibited a full understanding of the Gospel's meaning in our world. Christ calls us to express His love through all that we do. We are to meet the needs of others — spiritual and physical. Whether we are relating to one another the reality of Christ's life or giving a cup of cold water in His name, we are bearing witness to that love.

Our task requires personal involvement in the world. We cannot abdicate our personal responsibility to an institutional response. Unfortunately our tendency too often is to seek escape from personal involvement in problems confronting us by endorsing institutional solutions to them. We give money to the church's missionary fund, we donate clothes to the street mission, and we contribute faithfully to worthy causes, believing that these are the only avenues for us to carry out God's work. Yet, what is most needed is individual, personal involvement. We must make our lives relevant to others; we must involve ourselves personally in situations where we demonstrate the concern and compassion Christ imparts to us. We must engage ourselves personally in sharing with others our experience of God's love.

Just as our religious institutions cannot become a substitute for our personal responsibility to minister to human needs, they also cannot provide any insulated shelter from the trauma of the world. The church was never meant to be a fortress that protected its members from the perils of the outside world. Rather, the church is nothing more than those believers who gather to strengthen and encourage one another for their involvement within the world.

That, of course, includes churchly responsibilities of preaching, edifying, and instructing. But evangelism — our message and mission as Christians — is primarily an individual, rather than an institutional responsibility.

But how does this responsibility for carrying forth the message of Christ's life and earnestly seeking God's peace for the world become relevant at some point in each of our lives? What is it that we can do?

Our faith calls us to seek God's will for man and for the world. As such, we must look at our own country — look at the values that are guiding our culture and ask whether they are true to God's will and purpose. If not, they must be challenged with a prophetic word, and Christians must witness to the need for national repentance; that is, to turn from present ways unto the "way of the Lord."

In our democracy, the values and commitments of the nation rest fundamentally with the people. The corporate effect of the people's thoughts and actions eventually has its influence upon the shape of our society.

For us who are Christians, then, it is our basic responsibility to express the values and truths that we have acquired through our faith. Further, we must attempt to implant them within the lives of others.

Therefore, one of the urgent avenues for personal action is to influence public attitudes and values.

Public opinion drove a President out of office last year; the attitudes of the people in our democracy can change the course of our country.

So we must be diligent and responsible in the expression of our views regarding the state of our nation. We must attempt to mold public attitudes so they will become attuned to God's purposes. The leaven of the Kingdom of God must continually make its entry into the life of our nation; it can do so only through the witness of our lives.

When we, as evangelicals, look at the state of our nation, how should we react? What should our attitude be toward a people who are absorbed by materialism, controlled by greed, and motivated by the pursuit of selfish and corporate gain, with little regard to the value and quality of human life? How should we judge the way our nation uses its resources? Since World War II, for instance, we have spent over $1 trillion for military purposes — for weapons, soldiers, and the machinery of war. Today, about $67 out of each $100 of our government's tax revenues are given to the purposes of war — past, present, and future. Comparatively, we spend only $2.50 for all our efforts to assist the impoverished millions of the world. We witness the decay of our cities and the inhumane life that millions must endure. Yet, only about $1.84 of every 100 tax dollars are devoted to community development and housing. Recently, it was calculated that the people of New York City pay more money in federal taxes for national defense than they spend on the welfare of their own city. Yet, what poses the greatest threat to our country? Nationalistic rebellions against corrupt governments in distant lands? Or the unrest and hope-lessness found in the heart of Harlem?

We are called to be stewards of our resources. Are we, as a nation, utilizing our abundance in a way that pleases God and seeks His purposes for mankind?

When we, as evangelicals, conclude that our nation is not following God's way, then we must speak out. That must be part of our witness. And that is where each of us can express his personal responsibility.

The nation of Israel experienced situations similar to that of our own land. In their quest for stability and power, they were often tempted to trust in their military power as the ultimate source of their security. Hosea warned prophetically against this danger: "Because you have trusted in your chariots and the multitude of your warriors, therefore shall the tumult arise among your people." (see Hosea 10:13–14)

The question is not whether we should have an army, but rather, it is whether our trust rests solely in our military power as a means of insuring our security and peace. The Scripture does not condone such a trust.

You and I are confronted personally with this issue. Where is our trust? Do we believe that our military might is the final guarantee of our peace? Does our personal trust fundamentally rest in our chariots and warriors, or do we really believe that peace is a gift granted by God, and not a utopia insured with our armed might?

Our individual convictions on this matter, as Christians and citizens, will have an effect on our nation's destiny.

Our point of individual involvement, then, can begin with an evalua-tion of our own attitudes and values concerning the Christian commission to seek peace. We must look within ourselves and see if we truly possess

God's inner peace. We must look to our families, and to those close to us, and ask if we are pursuing God's peace in all these relationships. We must look to our communities; what are we doing about the frustrated needs of many who inhabit them? We must look to our country; are we as a people truly seeking God's path to peace? How are we involved in speaking forth our convictions, and causing our nation to change its course? Finally, we must look to the world; what have we done to alleviate the human misery and cultural chasms that destroy the foundations of any lasting peace?

Our personal involvement, then, must be characterized by an examination of our own thinking in the light of God's purposes, relevant action to bring peace to those situations of conflict that touch our lives, and the proclamation of God's redemptive love.

Changes in people will have to occur if we are to discover any true peace. People must permit God to transform their values, their attitudes, and their purpose in life. This, in part, is the meaning of conversion. The life which becomes oriented around the person of Christ is radically re-created. Such a life is no longer in complete bondage to his selfish goals. The focus of his life is seeking to do God's will. God's Spirit injects new life — Christ's life. Thus, values, attitudes and purposes become reformulated. The world is visualized through its Creator's perspective, and His peace is sought.

Thus, the mission of peace cannot be severed from the task of evangelism. Seeking peace requires witnessing to God's will, judging nations, orienting one's life to the purposes of His peace, influencing the thinking of the public, acting in love towards our neighbors, and proclaiming the power of Christ to remake human life according to the "fulness of Christ."

Today our situation is much like that which faced the primitive church. As a small band, they faced a pagan world. But they did not remain in Jerusalem, fortifying themselves against their enemies. They became the church dispersed, the church on mission. Brave small bands infiltrated all levels of society throughout the known world. The impact was revolutionary, changing the entire course of civilization as the message of Christ's life spread throughout the Roman Empire.

Today we also must leave our institutional seclusion and go forth into the midst of the world's suffering and turmoil. We go with love to bring peace. We cannot be bound by our institutions, our organizations, and our comforts — all those things that serve as spiritual security blankets. We must seek to bring fulfillment to every need — to bring peace to every conflict.

Peace will not come to earth until the total needs of mankind are met. Changed lives must implement the mission of peace through the changing of society.

We cannot protect the status quo. We know that peace is not static.

The Christian must realize that the impact of his message challenges and questions things as they are, and claims that new life is possible.

So we go forth into the world seeing new possibilities — grasping God's vision of what He can do. We have the certain hope that He can impart new life — new life to individuals, to nations, and to all creation. That hope is based in the Risen Christ. All history is consummated in Him. He is our Peace.

PEACE — NOT OF THIS WORLD

Dr. Ira Gallaway

As I was thinking this morning about what has happened here during these days, I was taken back to Paul's letter to the Romans, to two verses in the eighth chapter. I believe this is what is happening here and I praise God for it. Paul says, "Up to the present time we know the whole created universe groans in all its parts as if in the pains of childbirth. Not only so but even we to whom the Spirit is given as first fruits of the harvest to come. We are groaning inwardly while we wait for God to make us His sons and set our whole body free." Set free to minister for Him. I believe new birth is happening in this convocation, and I'm grateful to be a part of it.

We're living in a time of new birth in our church, and this is my faith, and this is my hope. Last night we saw a great presentation here in the Black Light Presentation. "The answer, my friend, is blowing in the wind. Is the answer blowing in the wind?" Young people look right at us and ask us the question, "Is the answer blowing in the wind?" Or do we believe there will be another day, another tomorrow, to re-present the love of Christ in our time? Shall we put off for tomorrow what we have but today to do?

I was reminded when I thought of this about an incident that involved the life of my son three or four years ago. He was not much of a track man. He runs because he'd like to train for football, and he's only won two races in about 10 or 12 years. He was in Junior High at that time and that morning he thought he would really do well that day. I wasn't at the track meet. I picked him up, as most busy fathers do, after the track meet was over, and when he came out I saw he hadn't done very well. You know, you can tell a winner from a loser. And I asked him, "How did you do, son?" He said, "The worst I've ever done." I said, "Well, what was wrong? What happened to you?" He said, "Well, you know, Daddy, I run the 330 yard race. It was staked here on the 440 yard course and I misjudged the length of the race. I started off easy, saving myself. I started running real hard too late, the race was over too quick, and when the race was over I had too much left. I hadn't used all I had."

Now I want to remind you of a statement that Rev. Nelson Trout made to the press in a press conference two or three days ago. I believe with Leighton Ford, that unless we see change in America, it is doomed. Already we have begun to see God judging us. God is trying to catch the ear of the American society through the strife in our cities. We've always

DR. IRA GALLOWAY, District Superintendent, the United Methodist Church, Fort Worth, East District.

felt that the only way America could go down was from the outside. I don't want to dignify Communism by giving it credit for inventing revolution within. Communists may appropriate it, but they did not originate it. Billy Graham has said that unless we get together, black and white, Indians, and all the rest, America will not last our lifetime, and I believe that is true.

When I first began to ponder the subject to which I was assigned, "Evangelism and Coming World Peace," there were two thoughts that came into my mind again and again — two thoughts that tended to make me despair about the magnitude and depth of the subject, and my own most inadequate knowledge and ability to deal with it in a helpful and positive fashion. One of these thoughts came from the words of Jeremiah: "They have healed also the hurt of the daughter of my people slightly, saying, Peace, peace; when there is no peace" (6:14). Across the world today, there is much talk about *peace, peace, when there is no peace*. I certainly do not want to add further confusion to the seemingly hopeless search for peace. The second thought came from the words of Jesus, "Ye shall hear of wars and rumors of wars" (Matthew 24:6), which, when coupled with the Biblical view of man fallen, and my own experience with this reality in my own, and other lives, makes me wonder if this is not a futile search, which will be unending and unfulfilled until the coming of Christ again.

But, the Bible speaks of Peace. Upon the return of the Ark under Samuel, the Judge, the stone of Ebenezer was raised and we read, "The Lord (hath) helped us — and *there was peace* between Israel and the Amorites" (1 Samuel 7:12, 14). In the Kingdom under Solomon we read, "And he had peace on all sides round about him" (1 Kings 4:24). The apostle Paul speaks of peace "You must live at peace among yourselves" (1 Thess. 5:13, NEB). Again, "Spare no effort to make fast with bonds of peace the unity which the Spirit gives" (Ephesians 4:3, NEB).

And, of course, our Master, the Lord Jesus Christ spoke of peace. In His farewell discourses, as recorded in John, He said: "Peace is my parting gift to you, my own peace, such as the world cannot give. Set your troubled hearts at rest and banish your fears. — I shall not talk much longer with you, for the Prince of this world approaches. He has no rights over me; but the world must be shown that I love the Father and do exactly as He commands; so up, let us go forward!" (John 14:27, 30–31, NEB).

While it may not be our destiny to see world peace in our lifetime, it is our privilege as disciples *to do as the Son*, show love toward the Father and our fellowman, that others will be drawn to Him who is the author and finisher of our faith, and of *our peace*. As fellow ministers and evangelists for our Lord, it is my deep conviction that this is the most we can do for World Peace. The Prince of Peace casteth out fear, and enables man to live in peace.

But how do we effectively do this? We who are here, most of us, call ourselves evangelical Christians. I suppose this means, in brief, that we accept the gift of salvation in Jesus Christ; we believe in rebirth and the forgiveness of sin; and, we believe that God's Holy Spirit is present to live in us and direct our lives as disciples and followers of our Lord. In other words, we take the Incarnation seriously. God was in Christ, and through Christ, God will, *if we allow*, live out His love and grace in our lives. But somewhere, there is failure! We don't seem to be "doing so good," and it is not enough to castigate and blame the radicals and the liberals. We live in this world too! It is also our responsibility!

Christopher Dawson, in *The Dynamics of World History* has a chapter on T. S. Eliot and the Meaning of Culture. He interprets Eliot as indicating that "a culture is the incarnation of a religion." (pg. 112). Dawson goes on to say, "It is the religious impulse which supplies the cohesive force which unifies a society and a culture. — A society which has lost its religion becomes sooner or later a society which has lost its culture." (pg. 132). If culture is the incarnation of a religion, and I believe that there is real insight here, what religion would you say was the religion of America — as you look at our "culture" today? Would a broad cross-section look at our culture — at the people of our nation — remind one of Jesus of Nazareth, who had no place to lay His head, who came as one to suffer and serve — not to rule? *I think not*! Have we lost our Faith, or at least perverted it?

Dr. L. Harold DeWolf wrote in *A Hard Rain and A Cross*, "Because we Christians do not want to get involved in the reconciling way of the Cross, the world itself moves," remember this, "The world itself moves, as if in a kind of ritual dance, toward death." *Not dancing toward peace, but death*! Because Christians won't pick up the towel and basin, because Christians are not willing to be servant-disciples, because Christians won't pick up the cross, because Christians won't follow Jesus as Lord and Master, because Christians won't do exactly as the Father commands! — the world *dances toward death*! I believe strongly in the necessity of prayer, Bible study, and the devotional life. But, sometimes I feel that Christians are far more concerned to spend time in sweet fellowship with each other than they are to spend their lives in seeking to touch and heal those outside the faith. An uninvolved orthodox-piety is a heresy. It is a part of the dance toward death.

As I look at history, through the eyes of reason and of faith, I believe this dance can be changed! I believe that at least our direction can be changed! I believe that we can move away from chaos and death, at least toward peace and life. This is my faith, because I believe in the providence of God over His creation, and in the love and grace of God toward His creatures. *I believe in* Jesus Christ, and that He is the Lord of all the earth, *my Savior and my Lord*!

Now we must be willing to learn from past mistakes if we are not to repeat them. This is not the first time the world has been here, that is, in chaos, adrift, seemingly with little hope for peace and life without fear. Man has traveled this road many times before. This is the story of Israel, and of Western man; the story of faith and unfaithful; the story of God finding it necessary to bring us back to first things; to bring us before Him in repentance that we might again live as redeemed men — with peace in our hearts.

Now I am well aware that any analogy you draw when comparing two historical eras is not without serious difficulties. There are always different factors at work in different cultures. With this in mind, however, I feel that we can look at 18th century France and England and there find some significant lessons for all of us. This was a time of Revolution, in both France and England. In France the crown was corrupt. The nobility fought the crown, but both kept in subjugation the peasants and working class. Prisons were full of political prisoners. In England the miners worked under deplorable conditions; child labor was the rule; the plight of the poor was dismal; debtors' prisons were full, the Church was corrupt; and there was no hope for a good life for the common man.

In France, and I have an uncomfortable and uneasy feeling when I remember this, the revolutionary cry was for *Liberty, Equality*, and *Fraternity*. This is much the same cry as the young radicals make today, and their intellectual heritage is much the same, with the refinement of atheistic philosophers through the intervening years. Professor Leo Gershoy of New York University says that the revolution in France "was the accomplishment of men who believed in full sincerity that they were working for all mankind . . . They insisted fiercely that the natural *liberties* of the individual be safeguarded by the law. They had invincible faith in the moral dignity of man, and in the competence of his reason to lead him into paths of righteousness. They were firmly convinced that social *equality* would follow the exercise of freedom in thought and religious expression, in economic enterprise and government. They believed that a new spiritual unity, *fraternité*, would bind together the regenerated citizens in the common faith of revolutionary idealism." Professor Gershoy says of Robespierre that he had the "loftiest sense of civic service to society with a deep strain of coercive idealism." His purpose was "to remake France in the light of its religion of humanity and humanitarianism, social idealism and revolutionary patriotism, and reliance upon the guillotine" (pages 68–70 "Americana," Vol. 12).

Shades of the S.D.S.! This philosophical purpose and foundation of the French Revolution seems to be so similar to that of the young radicals of today. And we should remember that the French Revolution was a success, as revolutions go; that is, it overthrew the established order. And you are wrong if you doubt that such is the purpose of the young revolutionaries today. They sincerely believe that the established order of our society, including our religion, is corrupt and must be overthrown, discarded, or destroyed. As a matter of fact, many of them sincerely believe that the Church is the most reactionary force in our society, concerned only with preserving the status quo and protecting the economic, political, and social rights of the affluent. So they revolt. *And all we cry is "Law and Order."* What have we done to bring the healing power of Jesus Christ to their hurt and anger?

Almost simultaneously, in England there was another revolution occurring. Lecky, the historian, avers that it would likely have been similar to that of France, except for another ingredient. That ingredient was a revival and renewal of personal religion through the Wesleyan Revival. John Wesley, a member of the establishment, a political conservative, became a prime mover of social revolution, without being a reformer. I consider that Wesley being a Methodist is incidental here. As a matter of fact he, himself, never was a Methodist. He died an Anglican priest. Wesley preached a radical Gospel of the dignity of man and love of God. He preached a life of holiness and total commitment. He proclaimed a God of love who had come to enter into the life of the lost and least, and his fellowman heard his message. Now, all of us need to dismiss from our minds that the Wesleyan revival was a continuous prayer meeting where everybody came to know Jesus and lived happily ever after. It was far from that. Along with Wesley's concern for personal sin and individual redemption, there was a like concern for prison reform, abolition of the slave trade, abolishment of child labor and the sweatshop. He preached a faith which was both personal and social, and the faith he preached changed England.

Now, there are humanists, in the Church and out, today who seem to say that when all men are made equal socially, economically, and politically then our problems will be solved. And I know, as well as you, that this is not true. But I also know that an uninvolved orthodox Christian faith, which believes that the number one responsibility of the Christian is to go to church on Sunday morning — and then desist from smoking, drinking, and dancing — is neither true to Christ nor will help bring peace in our time. *My number one problem* as a church administrator is Christians — orthodox Christians, ministerial and lay — who either do not want to follow Jesus Christ or do not know how. We are not willing to risk our lives to lay them out as servants for Christ's sake — *and so the world cannot see the* Father — who is the only one who can bring peace. The world looks at us, we who call ourselves Christian, and says that it does not believe in God. Or, if it does believe, in a sort of hangover faith, it does not believe enough to become committed disciples of Jesus Christ. I am convinced that the greatest obstacle to the evangelization of the world is professing, creed-proclaiming Christians, who have at best, "the form of religion without the power thereof" — Christians who think that belief is enough.

I am equally convinced that Christian leaders, especially ministers of the Gospel, are being called to become player-coaches or teaching-elders — to teach as Jesus taught the disciples — what it means to become a committed follower of Jesus Christ. The textbook is the Bible — the place of application is the world in which we live. Now I believe in evangelistic and prophetic preaching, and I sincerely attempt to do both; but, let us face the truth, except for a very few evangelists, such as Dr. Graham, the world out there — the unbeliever — is not interested enough to even come and hear what a preacher has to say. If we are to reach that world, it will be because committed laymen, who rub elbows with the uncommitted in the market place, take it upon themselves to be active witnesses for Jesus Christ.

The truly effective evangelists for our day will be increasingly laymen, who having been led to Christ, and trained and taught through the Scriptures, know what it means to be a witnessing disciple for Jesus Christ. And I know of few pastors willing to assume the privileged responsibility and pay the price of preparation and study to effectively teach the Scriptures.

I recently asked Dr. Harry Denman, Minister Evangelist in the United Methodist Church, why most pastors were not teaching several classes in the Scripture each week. Harry replied that it was because they did not know, *or read the Scriptures*, except in search of a text. Could this be true? Could this be true? Could we be so busy with the necessary housekeeping chores of being a Pastor-Administrator, that we fail to take time for the *most necessary* requirement of effective ministry — spending time with THE Book and before our Lord in prayer? I'm afraid that Harry is more right than wrong!

When I think of the plight and dilemma of the black man in America today, I have a burdened heart. On the one hand, he lives with the heritage of slavery, serfdom, and subjugation. He is told by many of his militant brothers that he must rise up, revolt, burn, destroy, and fight for equality and power. On the other hand, he is told that all men are equal in America. He is promised the "Great Society." The hope is held before him that *his time* is coming — that he will get his share of the pie — the economic, the educational, the social, the political pie. And, worst of all, he is led to believe that when all of this occurs he will have arrived in heaven on earth.

Now, in the first place, things are not moving fast enough to bring about this equality, and secondly, when, and if, it arrives — for individuals or any group it will not be the promised land. Perhaps without knowing why at all, he will still find himself unfulfilled — that life has not been made meaningful as he had anticipated. And so he will conclude that he just hasn't received enough, and continuous revolt and despair are his lot.

As a matter of ironic information, he will be no more happy, fulfilled, or joyous than the average secular, affluent man in the pew in your church who is only half-committed to Jesus Christ. He will be filled with the same disease which will destroy any man — living for self and not for God.

Now, there have been particular problems in every age to which Christians were called to give their attention and to invest their lives in solving. Always, these problems have involved hatred, bitterness, alienation, fear, lostness, etc. The role of the Christian has, in every age, been that of reconciliation. Our own first need is reconciliation, and, then, we of necessity, if we are to live as Christians, must become disciples of reconciliation. Our lives must be *invested* in the places and circumstances where people hurt and suffer. Not that we have any patent social or political answers, but that we care, *as Jesus cared*, and *cares for us*; and we hurt when others hurt, we suffer when any man suffers. If you are a Christian today, you are bound to have a burdened heart. With Jesus, you look over Jerusalem and weep, *because you care*.

The story is told of a greeting in a certain tribe in Africa. One native meeting another asks, "How are you?" The reply is, "I am well if you are well." Or I hurt, if you hurt. If you have problems, I have problems. I care!

I see very little willingness on the part of most so-called evangelical Christians to so invest their lives and identify with the black man, or the young drop-out social revolutionary. Yes, I hear us saying, "*Law* AND ORDER," and, if necessary, we believe that force *must* be used to make the land secure and keep down revolt. Professor Arnold Toynbee in "An Historian's Approach to Religion" says, "We can, however, foresee that, when world-government does come, the need for it will have become so desperate that mankind will not only be ready to accept it even at the most exorbitantly high price in terms of loss of liberty but will deify it and its human embodiments, as an excruciated Graeco-Roman world once deified Rome and Augustus. The virtual worship that has already been paid to Napoleon, Mussolini, Stalin, Hitler, and Mao indicates the degree of the idolization that would be the reward of an American or a Russian Caesar who did succeed in giving the world a stable peace at any price; and in this baleful light it looks as if the ecumenical welfare state may be the next idol that will be erected in a still-discarded Christianity's place."

I am firmly convinced that the only healing agent for the divisions, the hatreds, the hurts in our world is the unconditional witnessing love of Christians who are willing to take on the role of being servant to God and servant to our fellowman. I'm sure that I do not know all that such a role calls for, but I have the definite suspicion that the Cross is somehow involved. Perhaps, just perhaps, if we were willing to lay down our lives — in such a whole-hearted fashion as Jesus did — many unbelievers would come to believe in God the Father, and in His Son, Jesus Christ. Again,

I am equally convinced that unless we Christians are willing to follow Jesus to the Cross, our destiny is slavery under despotism, and the only peace which we shall enjoy will be the security of the police state "as the world dances toward death."

Now, I make no plea here today for the coddling of anarchists, or revolutionary militants of whatever color. I do plead, however, for Christians, Christians who, having been reconciled to God, now choose not to hate any longer. I plead for Christians who are concerned, not to *protect* their lives, but to *invest* their lives as servants of God and man, to the end that peace may come, to the individual and to his segment of the world. This may take some of us away from our secure pulpits, or denominational jobs. This may change some of our professions and lower our incomes, but of what importance should this be? The question is — *are we willing, each of us, to do exactly as God commands?* The world will not know that we love the Father, unless we do. The world has no other chance to know peace, other than the peace offered through Jesus Christ.

"Peace is my parting gift to you, my own peace, such as the world cannot give. Set your troubled hearts at rest, and banish your fears. — I shall not talk much longer with you, for the Prince of this world approaches. He has no rights over me; but the world must be shown that I love the Father, and do exactly as he commands; so up, let us go forward!" (John 14:27, 30–31, NEB).

Now the peace of God be with you all (see Romans 15:33). Amen!

EVANGELISM AND THE
JOURNEY OUTWARD

Dr. Harold J. Ockenga

Billy Graham is one of those individuals who are few in number, and I'm very glad to take directions from him. He's most generous in what he says. I know it comes out of a very warm and loving heart, and I want to say that I think you're one of the most responsive audiences that I've ever listened to or participated in. I've never heard quite so much clapping as I've heard here this week.

I'd like to suggest one or two things in the beginning. One is a word of appreciation. As I listened to these addresses I've been profoundly moved. I've been moved emotionally, moved to tears on one or two occasions, moved to real vicarious indignation on other occasions, and moved to a sense of sympathy for the things which are being espoused here. I especially felt moved by that address of Leighton Ford in its balance and in its burden. I admired more than I can say the beauty, the academic quality, and the turning of a phrase of that address by Dr. Paul Rees, our long-time friend. I felt the passion of Tom Skinner's address. And so I've entered into each one of these addresses this week with a great deal of understanding, and sympathy, and empathy. They moved me profoundly.

I'd like to say one other thing. I've never seen a chairman enjoy chairing a meeting like this any more than Dr. Oswald Hoffmann has done. He just seems to enjoy every moment. This can be a great burden to someone, you know, but I don't think it's been any burden to him.

And as for Billy, I can't add much to what you all feel, but I certainly believe that he is one of God's great of the ages.

Now, the second word I'd like to say is a word of admonition. We have had different emphases here and they have been in balance. I don't suppose any of us can espouse everything which has been said by any means at all. We've held our reservations on some occasions. We've felt the thrust, of course, of the great propositional truth given to us in divine revelation, and we've felt the thrust of the experiential that's been given to us through encounter and through the personal experience of the individuals who've been involved. It would be very easy, you know, to move into one area or into the other. When I was listening to one speaker, I sort of felt that we were so subjectivistic that we almost bordered onto heresy.

DR. HAROLD J. OCKENGA, President, Gordon College and Conwell Divinity School, Wenham, Massachusetts.

When I listened to another speaker, I felt we were moving very definitely into the area of the right.

Now there has been a time in American history when we have considered Christian thought and Christian action in two ways, but each one of them has been in the interpretation of a circle — if we take a center point and then construct a circle around about that point. One has been, I might say, the left wing movement of theology and sociology in which the social gospel has been the center, the sociological need has motivated the action; and the circle would include largely the application unto all of these problems. We've called it the social gospel, we've called it the liberal movement, we've called it by other names, modernism, etc., and oftentimes some of us have criticized.

Then on the other hand there's been that movement whereby we place propositional truth, divine revelation, the content of theology, the person of Christ in the center, emphasize regeneration, personal piety, and the transformation of individual lives. This was the center and our whole relationship revolved around that center.

I don't think either one of these is the exact interpretation of historical Christianity. I think we evangelicals, for a period, in reaction against the social gospel of Walter Rauschenbusch, and those who followed him like Harry Ward, and many others we might mention, reacted a little bit too far to the right in this and made ours a circle which was self-contained, and that probably lasted for several decades. But some time ago there was the enunciation of what was called the "New Evangelicalism," and I think this could best be illustrated by an ellipse. In an ellipse you have two fixed points on which you construct your ellipse. One is that great truth, or that great point of divine revelation and propositional truth and theology, and the integration of one's faith around the objective. The other point is the subjectivistic, the personal encounter, that which is involved largely in the horizontal relationship. Both of these are absolutely essential to the Christian faith and it's only this week, as we've had the objective balancing the subjective, that we can guard ourselves from those errors and aberrations of Christian history.

It's only as we have divine revelation and propositional truth as the object of our faith centering in the person of Christ, and then the encounter and the experience as our own knowledge and our own entering into the existential realization of it, that we can possibly adapt both of these unto the whole realm of life and every area — whether it is economics, or family life, or educational life, or entertainment, or politics, or diplomacy, or whatever it may be — because we do not preach our Gospel in a vacuum. It has to do with every one of these areas. And I'm so glad that this conference has blazed a trail to emphasize both phases of our Christian truth and our Christian life.

I'd like to say one other brief thing by way of introduction. A word of apology because I feel a little bit weary, and I rather judge most of us feel the same from a good many of the things that we've gone through in the course of the week from early morning till late at night. If my voice gets a little bit raspy today, I hope you'll realize that this is the cause of it.

As I've been listening to these addresses and the encounter that has taken place personally and in group action, more and more I've come to feel that I wanted to say something different than I had planned. I was going to talk about evangelism with a definition, and then a description, and then something of differentiation in it, and then state that the moral incumbency of the Great Commission stands. It is unchanged, it will stand as long as the age stands, until Jesus comes. I was going to say that the outward look is going to reach into the future by our expectancy inspiring us in the hope of the advent of Christ, which is an eschatological hope, an eschatological experience, and an eschatological action. Jürgen Moltmann in his book tells us that those of us who have that hope will be the ones who take the pioneering action in the evangelical and sociological field.

And then finally, the equipment enables in the person of the Holy Spirit, and the unction that falls upon us from Him for this age. And that, I believe, Dr. Lindsell has adequately covered this morning.

But I'd like to turn your attention in these few moments now, by way of conclusion of this conference and the positional papers, to a text of Scripture that I think is particularly appropriate to us. It's in 2 Chronicles, chapter 7 and verse 14. "If my people, which are called by my name, shall humble themselves, and pray, and seek my face, and turn from their wicked ways; then will I hear from heaven, and will forgive their sin, and will heal their land."

This text is in a passage of Scripture that describes the dedication of Solomon's temple. If there was any occasion in the Old Testament where there was a national occasion and a nation dedication, a national prayer, and a national relationship of a people unto God, it certainly was this time; and surely, if anything, this conference has had national, if not world-wide significance.

Let us remember as we see this whole passage of Scripture, that David had prepared for the temple, and Solomon had erected it at enormous cost. That cost, if computed in modern values, would be somewhere around 4 billion dollars, which would make it one of the wonders of the ancient world. And when it was done Solomon made his brazen altar which was 7 1/2 feet wide and long, and 4 1/2 feet high. He stood before it in the midst of the representatives of the people and then he knelt and made a magnificent prayer in 2 Chronicles, chapter 6. In that prayer he used the word "if" nine times and then dismissed the people after feasting, and the giving of gifts, and the recognition and worship of the Lord.

Chapter 7 tells us that God appeared to Solomon at night and told him that He had heard his prayers, that His eye would be upon that place, and then He said, "If my people, which are called by my name, shall humble themselves, and pray, and seek my face, and turn from their wicked ways; then will I hear from heaven, and will forgive their sin, and will heal their land."

Now let us remember that in the Old Testament, the presence of God was symbolized by the tabernacle in the holy of holies, which was symbolically the dwelling place of God above the mercy seat. Later, in the temple that was erected by Solomon, the condition — which was a Biblical condition — that Solomon put in his prayer was that if they would pray toward that place, that is toward the present dwelling place of God, with repentance, etc., that God would hear and that God would forgive, and that God would heal.

And it is illustrated, I think, by Daniel when Daniel was in captivity in Babylon. You recall it says that he opened his window toward Jerusalem and bowed down and prayed toward Jerusalem, because that was the symbolic dwelling place of God.

Since of course the veil of the temple was rent from top to bottom, and since Jesus by His own flesh entered into the temple not made with hands and now the shadows have been done away with, and those that have been forerunners of the true have been abrogated, we enter into the presence of God immediately through our Lord Jesus Christ. And He has given us the great promise that where two or three are gathered together "in my name, there I am in the midst of them." Therefore we don't pray to Jerusalem, we don't pray to the East, we don't have any specific place for the dwelling place of God, but we know that God is present now, where two or three are gathered together, and much more in the great congregation where multitudes have gathered together in His name. Seventeen thousand were gathered together last night, and it was in the name of the Lord. In a sense that was a true church there in the Armory. This is a true church here and wherever you have husband and wife and child kneeling at a family altar, there is the true church.

Now you see the condition that was given there was that "if my people will pray toward this place." Now that meant that they accepted that God was there, that He existed, that there was a certain revelation of a self-existent God manifested in symbolic ways before the people. In our day, unquestionably, the condition laid before us is that we will seek the presence of God in and through the Lord Jesus Christ in His church, wherever that manifestation of the church may be. Now when that is given, then the promise stands, "I will hear. I will forgive and I will heal."

You see, we don't have to have a vast number of people praying. All we need is a remnant of God's people. That's all that was needed in the days of Elijah. That was all that existed in the days when the Lord Jesus Christ came. There was a remnant that looked for redemption. That's all that existed in the days of St. Paul according to Romans 11, and that's all that's necessary today — a remnant of God's people, who will pray, who believe that when they pray according to His will they know that God hears them, and when He hears them He will answer. And He says, "I will hear."

What a remnant is represented in this group this morning! What a tremendous group of people we've got in America who are believing people, God's remnant, and who are ready to seek His face. Then to know that He will forgive our iniquity as the promise is "Let the wicked forsake his way, and the unrighteous man his thoughts, and let him turn unto our God for He will have mercy and will abundantly pardon." God will forgive.

And then to know that God will heal. What a promise that is to a nation that's torn by racial strife. A nation that's facing revolution from within. A nation that's rocked by violence and crime and by all kinds of addictions to things which are ruining individual life. To know that God promises that He will heal. This is the promise that we have before us this morning.

Now I should like to suggest to you here very briefly in these few moments this question. Are there things from which we should repent? Is there a divine indictment which may be drawn against us today, such as could have been drawn against Israel of old? Then is there an invitation for us to repent and to turn unto the Lord? Then will there be a divine intervention?

Now we could move into great detail in this but it's going to be impossible, so I'm only going to suggest certain things that have become to me very deep matters of conviction.

The first thing is that there is an indictment that might be drawn against us as a nation and as a church, and I think that indictment has partially been drawn in this conference this week. Let's not for a moment compare ourselves with other nations or with other periods of history. It is perfectly true that if we did that then America would still be on a very high level. If we, for instance, compared America with Germany between 1914 and 1918, or rather from 1918 to 1933, those years of shame and of disgrace in the German nation. Or if we compared ourselves to certain aspects of the Communist nations and what they do in their brutality and sadism. But you see that's not the way that God looks at us. God looks at us, according to Scripture, according to the light that we have. "Remember he that did things worthy of stripes, and knew it, shall be beaten with many stripes, and he that knew not to do things worthy of stripes and did them shall be beaten with few stripes," Jesus said. This is the Biblical law that according to our light we shall be judged.

Now we have had a great philosophic heritage come into this nation from the early times. This has been the view that God is there; that God has revealed and written His law in the warp and woof of nature, and of human nature, and of history; that man has been made in the image of God and is of infinite value; that man is responsible to God according to the law; and that this has been expressed in the communities' relationships. As a result, we've had in our background what has been called Christian civilization, and well might it be called Christian civilization.

All of this is our heritage. We've had a heritage of great physical and material resources, of people that have come out of Europe seeking freedom, of the ideology of these movements. They've been written into the warp and woof of the charters of the early colonies, in the constitutions of the states, in the Declaration of Independence, and then into our own constitution. All this is our heritage. We have it and we're going to be judged according to the light that we have.

Now that means that when we're examined today and there's injustice, and we say that we believe that all men are created equal, then we shut them out of housing areas, and employment, and education, and other areas, we ourselves are inviting judgment upon ourselves, because we're acting inconsistently with the light that we have. Then when we talk about pride and we say we are the people — I admit that I belong to that group that they call "the wasps" you know, that they say still have control of America, and there's a certain comfort that lies in that — we have to recognize these minorities, their rights, their privileges, and all that ought to come here. And we could be indicted along this line as far as our church life and our American life is concerned.

When it comes to the matter of lawlessness today, we have — even in the theologians of the church — the attitude that we "do every man what is right in his own eyes," not that we have an authority under which we walk as the aegis that controls our intellectual and moral and social judgments. And this attitude reaches not only out of our intellectual and our moral concerns, it reaches now into all the activities of life itself until you talk about the new morality, and the new theology, and the new sociology, and all of these things. And there is a rejection of that which is the traditional viewpoint of western civilization and also of Christian history.

Then there's the modern means of drunkenness and inebriation. The Scriptures speak about this and these people shall not inherit the kingdom of God, and yet you go where you will today, and this is a way of life. It's a way of life in society, in the clubs, in all of the organizations, in the diplomacy, in the government, in every way. It's a way of life.

Then there's the promiscuity that's manifested in the new morality. The time won't permit us to go into a discussion of it, and it's causing this wave of infection of venereal diseases that the head of the contagious department of the government says is like a great flood that's going over the great metropolitan areas of America today.

And there's the prodigality. Look at the dinners that we eat day after day and throw part away, because we can't possibly eat half of what they serve us. Then two-thirds of the world is hungry. As Frank Laubach says, they live underneath a glass platform, they look up, and they see what we're doing up here. They no longer are willing to stay down there, being deprived and without. They're going to revolt against these things. There is an indictment that can be drawn against us in the church, and in America, in this particular day.

You see, when that indictment is drawn, then we turn to Scripture and read the prophets, and read John the Baptist, and read Jesus, and what do we find? Isaiah 1 describes, as you're familiar with it, how that the whole head is sick, how that the body is sick from the sole of the feet to the top of the head. There's no soundness whatsoever but wounds, and sores, and putrefying running sores. And then he says as he pleads with them to turn from their anti-social acts, "Come let us reason together. Though your sins be as scarlet, they shall be white as snow."

Jeremiah says, "Turn from your iniquities." He said, "I'm married to you as a backslider. Say not the temple, the temple of the Lord, but let righteousness flow down as a river."

Micah the same. John the Baptist, you know, says, "Turn, turn. If you have two coats, give to him that hath none. Be content with your wages, do no violence," etc. Jesus came saying, "Repent, repent, for the kingdom of God is at hand." And then told men what to do.

You see this passage of Scripture says to us that if God becomes angry with Israel and delivers them over to their enemies, "Then," says God, "if they turn, and if they bethink themselves, and if they confess, I will hear from heaven and forgive their sin and heal their land."

What it simply means is this. That we too will stand under the judgment of history, as Butterfield has said, John Baillie has said, Walter Keil of Erlangen University has said, and others in their books. We will stand under the judgment of a holy God who has written His moral law into the warp and woof of history as Germany discovered, as England did in a measure, and as Russia did. We also will so suffer if we do not turn and repent and think again about these great things.

This is the challenge which is put before us in an hour like this. It's an indictment which is drawn against us because God is angry. He hath whet His bow, He hath drawn His sword, and judgment is certainly imminent for our nation if we do not turn.

Is there invitation? Remember what it says here. "If my people." Nine times Solomon said it; six times, in the response, God said it. "If my people will bethink themselves."

Now to bethink yourself is to think again, and to think again is the New Testament word "meta," after, and "nous," knowledge, "metanoia," to think again. When we think again we repent. That's the translation of that word. We change our mind, and, of course, sometimes it's catastrophe, or it's sorrow, or it's suffering that makes us change our mind. That's the way it was with the prodigal son. That's the way it was in Germany after World War II when it lay in ruins. That's the way it is in many areas. It's this that brings us to repentance.

But you see, the Scripture says to us that if now we'll change our minds about these things, terrible times may be averted. Thomas Jefferson, writing his history of Virginia at Harper's Ferry said, "I tremble when I remember that God is just, considering the slave," and he also added that he thought that every drop of blood that had been drawn by the lash would also be drawn by the sword. This is a reflection concerning the justice of God.

Let's remember then that in this hour when we change our minds, we change our minds for the better, and we seek to turn and to do those things that are right, both individually, and in the church, and also we need to repent within the nation, and to turn.

Then Solomon said "and confess." We've sinned, we've done amiss, we've done wickedly. Confess one's evil, his wrongdoings, his sin.

I don't take responsibility for many of the things that have happened in this nation. I find it very difficult to find personal guilt about some of the areas of race condemnation. I find it difficult to find responsibility in many of the other things because, in many ways, I made no conscious contribution to many of those ills. But take a look at Daniel again for a moment, as his prayer is recorded in the 9th chapter of Daniel's prophecy. This man was one of the three most holy men of the Old Testament, "Noah, Daniel, and Job," it says. Remember Daniel said, "O Lord, *we* have sinned." Then he confessed the sins of the people and he confessed them as his own sin, identifying himself with that sin, and he cried, "O God, hear, O God, have mercy, O God, forgive," because it was his sin he felt, as he identified himself with the sins of Israel that had driven them into captivity.

"If my people will bethink themselves, repent, if they will turn (that's convert for the better), if they will confess (identify themselves with the sins of the day and of their people and confess them unto God), then," He says, "I'll hear and I'll forgive and I'll heal."

Now because time's going, I'm going to leap very quickly unto what I believe is the proffered involvement, the undertaking that God said that He would give, tracing your studies, what He did through Abraham, what He did through Moses in dividing the Red Sea and overcoming the Egyptians, the ten plagues, and the mighty leadership through Moses in dividing the Red Sea and overcoming the wilderness. Think what He did through Joshua; think what He did in the days of Hezekiah, which Dr. Lindsell mentioned; or in the days of Elijah, opening the eyes of the young men to show them that the powers that were with them were far more than those that were against them; or in the days of Jehoshaphat. Just remember for a moment what God has done and then remember this: God is the same yesterday, today and forever, and God offers today, if we'll meet the conditions that are involved, that He will undertake for us once again with that omnipotence, and with that goodness, and with that grace. He is still exactly the same.

It's interesting that in history progress is made by waves. Progress never comes just steadily; it moves in waves. When the waves come you have a gathering of momentum and then there's the backwash that comes from the trough in which is all the debris and all of the flotsam and jetsam of the beach. Then finally the swell comes, and then the wave breaks upon the beach. And then it withdraws and there's a trough again that takes back all of that flotsam and jetsam and then once again comes another wave, the swell, and it breaks and underneath it all the tide moves in.

That's exactly the way history moves. It never moves steadily and consistently. It moves in waves and that's the way the church moves on and will move on to that glorious climax that is yet to come, in the advent of our Lord Jesus Christ. And those waves that come are the waves of spiritual quickening.

Now let's remember that there are providential preparations for them, and those providential preparations are negative and positive before the swell comes. The negative one is that there's a time of doubt, a time of unbelief, a time of sin and indulgence and despair, a time of satiety with the physical and the material things of the world, and if I know anything about our day, this is the kind of situation we're in. Nations don't keep their covenants and word, there's a building up in business now of credit associations to find out if men mean what they say and can be depended upon in their word. Individuals are breaking their moral standards and doing what is right in their own eyes. This is the condition in which we are everywhere with our crime, violence, promiscuity, inebriation, and drug addiction. These things are there.

Then, let's remember there's a positive preparation. There comes a swell before the wave breaks and that swell is the satiety that men get with materialism and earthly pleasure. The hunger for God that comes out of the depth of a man's being, for deep calleth unto deep. The resorting unto prayer and groups for Bible study, and the seeking of God's presence, until finally there's a mighty rising swell on the part of men in their expectation of what God's going to do, and then there comes the mighty wave that crashes in.

Now if you know anything about history, it broke in the 12th century under Francis of Assisi and others. It came in the 15th century in part under Savonarola, in the 16th century with Luther, Calvin, Knox and others. In the 18th century with Wesley, Whitefield, Toplady and others. And it came in the 19th century with Moody and Sankey and also in a measure with Billy Sunday. And the question is, will it come today? Will there be the swell? Will it come?

Now I'd like to suggest to you just a few things as we draw to a close this morning that we can do to prepare for a quickening that can turn us back to those areas of truth and experience which will revive our Christian faith and experience. What are they?

Well, the first thing that I would mention is united confession. Some 26 years ago we organized the N.A.E., and I stumped the country for two years in reference to that, and met with hundreds and even thousands of ministers. Those were days of acrimony, days of division and fragmentization, days of bitterness in the fundamentalist-modernist controversy. And whenever we as a group got on our knees and confessed to God our sins, our abandonment of Biblical objectives, our failures to pray, our lack of love for one another, our unwillingness to bear the burdens of our brethren, the Spirit of God came upon us in a remarkable way.

I believe today that what's represented here in this group needs united confession of our divisions, our unbelief, our fragmentization, our suspicions, all of these things which have marred the evangelical cause. You know, we divided 25 years ago into the American Council and the N.A.E. If that hadn't happened, there could have been a united front that would have taken in perhaps all of the evangelicals. What we need today is for the Lutherans, the Southern Baptists, and all the evangelicals in the great denominations to come together. We need a re-examination of that division to recognize that there ought to be a framework today for the continuation of that which is carried on right here in this Congress. And it could be done.

But we need unity. We need confession, united confession. And that ought to take place at the grass-roots level, as well as in an area like this.

We need united praying. We need to "lay hold" as the Herrnhut people did in 1727 and started the modern missionary movement. We need to lay hold as Sidney Lampier and the noonday prayer meetings did before the Finney revival across this nation. We need to have united praying in order that there can be the release of power. We should pray for the gift of the Holy Spirit, and we ought to believe that we can have revival.

We need also united believing. Now there's a difference between the kind of faith that we exercise to be saved, and the kind of faith that's a gift of the Holy Spirit. If we can unitedly believe that God will do this, and take the Scripture teaching that revival is possible, even until the advent of our Lord Jesus Christ, as Peter said, "Repent . . . and be converted and He shall send you Jesus and times of refreshing shall come from the presence of the Lord" (see Acts 3:19, 20), then we can have those times of refreshing — right up to the time of the coming of the Lord Jesus Christ. Don't think that the days of revival are past.

And then there's united action where together we can stand and where, not the mathematics but the geometry of the Scriptures cares; where one shall chase a thousand, two shall chase 5,000. That's geometrical increase. That's what takes place in the great campaigns of Billy Graham and others.

We need united thinking, united confessing, united praying, united believing and united witnessing for Jesus Christ. That's what we're finding in the student movement of Bill Bright and Crusades for Christ. They believe, they really believe today that they can evangelize the world through having these people in the nations disciple others.

Now what will happen? Well you know, if you know history, what happened after all the great revivals. What happened in Europe after the Reformation was the birth of the modern era. What happened after the evangelical revival? You had John Bright and the Earl of Shaftesbury, Wilberforce, and the movement against slavery, long hours, child labor, and all these things that took place. What happened was the coming of the Victorian era and morality, and if we can have revival today, it will not only infuse radiance and power and life in the individual, so it will be an antidote for our loneliness and for our isolation, but it will also mean that the masses of men will be moved. And out of the masses, which are the reservoir of the anti-social actions of the day, will come those great movements that can be for the glory of God and for the transformation of society itself.

That's the repository of your future, ministers. That's the repository of missionary work. That's where we'll get our Christian education leaders, and the support of our Christian institutions. It'll come out of this kind of turning unto the revealed truth of God, centered in the person of our Lord Jesus Christ, and the encounter with Him that's translated into horizontal relationships to men.

Oh, the time's later than you think. That bulletin of the atomic scientist in 1951 went to 3 minutes to 12. It's back to 8 minutes of 12 now, but when I read of what's happening along the Nile, when I read of what's happening in Southeast Asia and think of what could happen, when I realize all of these things that are coming to pass in the fulfillment in this day of the prophetic word, I say the time is short. And just like those people in Pompeii who have been dug up by the archaeologists, and we see them in their various positions in their homes and in their businesses, and they were inundated by the ash when Vesuvius overthrew them (although they'd been warned), the day may come when we too will find that if we keep on as usual there will come that holocaust, there will come that conflagration, there will come that apotheosis of judgment upon us some day too.

Therefore remember, God says, "If my people (and that's you) will humble themselves, and pray, and seek my face, and turn from their wicked ways (individual and social) then will I hear from heaven, and forgive their sin, and heal their land."

O God, heal America today.

EVANGELISM IN OUR MODERN COMMUNITY

Evangelist Tom Skinner

Thank you very much, Dr. Graham, Dr. Hoffmann, and each one gathered here at this U.S. Congress on Evangelism. It is my privilege to have the opportunity this evening to share with you. One of my main reasons for being at this convention is because I believe this U.S. Congress on Evangelism can provide the momentum and direction for evangelism in our country. I firmly believe that if the Spirit of God is allowed to have His way in our midst, it can make the most fantastic impact that our country has ever known in terms of the Gospel of Jesus Christ. And that's why I'm here.

This day has already begun as an eventful day in this Congress, with tremendous challenges being presented to us in terms of the presentation of the Gospel of Jesus Christ in the "now" of revolution. As a result, a majority of the black delegates here at this convention are earnest in seeking to have dialogue, confrontation, and fellowship with those who have met here, in terms of what it means to communicate the Gospel of Jesus Christ to the black community.

What brought on the revolution? What is the role of the church in this hour of revolution? I am convinced that the most volatile, the most explosive, the most fantastic revolution taking place secularly in American society is the black revolution in America. There are large numbers of people who are asking, "What does the church have to say? What is the Gospel in this hour of conflict and confusion?"

If the Kerner Report is to be believed, they tell us that we are two societies separate and unequal. What does the church say to this? What is the message of evangelism in this hour? Where does the Lord Jesus stand in the midst of this hour?

I believe to understand it clearly we must begin to understand something of the roots of this hour. They go back to about 1619 when the first ships landed in Jamestown, Virginia and on them there were approximately 40 black people. Notable among them was a couple known as Isabelle and Antony who sired the first black family on American soil in 1624. So that black people have been an integral part of American society from its very inception.

Between the years of 1619 and 1660 there was relatively no problem in terms of the races living together. Our country had then what was known as indentured servanthood where a person who wanted to come

The REV. TOM SKINNER, Evangelist, Brooklyn, New York.

to the new world but could not afford to pay his passage, or a person who was a prisoner in the old world, sold himself to some one for seven years, worked off his debt and then was set free. There were both black indentured servants and white indentured servants and both black and white people held those servants. Black and white people lived together, ate together, sued each other, went to court, fought each other, married each other, made love to each other, and had children by, for, and with each other, and there was no problem.

But by 1660 there developed the cries that it was difficult to control the white indentured servants who ran away before their contract was up. They could easily assimilate into the rest of society. It was very difficult to recapture them. But if black indentured servants ran away, they could be very easily recaptured because of their high degree of visibility. Therefore, it was decreed that only black indentured servants would be used.

By 1701 this became permanent, and slavery became a way of life in American society. As with any institution growing up in a society, there must develop rationalizations in order to support it, and there were three segments of our society that upheld slavery. There was the economic system — slavery was a cheap form of labor. They soon discovered that with slave labor they could compete with the foreign cotton markets. But what is supported by the economic system in America is usually supported by the political system, because politics and economics are synonymous. If you watch the Dow Jones average in times of political bad news, it goes down. The stock market goes up when political news is good. Our country was no different at that time.

The third system that upheld slavery was the religious system. There were large numbers of churches who said that slavery was a divine institution ordained by God, and there were others who sought to find Scriptural means to support slavery. There were others who said that the slave was not a real man, he was sub-human, therefore the Gospel of Jesus Christ and all that it said did not pertain to him.

Slaves were not allowed to develop their own children or their own families. The slave master rather developed on the plantation what was known as a "stud." He was a healthy male slave whose sole job was to impregnate a healthy female slave to bear healthy children. When the woman became pregnant he would move to other quarters to do the same thing, so that within the course of 10 years he could have brought into the world 100 children but was never allowed to father any of them. No child who had been around the plantation could say "Mommy" or "Daddy" because they didn't know who they were.

Their emancipation came. In 1865 the black man was free, but all the emancipation did was to say what he was not. It never said what he was. Emancipation said, "He is not a slave," but it never defined him as a man. Society then turned to this former slave and said, "Now that you are free you are to settle down, become the husband of one wife, the father of your own children, and you are to assimilate into American cultured society." And they expected him in one night to change what he had been taught to do for 250 years another way, and the amazing part about it is that he began to do it. Through programs of self-help and self-determination, he began to pull himself up by the bootstraps so that by 1876 dozens of black people had been elected to the United States Congress, United States Senate, and the state legislatures in the states of South Carolina, Alabama, and Mississippi. And Florida and Louisiana were controlled by black politicians.

By 1877 there developed cries from certain sectors of society that this former slave was moving too far too fast. They said that he had only been freed for 12 years. "Does he expect to have all of his marbles in 12 years? These people must learn that these things take time. They must learn to be patient. The course of change is not easy." It is very strange that 100 years later that same cry is still enunciated in American society.

Mr. Hayes, in order to be elected President of the United States, had to enter into negotiations with politicians that if elected he would withdraw troops from the South and allow southern politicians to deal with the black man in their own way. He was elected, the Compromise of 1877 took place, troops were withdrawn from the South, and there began between the years of 1877 and 1925 public attempts to eliminate the black man from public political life. During that period of time more than 5,000 black people were lynched without one person ever being brought to trial, or being convicted for it. His homes could be burned, his women raped, his children beaten, and he could not find recourse in the courts of law.

But 1914 came and World War I. The black man put on an American uniform and went off to defend America as the land of the free and the home of the brave. Now you must give him credit. He had been denied his rights, he had been disenfranchised, he had been relegated to fourth class citizenship, yet he put on an American uniform and went off to fight for the principles of a democratic country who had so nobly denied him those principles. And you must keep in mind that even in the present conflict in Vietnam it is not the black soldier who is burning his draft card and running off to Canada to avoid his responsibility in the Armed Forces.

As a result of being stationed in the large cities in the North: New York, Chicago, Detroit, San Francisco, Philadelphia, the black soldier began to send word back to the South where 90 percent of the black population lived that if black people would migrate north they would find a better way of life, greater economic opportunity and more social justice. So between the years of 1920 and 1950 there was a mass movement of black people to northern cities. Such songs as "So Long, Dixie" began to be developed, and the North became the so-called promised land.

But when they arrived in the North they soon discovered that the patterns of segregation and social injustice were not too different. They soon discovered that they were forced to live only in certain communities. They could buy or rent homes only in certain neighborhoods. They discovered that whenever they moved into certain communities in large numbers, whites moved out in equally large numbers. So integration began to be defined as that period of time when the first black family moved into a community and the last white family moved out.

And as a result the black man soon discovered that he was disenfranchised even there.

In the early '30s they began to sow the seeds of discontent and rebellion that have brought us presently to this hour of revolution. It is a revolution that breaks itself down into three areas: First, it is a revolution of identity. The black man is trying to discover who he is, thus his rejection of the words "negro" and "colored" for the word "black." Negro and colored, in his estimation, being the white man's definition, black being his own. But more than that, it is an attempt to find himself, to discover his place in the world. One of the great tragedies that I faced as a young person growing up in Harlem was trying to find out who in the world I was. I knew I was black. I knew that I lived in a black community. Harlem was a 2 1/2 square mile area with a population of 1 million people. There were 4,000 people in my block alone. Forty-three percent of the kids were born out of wedlock and 57 percent grew up without their fathers, producing what the sociologist called "a matriarchal society" which simply meant that the kid's old man wasn't home.

And in the middle of that I was trying to discover who I was. I looked at television and I found very few personalities with whom I could relate. Oh yes, they showed me Step-an-fetch-it who went out on the stage and made a fool out of himself, or they gave me Rochester who was Jack Benny's sidekick and they said, "Tom, that's you," and I said, "No way."

I started school and they gave me a Grade 1 reader. In it there were stories about Dick and Jane and Sally and a dog named Spot who said, "Bow-wow," but none of them were black with the exception of Spot who was integrated. But I soon discovered that there was no person with whom I could relate, nothing that gave me a sense of identity.

The black girls in my community grew up without a sense of identity. From the time they were one year of age their mothers began to take them through a long process called "combing" in order to help them adjust to the American concept of beauty. You see the black girl's hair is different from the white girl's hair. Black people's hair is thicker and coarser than white's, but yet the American concept of beauty, of course, is white people's hair. The mother begins this long combing process when the child is very young to try to straighten the child's hair out so that it will be accepted in the American concept of beauty. And it's one of the most painful processes. So that one of the worst things that little Janie would like to hear from her mother is, "Janie, come and let me comb your hair." You would think, after the many hours of braiding and plaiting, that when little Janie hit the street she would be so overwhelmingly beautiful that the whole world would be stunned by her beauty, but the fact was that she was merely made acceptable. Janie began to reason that if she had to go through all of that in order to be acceptable, then she must have been awful ugly before the combing started. Or when she watched television and she saw the young girl come on flinging her hair around and saying that her hair was soft and beautiful because she had just finished shampooing it, little Janie knew that she could wash her hair in any shampoo on the market and it wasn't coming out looking like that.

She also knew that she couldn't dream of ever becoming Miss America and so the search for identity went on.

Second, the revolution is a revolution of community where black people are seeking now to possess power in their own community. Ninety-nine percent of the businesses in the black community are not owned by black people. The majority of the politicians who hold office representing the black community are not black. And so there is a tremendous upsurge to bring together community, and this is what the revolution is all about.

Third, it is also a revolution of power. Large segments of the black population feel powerless in American society. They feel powerless to deal with the status quo. They feel powerless to deal with the Establishment, and out of it is coming a frustration and rebellion. You must keep in mind that during all those years of slavery and all those years of struggle, for the most part, the evangelical church in America remained strangely silent. Now that's what the revolution is all about.

But in a sense it is a revolution that is the outgrowth of so many other problems that have developed as a result of what took place back in the early chapters of Genesis where one man stood and clenched his fist in the face of God and in essence said to God, "I will be the captain of my own soul, the master of my own fate. I choose to run my own life," and it was through Adam's independence that he injected into the entire human race the problems of identity, and community, and power. Because the Bible says that when Adam sinned and transgressed, when he decided to be independent, he lost fellowship with God and no longer knew who he was, and no longer knew who his neighbor or his brother was.

Cain rises up and slays his brother Abel and then has the audacity to turn around and ask God, "Am I my brother's keeper?"

But in the midst of this, if this is the situation we face, we're facing an explosive situation in America, and make no bones about it. We are in the midst of a revolution, and the black brothers on the street are not playing when they say that unless they get justice they will burn the system. Now the question is, where does the church stand in the midst of that revolution? What is the message of evangelism? What is the message of the church? What do we have to say to 25 million people who feel shut out of American society?

May we begin by considering what the role of the church is. I would like to suggest to you, in the first place, that in this hour of revolution it is the role of the church to reflect the life of Jesus. I'm tremendously impressed as I read the book of Acts. I read of Peter and John who go out on the streets of Jerusalem and begin to declare the unsearchable riches of Jesus Christ, and the Bible says that they were arrested by the Sanhedrin. The Word of God says that when they saw the boldness of Peter and John and perceived that they were ignorant and unlearned men, they took knowledge of them that they had been with Jesus.

The New Testament church also grew up in a time of revolution. It grew up in a time when the Romans were exploiting the Jews. It grew up in an hour when the seeds of revolution were being sown by Jewish nationals who were saying that there was only one way to get those Romans off your back and that was to burn them out. In the midst of this, there arose this radical group of disciples who had been with Jesus for 3 1/2 years, who had walked with Him, had seen Him live His life in total dependency upon His Father, had seen Him crucified, had seen Him after He was resurrected, and had seen Him ascend to His Father. Filled with His life, they went out and they impressed people that they had been with Jesus.

My black brothers in Harlem and Watts are not so sure that the church in the 20th century has been with Jesus. They're not so convinced that we present Christ, or that we are the vehicles through which Jesus Christ has chosen to reflect Himself.

But you see, it is the purpose of God in this hour of revolution to take you and me as the church, and make us the vehicles through whom He expresses Himself. It is therefore the responsibility of the church to be able to say to a revolution that we're not here necessarily to take sides with the revolution, but we're merely here in the midst of this revolution to say to you what the principles of the Kingdom of God are. The early disciples simply went out and they said, "Yes, there's a revolution. Yes, some of it is right. The Jewish radicals are right about what they say to the Roman Empire, but what are they going to replace the Roman Empire with?" They came forth saying that the Roman Empire and the Jewish radicals had no real answers. They said that real revolution lies in allowing the common clay of your humanity to be saturated with the deity of Christ, and for you to go out in open display as a living testimony that it is possible for the invisible God to make Himself visible in a man.

Romans 8:28 tells us that the role of the Christian, the role of the church, is to teach that everything in our lives works together for good, to those who are called according to His purpose. Romans 8:29 tells us that we are to be conformed to the image of His Son, that He might be the first-born among many brethren. In other words, it is the intention of the living Christ to saturate us with Himself, and then to put us out in open display in an explosive world, not to take a political position to the right, the left, or what have you, but to simply declare that we are the vehicles through which Christ chooses to express Himself; and in this hour of revolution we come to proclaim the principles of the Kingdom of God.

Where does the church get this authority? Where did Peter and John get this authority in their explosive situation? In Acts 3 we are told that Peter and John were on their way to the Temple to pray, and the Bible says that there sat at the gate of this Temple a man who was lame from his mother's womb. He had never walked in his entire life, and the man would hold out his hands to beg money from various worshipers as they went up to pray. People would drop a few gold and silver coins in his cup, but all they managed to do was to make the man a little more comfortable in his misery. They would walk up and they would worship the Lord, they would pray to the Lord, and they would thank God that they were the last of the Mohicans holding on to any New Testament truth, while all the liberals were contaminating the Word of God. They would walk out rejoicing in the fact that they were the last of the people upholding the true Word, they passed that man sitting there, and they would shake their heads. And they would say, "Wasn't the service wonderful this evening? Wasn't that a great Word?" And they would rejoice with each other, and meanwhile the man sat there.

Finally Peter and John go up one day to pray and the man holds out his hand to beg alms of them, and Peter uses those classic words, "Silver and gold have we none. But such as we have, give we unto you. In the name of Jesus Christ of Nazareth, rise up and walk." And the man rose up. What Peter and John were saying is simply this, "For 3 1/2 years we have walked with a man who lived His life in total dependency upon His Father. For 3 1/2 years we walked with the only man who ever walked the face of the earth as God intended man to walk. For 3 1/2 years we handled the Word of life. For 3 1/2 years we saw a man make Himself available to His Father." If you check out the life of Jesus you will discover that that was the evidence of His perfection. He was not perfect because He carried around in His pocket a bunch of rules and regulations. He was not perfect because He sought to conform to the cultural "mores" of His time, but He was perfect because He never made a move without His Father. Which is precisely again why Jesus says, "I come to do only those things which please my Father." Which is again why Jesus said, "Don't believe me just because I perform miracles but believe me because the miracles which I perform, my Father does them in me. If you ever see me do something that my Father isn't doing in me, then you have a right not to believe me. As long as that which I do is what my Father's doing in me, then you better believe me."

Peter says, "As Christ was available to His Father, His Father was available to Him. We have made ourselves available to Christ, and Christ has made His aid available to us. Because we're available to Him and He is available to us, we now tell you in His name to rise up and walk."

In the middle of this revolution the church will have to go to a crippled people, a people who are crippled economically, a people who are crippled socially, a people who are crippled politically, a people who are crippled psychologically, a people who have been robbed of the opportunity that you've had for so many centuries to hear of the unsearchable riches of Jesus. You yourselves will have to go to the Cross to repent of your negligence. Then being filled with the Holy Spirit, go to a black population that is burdened down, and cry out to them in the name of Jesus, because you are available to Him, to rise up and walk.

The next role of the church is to live oblivious to public opinion. Peter and John were arrested, and they were told never again to mention the name Jesus or they would be put to death. And Peter and John answered and said, "Whether it is right in the sight of God to listen to you more than God, you judge, but as for us, we cannot help but speak the things which we have seen and heard." In other words, a church that is filled with the Holy Spirit and really wants to do the job of evangelism is a people who live oblivious to public opinion. They take their orders from God, and when they know what God wants they go ahead.

One of the great problems that we face in race relations in America is that great numbers of us as Christians know where we ought to stand. We know that we should speak. We know what we ought to say. We know that we ought to preach against racism as sin against God, but many of us have refused to do so on the grounds that it is not popular, on the grounds of what our neighbors would say, and on the grounds of what the parishioners would say. I've had large numbers of pastors tell me, "Tom, I know I ought to take a stand in my church, but my Board of Trustees would vote me out next week." I've had large numbers of church leaders tell me that they would be glad to take a stand, but their financial support would be cut off if they did. There are others who say, "Tom, I know I ought to stand in my neighborhood, but my neighbors would turn against me." Young people are saying the same thing. But what Peter and John are saying is, "We know what God has said, we know what the principles of the Kingdom of God are. For 3 1/2 years we took our orders from the Lord of heaven. He now indwells us and if you think we're going to be quiet you're out of your mind. We're going to speak for Jesus."

It is the role of the church to produce a relationship that is thicker than blood brother and sister. The Bible says in Acts 4:23 that when Peter and John had been threatened, "Being let go, they went to their own company, and reported all that the chief priests and elders had said unto them." They went to their own company, which meant that they had a fellowship and a relationship that was thicker than blood brother and sister. And again the Bible tells me that when these men were filled with the Holy Spirit, the multitude of them that believed were of one heart and one soul.

People ask me, "Tom, what is the answer to the race question in the church?" The answer, my friend, is to be filled with the Holy Spirit, because when we are filled with the Holy Spirit we see ourselves as one in Christ. But more than that, the multitude of them that believe are of one heart and of one soul. One of the great things right here in this convention is the large number of black Christians who are attending. They desire more than anything else genuine fellowship. Now don't get me wrong. By fellowship I do not mean retiring to the basement of a church for a time of fellowship, namely cookies, tea and coffee. I don't mean that. But by fellowship I mean where we pour ourselves into each other, where we share with each other on an equal relationship.

There are large numbers of us black Christians who have discovered that fellowship in the minds of some of our brethren usually means a paternal relationship. If we act as they expect us to act, if we say what they want us to say, and if we believe what they want us to believe, then we can have fellowship. My friend, that is not fellowship, that is psychological slavery. But what we need is fellowship, fellowship that says, "I respond to you as my brother. I respond to you as my sister," and as Bill Glass pointed out, the kind of fellowship that says, "I am prepared to lay down my life for you."

This was the kind of relationship they had and, my friend, there is no possible way by which we're going to penetrate the black communities and the black ghettos of America until we can again begin to show, in a demonstration of love and responsibility and fellowship, that the body of Jesus Christ is one. Those of us who preach from the streets of the black communities are increasingly embarrassed as we must answer the question as to why churches are segregated in America. Why is it that we preach the same Gospel and there are certain churches we can't fellowship in? Why is it that even though we preach the same Gospel there are certain pulpits we are not welcomed in? Why is it that even though we preach the same Gospel, there are certain Christian institutions in this society that actually have written in their constitutions that no black person can attend that school? We continue to be embarrassed by the lack of genuine fellowship on the part of those who name the name of Jesus. It is the kind of fellowship that if you attended my church and you were slighted that morning or you were not allowed to enter, my church would not hear from me tomorrow or next week, but they would hear from me that morning, in that service, because my brother has been turned away.

If the revolution develops to the point where you happen to be present in my community when a volatile situation develops, and the situation calls on the part of the black radicals to eliminate all white people present in that community, and you and I are together, that kind of fellowship says that I will take upon myself the responsibility of standing between you as my brother and between the radicals as the foe, because you are my brother in Christ. Never mind your political point of view or your social position. But this kind of relationship calls upon me. My Master, my Christ demands if I'm available to Him that I be willing to lay down my life for you. But the issue is this. Will you reciprocate?

When I move to your community and buy a home and I'm being given a rough time, will you take a stand? If my daughter falls in love with your son and they decide to get married, will you allow them to marry in peace? Will you reciprocate by accepting me as a brother? This is what black Christian brethren are crying out for, a genuine relationship.

The church must begin to take a stand in those areas of racism that pervade our own institutions. You must begin to investigate your own mission societies that have continued to refuse to send black missionaries to the foreign fields. You must begin to investigate those colleges and universities that are not opening their doors to black people. Now I know that there are many college presidents who will say, "If they come, the doors are open." But you see, it's like your coming to my house for 10, 15, 20 or 30 years and knocking on my door and I refuse to let you in. Day after day for 30 years you keep knocking and knocking and I don't open. And then finally one day I hold a meeting with my family and I'll say, "Now the next time that fellow knocks we'll let him in, but we won't tell him."

Many institutions in American society say that they're open but they haven't communicated it to us. They haven't come to the black community and said, "We are open. We'll provide scholarships. We'll provide the education to train you, to go out and reach your people in the name of God." This is what we need to hear.

You need to begin to speak to those institutions in your society that have been closing the doors. But may I say a word about the fact that black Christians who are seeking to reach their people for Jesus Christ need to have available to them your resources and your facilities. You must keep in mind that because you are the majority in America, God has blessed you with the colleges, and universities, and Bible schools. But keep in mind that right now in the United States there are less than 100 black students studying in all the white evangelical Bible schools put together. Keep in mind that God has blessed you with those facilities and if we are to reach our people, you must open the doors. And not only do that, but also seek to provide black faculty, black curricula, black recruitment, so that we can go back and communicate the Gospel to the black community.

You own the Christian radio stations so that if black teachers, and black Bible scholars, and black evangelists are to be heard, you have to open the door. You own the evangelical magazines. There are no black evangelical magazines. You own them, you write them, you control them. You must begin to use your media to provide news of what God is doing in the black community. The honest truth is that if we read most of the evangelical magazines today, the impression is that God is only working among white Christians. There's much that God is doing in the ghetto. There is much that God is doing in the black community. There is much that God is doing on black college campuses. It is up to you to begin to speak to the editors of Christian magazines to cover what God is doing in the black community so that people in the black community as well as the white community will not get the impression that Jesus Christ is merely an Anglo-Saxon middle-class Protestant Republican.

Allow me to make it plain that if you're going to share with us and we to share with you, this sharing must be with no strings attached. One of the great problems we have faced as black brethren is that oftentimes in order to communicate the Gospel there has been a certain amount of games we have had to play with our white brethren. We couldn't be ourselves if we were going to communicate.

But you must express to black Christians — and there are large numbers of them — faith in their leadership as you have expressed in your own. Just as you continue to do works of God among your own people without necessarily wanting to pull the strings, simply because you believe God's got His hands on a particular group, or certain men, you must begin to have that kind of faith in the men that God is raising up in this hour to communicate the Gospel in the black community. But you see there are large numbers of us as black Christians who preach and teach under great pressure. There are large numbers of stations that are beginning to pressure black evangelists who are preaching on the radio if they begin to speak about certain issues. There are several of us who broadcast on certain stations and there are several Christian stations who have preempted some of the black evangelists, because they felt they were getting a little bit too militant.

But, my friend, why is it that you allow certain evangelists or certain teachers to speak strongly against Communism, strongly against social disorders, strongly against sex, strongly against movies, strongly against night clubs, strongly against mini-skirts, and you will not allow black people to speak in the name of God against racism?

I plead with you. I plead with you as a brother in Christ, as one who is willing to lay down his life for any other brother in the body of Christ, I plead with you to respond to the needs of black Christians in this hour and to respond to the need to communicate the Gospel in a community that has been neglected. There is no community on the North American continent that is so hurting and so lacking the Gospel, and in such desperate need for all that Jesus can mean as the black community. I plead with you on the grounds that to deny a brother a place to live because of the color of his skin is one thing, he can recover from that; to deny him a job based on his qualifications is something else, because he can recover from that; to deny him economic opportunity because of the color of his skin is something else, he can recover from that; to deny him social position because of the color of his skin is something else, he can recover from that; but to tell me that I can't hear of the unsearchable riches of Jesus, to deny me the truth of Calvary, to deny me participation in the body of Christ, to deny me the privilege of being a joint heir with Jesus to be seated together with Him in heavenly places, to deny me the right of participating in every spiritual gift in heavenly places is a blow that I can never recover from.

May I say a word to my black brethren. All the blame is not to be placed upon our white evangelical friends. A lot of blame lies squarely with us as well, because over the years we've allowed envy and jealousy to split us. Then large numbers of us black Christians have had the privileges of being the first to join various evangelical organizations as editors, or evangelists, but some of us have not used those positions of influence to change the minds of our white brethren as to what their attitude should be. And there are many of us black Christians who were so busy seeking to court the favor and prestige of being associated with our white brethren, that we forgot the bridge that brought us over. We forgot the black brethren who were struggling, and we did not use our influence to bring them.

Now, of course, much of this is a carry-over from slave days. The slave master had what was known as a house slave and a field slave, and the master convinced the house slave that he was better than the field slave because the house slave lived in the house, ate the food cooked in the house, and dressed in house clothing, while the field slave labored all the day long in the hot sun and ate out of the pail with the other slaves.

The house slave watched the field slave to make sure he didn't get his job and the field slave watched the house slave to try to get his job, and the master watched no one. But it still lives with us, the slave mentality is still present. There are some of us who've had the privilege of moving into the ranks. There are large numbers of us who've had the opportunities as black Christians to get close to the positions of power within the evangelical establishment. But we have not used that influence, we have not used that position to further the Gospel of Jesus Christ among our own people, and much of the ignorance that exists with many of our white brethren must lie squarely with large numbers of black Christians who refuse to open their mouths.

Finally, to my black brethren, we must never cease to tell it like it is. We must never cease to seek to educate, to train, and to inform our white evangelical brethren, because much of their lack of knowledge is not due to deliberate prejudice but due to the backgrounds from which they come. Therefore we must caution ourselves against bitterness, against malice, and against hate. In the spirit of love, and in the Spirit of Jesus Christ we must seek to fellowship with our brethren, and to win them, to school them, and to educate without malice and without bitterness. We must not fall into the same trap. We must be careful that the very things that we speak against we do not fall into. And I suppose the best example is to take back to our positions in life the individual Jesus Christ for whom we are to communicate, because in the middle of this revolution He stands as the only answer.

But what does Jesus Christ have to say to it? I suggest to you that if Jesus Christ is going to penetrate this revolution, and if He is going to be exalted as the risen Christ and draw men to Himself, then we must be careful as to the kind of Christ that we possess. One of the things that turned me off about the Christian church was that the image they gave me of Jesus was that He was a softie, that He was a nice little patsy. The pictures I saw of Him, He came out with nice smooth hands as if they'd just been washed in Dove. I got the impression that Jesus was some sort of soft, effeminate individual, and I said, "I can't respond to Him. He looks so soft, as if we could beat Him up on any street corner at any hour," until I discovered that the Christ which leaps out of the pages of the New Testament was no softie.

The Christ that leaps out of the pages of the New Testament was a very gutsy, contemporary man with hair on His chest and dirt under His fingernails. He was the kind of Christ who could look the Establishment in the face and when He knew they were wrong He could face them and say, "You generation of vipers, you hypocrites, you filthy separatists. You're like dead men's bones." But that same Christ could be moved with compassion to weep over a city. That same Christ was radical enough to walk into the Temple where the house of His Father was being desecrated, and He could wrap cords around His hands, and He could knock over the money counters and drive the moneychangers out, and with a holy fervor stand there and say, "My Father's house shall be a house of prayer."

But the same Christ could look down upon an adulteress and tell her to sin no more. That Christ is the Christ who belongs to the common clay of our humanity. We must be willing to make ourselves available to Him. We must not present Christ as the maintainer of the status quo. Jesus Christ is not the head of the Pentagon, He is not the president of the New York Stock Exchange, He is not the defender of the capitalist system. He is neither capitalist nor Communist, He's no more Republican than He's Democrat, He's no more militaristic than He's pacifistic, He is no more leftist than He's rightist or conservative. He is the Lord from heaven, He must be worshiped as Lord, He must be preached as Lord, and we must respond to Him as Lord.

The time of Jesus Christ was no different from ours. There was a revolution going on. The Romans had exploited the Jews and there rose in the hills of Jerusalem a young radical by the name of Barabbas. And Barabbas looked out among his people and he said, "Brothers, there is only one way to get those Romans off our back and that is to burn them out." Barabbas gathered around him a group of radicals who began to throw fire bombs and Molotov cocktails in those nice Roman suburban homes and burned them down. And Barabbas was arrested as an insurrectionist.

But in those same hills was another radical, another revolutionary. His name was Jesus. He had no guns, He had no ammunition, He had no tanks, He never used guerrilla warfare. But He came preaching a thing called the kingdom of God and in essence Jesus would have agreed with Barabbas. He would have said, "Barabbas, you are right. The Roman system stinks. It is racistic, it's prejudiced, it's bigoted, it's militaristic, it's materialistic, it's polytheistic, it's Godless. You're right, Barabbas, the system is no good. But, Barabbas, what are you going to change it with? When you burn it down what are you going to replace it with? Don't you understand that you're going to replace that stinking Roman system with your own messed-up kind of system? And there is no difference between a Roman leech and a Jewish leech. There is no difference between a corrupt white man and a corrupt black man. I have come, therefore, to create a new kingdom. I've come to start a new race and it's going to be built upon me, Barabbas. It's going to be built upon the fact that I'm the Christ, the Son of the living God. It's going to be built upon me as the second man, as the leader of a new creation."

Jesus went around preaching that, and before long lame people started walking and blind people started seeing. A tax collector left his job and went after Him. A fisherman dropped his net. A doctor went after Him to pay his allegiance to Him, and great throngs of people came from miles to behold the man who was believed to be the Christ.

But they had to arrest Him too. And they arrested Him for insurrection. So now Pilate has got two radicals on his hands. Around festivity time Pilate stands up and says, "Look, I've got two revolutionaries, and I have the disposition at this time to let one go. Whom should I release unto you? Should I let this man here go, Barabbas, the insurrectionist, the anarchist, the murderer? Or should I release unto you this man Jesus? I don't find anything wrong with Him. I've examined Him. You've accused Him that He has committed blasphemy, but I find nothing wrong with Him. But whom should I release to you?" And with one voice they cried out, "Give us Barabbas. Give us Barabbas. We will not have this man Jesus rule over us."

Now the question is why in the world did they want Barabbas? Why would they want him released? He was the insurrectionist, he was the anarchist. It's very simple. If you let Barabbas go and Barabbas goes in the hills and gets some more guerrillas and starts some more warfare, you can always put down his riot. All you have to do is to call in the Federal troops or the National Guard and put some helmets on the police and they can put down Barabbas' conflict. They can bring it in to him. They can just roll the tanks into the middle of the city and you can bring it in to those rebels.

But how do you stop a man who's got no guns, no ammunition, no guerrillas? How do you stop a man who just tells a blind man to see, and he sees? How do you stop a man who tells a dead man, "Come out of the grave," and he lives? How do you stop a man who takes a few loaves and a few fishes and feeds 5,000 people? How do you stop a man who's got no army but thousands of people are going after him? So they said, "We've got to crucify Him."

Don't you understand, my friend, that every time you turn your television on, and you see a riot, and you shake your head, and you say, "Those dirty, no good people. Why don't they learn to have law and order?" And you turn your television off. Don't you understand you have said, "Give us Barabbas"? Every time your community starts changing to another color and you pack up your congregation and move out, and then sell your church building to a liberal church (and all the time you've been preaching against them) to get away from black people, you have said, "Give us Barabbas"? Don't you understand that every time you say, "We refuse to support, we refuse to get behind black men of God who are communicating the Gospel to their people," you are saying, "Give us Barabbas"? And every time you refuse to join hands with those of us black Christians who love the Savior and who genuinely want fellowship, you are saying, "Give us Barabbas."

So they nailed that radical Jesus to a Cross, little realizing that they were playing into the hands of God. And the Bible says that when He was nailed to that Cross my sin was nailed on that Cross with Him. He shed His blood on that Cross to forgive us every sin, and then rose from the dead to live again. They thought that they had gotten rid of Him. They nailed Him, they buried Him, they washed their hands, and they said, "That's one radical that's off our hands." And then three days later Jesus Christ pulled one of the greatest political coups of all time. He got up out of the grave, and when He arose from the dead the Bible calls Him "the second man," the leader of a new creation. And it was that Christ whom I as a gang leader on the streets of Harlem — with 22 notches on the handle of my knife, which meant that my blade had gone into the bodies of 22 different people — heard about that night while mapping out strategy for a gang fight. I responded to that Christ. I gave Him my life and ever since that moment He has saturated my humanity with His life so I no longer have an identity crisis. I know who I am. I'm God's son, I'm a member of the family of God, and as God's son I'm a member of the royal family of God which puts me in the best family stock there is in all the world. The Word of God tells me I'm a joint heir with Jesus Christ which means that I'm connected to Him, to inherit every-thing that God has, and I'm seated together with Jesus Christ in heavenly places which puts me in the highest social level in all the world.

I did not always think of Him as that. I did not always look at Him as that because when I was first confronted with Christ, I said He was nothing. When I was told about Him I examined who He was and I said He was nothing. I heard that He was just a simple carpenter who sawed wood and planed it out, sanded and built cabinets in people's houses, and put doors in people's houses. I felt that He was nothing. He had no status, He was nobody real, He was nothing.

I was told that He had never been to any institution of learning, He had no degrees behind His name. I said He was a nothing. I wrote Him off as the illegitimate bastard child of some woman who sacked out in the hayloft with a man and tried to blame it on God, and I said He was nothing. When they told me about Christ, I wrote Him off as a white man's God who could do nothing for me until one night I met Him, I encountered Him. He revolutionized my life and as I stand here I'm not a spokesman for the black community, I'm not a representative of the black community, but rather I'm a representative of the kingdom of God, and I happen to be black.

I say to you at this U.S. Congress on Evangelism that there are 25 million people out there waiting to hear what we're going to do here, waiting to decide whether the Gospel of Jesus Christ is really for all people, waiting to decide whether you are prepared and I am prepared to enter into genuine fellowship, so that if the revolution ever comes to the place where we have to lay down our lives for each other we will be willing to do it. There are people who are crying out for us to prove that it is possible for the common clay of a man's humanity to be saturated with the life of Christ, and for us to prove that the invisible God can make Himself visible in a man.

I pray that we will not fail in this hour of crisis.

THE COMMUNICATING POWER
OF THE INNER PILGRIMAGE

Mr. Keith Miller

I'm here representing small groups. When I left home in Austin, Texas earlier this week, I knew God would be pretty busy with all the prayers of the evangelicals here so I prayed ahead of time that He would meet me right now on this platform.

You know I've never really believed in mass evangelism. I've been saying this for years to myself. But you know it's harder and harder for me to say this since I've gotten to know Billy Graham. My wife also has been pretty cynical about this. We went to Dallas about eight years ago and a man interviewer on a program introduced me to Billy. We sat next to each other at dinner and the interviewer said, "Keith Miller's interested in small groups." Billy was very kind and looked at me, and I think he thought I meant a group about like this.

But my wife, who was very cynical about mass evangelism, went to the meeting with me that night and made a public profession of faith.

I do have something to blame Billy for. One of my children has picked up, because of going forward in one of your movies, two four-letter words, and I don't think she'll ever get rid of them and I must be honest to tell you this. These words are "love" and "hope" and we're very grateful to you, Billy, for what you mean in our family.

This week I came here with a lot of ambivalence because I've never been an evangelist, which, if it's not already obvious to you will be soon.

I wonder if in America there has ever been under one roof as many talented and gifted people who love Christ, who can communicate persuasively the Gospel of Jesus Christ, as there may be in this room tonight. This is an exciting thing, and it just scares the tar out of me.

I'd like to tell you what I've seen happening this week, because I'm a witness to you. Monday night Dr. Hoffmann hit an anvil and it grated on my nerves at first. And as he hit the anvil he said, "This meeting will be about committing your life to Jesus Christ and about going with Him." And then he said it again in another way, and then in another way, and somehow sitting back there I was disappointed. Not in his presentation. He's magnificent and I couldn't disagree with anything he said, but I had some other problems I wanted to deal with. But as this week has moved on I'm so glad that Dr. Hoffmann struck that note, because it's becoming the center of a strange living mosaic which God seems to be making out of the various addresses I've heard so far.

MR. KEITH MILLER, Author, Austin, Texas.

Leighton Ford began by painting us a moving picture of an age in which we must change, not the message, but our pattern of ministry. And he showed us a revolutionary atmosphere, as he can do very quickly and deftly. Then last night Tom Skinner did a thing I've never seen done before. He brought a revolution into this room, a powerful and loving one, and at least one evangelical money changer was chasing his spiritual nickels all over the floor of the auditorium after that.

After the meeting, this place was half full of people who wanted to come and talk about the problem of being Christ's people across some lines, but there was one question which kept coming from the floor to the stage, a question people said three or four times in different ways, "What must we do? Tell us, what must we do?"

As I sat up here listening to this and the people on the stage were patiently trying to give us answers I couldn't help thinking of Dr. Walter Hearn, the biochemist who's a very sharp lay speaker. He gave a talk several years ago on how to go out and witness "right now," and one of the little ladies — you may not have them in your church, the little ladies that sit on the front row — came up, she was always there, every Sunday, and she came rushing up to this sophisticated Dr. Hearn and said, "Oh, Dr. Hearn, my cup runneth over. What must I do?" And Dr. Hearn looked at her and said, "Well, Madam, why don't you go slosh it on someone?"

In various ways this was the answer which came back, from the men on the stage, but as patient as they were, I sensed they were frustrated with us. "You really don't understand," I heard them say underneath their answers. And behind those answers I heard a common theme, "We don't want to participate with you in another program, even a great one. We want to live with you in an open style of life in which color will soon not even be relevant to our commonness, but only our mutual problems in living and working in Christ's overgrown vineyard in a crazy and mixed-up world."

Last night a bunch of us wanted to go out after that and tell our churches. And this morning fortunately God sent Dr. Rees to us to remind us that His servant Ezekiel sat for seven days watching, listening, and identifying before he jumped up and did any counseling at all. Those of you who want to rush home and do something about this, let me tell you we're in a majority here that feel this way, at least we were last night, but at home you'll be in a minority. I want to talk about this tonight — what might happen to you.

And Dr. Rees said that to approach this great task that God had given Ezekiel, he first had to go into an inner pilgrimage with God and get close to Him. Then my dear friend Ken Chafin, who followed said that until we walk out into the world and face starkly the threat of change (and he spelled it out in no uncertain terms), we'll never have a need strong enough spiritually to drive us back in the closet, to have an inner journey with Jesus Christ which will give us the power we'll need to risk and to live a vulnerable life in the world.

Now I'd like to pick up at this point and talk to you. The topic I've been assigned is "Communication from the Inner Pilgrimage," from the inner journey. Because I think there's more to the inner journey than just prayer. We've always said the inner journey's a journey of prayer and the outer one is of action. I think there's a power of communication through the inner pilgrimage that brushes aside defenses, and goes through color, and goes into the heart. I believe that some of us can learn to live a vulnerable, life-size life. We can be brothers with a minimum of Mickey Mouse.

I've got to stop a minute because I'm really tired. We spent four hours last night talking about getting the Gospel out on the street.

Hebrews 1:1 (NEB) is my text and I'm piggybacking on Dr. Hoffmann and several others over the time. "When in former times God spoke to our forefathers, He spoke in fragmentary and varied fashion through the prophets." But the author goes on to say that in Jesus Christ, God has opened the door and showed us His inner heart, His hopes and dreams, and plan for the redemption and fulfillment of human life. He has showed us something of His own dream for an inner pilgrimage with each one of us.

Every generation seems to experience at least one central, pervasive human problem that's invisible like the Spirit blowing through a generation, and this problem I think covers everything it touches. Around this problem cluster many of the more obvious social dilemmas we've been talking about which are really, in my opinion, only symptoms of this central, deep problem that goes underground through a generation. Great renewal has taken place historically in the church when the church has begun to see the way; the healing Gospel of Jesus Christ is speaking specifically to that generation's problem as it's experienced by the common man.

But if this is true, how in the world would one go about finding our generation's pervasive human problem in the midst of the thousands of cries for help from all around us? During the past 10 years I have collected almost 4,000 anonymous answers from lay leaders, ministers, and their wives. In large meetings like this, and in small retreats, after we'd begun to feel a little safe with each other, we passed out slips of paper. To insure safety for the people the answers are anonymous. Everybody has to write, you can't cop out by not writing. You have to write, "I think this is a stupid procedure," if you don't want to write an answer and then fold it and turn it in.

The question was, "What is the most pressing personal problem that keeps you from living close to Jesus Christ in your own life where no one sees you?" Now this can be anything among ministers and laymen — these are church leaders all — from disbelief in the Trinity to masturbation, and you would be amazed at the percentages of everything between.

A while back I correlated a random 1,000 of these answers and discovered that only about 1/2 of 1 percent of the problems could be considered in any real sense technically theological. Yet at that same time, of the materials that I examined in terms of sermons and Sunday School materials, 90 percent of the material was aimed at an interest that occupied less than 1 percent of the concern of these people. I am not suggesting the replacing of theological sermons or teaching, but only mentioning the fact that people's crying needs are often being ignored in our own communication within the church. I write concerning these problems, and this is evidence to me that there's a need.

But out in the non-Christian marketplace the situation's just as bad. The world's communication media seem to be accentuating the common man's inner problems. Because of the skill and pervasiveness of modern advertising in America, particularly on TV, we know more about each other's homes and personal habits than any generation in history has. I know approximately what kind of cereal you eat, I know what you shave with, I know what you wear in every room in your house. I've seen it all on TV. We have created a fantastic illusion of intimacy and freedom, but along with this illusion of honesty has come a strong drive to look neat and cool, adequate in all circumstances. Kids and the rest of us learn from the most beautiful models in the world how to hide our true feelings, if they might be considered unattractive or inadequate, and apparently we'll buy anything that promises adequacy or its appearance. Look at us.

There seems to be only one area in my life which TV has not penetrated and that's inside my mind behind this facade, this mask, that I'm showing to you. In here on the inward journey I'm alone and uncertain about me, and about you, and about how you feel about me, and yet I'm committed to Jesus Christ as much as I consciously can be. And since we all know how to appear happy and well-adjusted from the time we can sit in front of the tube, any restless sense of incompleteness or loneliness that I feel is even more poignant. I think that this deeply personal restless incompleteness is near the root of our generation's major pervasive human problem of depersonalization. But, strangely, the problem is almost worse for us committed Christians, because we are subtly trained that if we are restless or lonely it may be a reflection on the depth of our commitment. Or if we express such feelings non-Christians might not want our faith, so this kind of honesty "would hurt our witness for Christ" is the way the line goes. So of all our generation we evangelicals are sometimes the most frustrated and lonely, with our problems of the inner pilgrimage.

This lonely, restless and sometimes frightening sense of unfulfillment spans all the age groups, all the divisions of our day. The young people feel it acutely and are rebelling, reaching in all directions for the personal; so do the old people, who are demanding security and feel they are shunted aside and being impersonalized. Men feel it and rush after sex and power, and so do women. Rich people and poor people feel the creeping impersonals in their lives which threaten to squeeze them against the wall and squash them like a bug, and no one will ever know. The problem is one of identity, as Tom said last night, and the black man is deadly serious, as I think we can see, in this depersonalization which he seems to think is uniquely his experience in our time — even though it's because of what Tom called "his high visibility."

But if this is true, that the issue is restless unfulfillment within our lives, how does one begin to communicate the Gospel with integrity in a way that can be heard by a restless generation that's shifting so much they don't stand still and seldom come to meetings like this? The church's answer has often been proximity, fellowship, involvement, and then preach the Gospel. But somehow it isn't working even as it once did. Real fellowship, which is personal, cannot it seems, as Tom told us last night, be programmed in the church basement with Kool-Aid.

If restless, lonely incompleteness is the disease, then I believe the answer will have to have built into it restless, lonely, incompleteness just as a serum has to have something of the essence of the disease in it. If the problem is deeply personal then the answer must be not fellowship, but something deeply personal.

But how in the world do we, who have been trained to look victorious, learn to bring our own inner problems into the communication of the Gospel of Jesus Christ in a healthy creative way? It's against everything we've been trained to do. Why I've even heard many ministers say from the pulpit, "Please excuse the personal illustration." It's lucky God didn't feel that way, or we wouldn't have had Jesus Christ. And yet I understand this reticence. I've been trained to look successful and happy and not talk about myself. It's culturally not considered good taste. But inside, from the time I was a little boy, I've often been very anxious. I've been somehow lonely and had terrific feelings of inadequacy. I worried about what people thought of me, and if you were small enough I'd whip you if you accused me of it. I denied that I cared at all. I've often been anxious about the future for my own self and for my children, I've been frustrated in many of my closest relationships, and I still almost desperately avoid failure.

The rest of you out there in the world appear to be so self-assured. When Jesus Christ became more than a word to me, and I saw that here was something real, I tried to commit my life to Him, and I began to talk about Him. I tried to communicate with the self-assured people I saw, and virtually nothing happened that lasted. I would sigh

inwardly and go on alone, aching for someone to hear this song that I
heard in my inner pilgrimage, and to love what they heard the way I
loved it. I looked for books that would help me in the strange contradictions in my real life behind the facade, and in my inability to move
people toward the God I was beginning to know and love in Jesus Christ,
and I poured over the Scriptures. But only a few writers in all of history
seemed to reveal their own inner contradictions, so that I could study them
and identify with them.

And do you know who these men were? It amazed me. We have
done something — we have selective blindness psychologically — with the
Scriptures. We don't read the *Bible*, we read what the *speakers* tell us is
in the Bible, and we go back and look and say, "Sure 'nuff." According
to the Protestant Reformation the *Holy Spirit* was to be the teacher.
We're reading often in another century's theology, and now men and
women are being reborn, being started out, who've never known about
all the things they're supposed to see in the Bible, and they're seeing a
new bunch of things. And this is the way renewal happens.

But two of these men who were very personal are Paul and
Augustine, and I always thought of them as theologians. Do you realize
that Paul may have been one of the first men in history, in antiquity,
to open himself in a personal way in his speaking and writing? He
was awful according to our standards for a preacher. He bragged. He
said, "I'm the best Jew that ever came down the pike." That's a loose
translation. He said, "I've got the best education." What would you do
if a minister started out like this? Not only that, Paul said, "I'm the best
Christian. If you don't know how to operate, look at me till you get on
your feet." Can you imagine that coming from the pulpit? And he had a
lot of courage, he wrote it down. He told his followers in detail, great
detail, about how he suffered. "I've suffered more than any of you. Whipped. Look at those scars. Thirty-nine times." We all know how many
times. "Shipwrecked. Cold water." Look at this guy! He got mad at Mark.
He said, "If you're not even good enough to follow me on the second
missionary journey, stay home." Paul was frustrated by his own inability
to follow his preaching, and he told us so in writing. So much of the time
he seems to have been talking about himself. We don't read those passages that way now. Every time he got into trouble what did he do? Did
he give them an explanation about the Cross? He started telling his personal testimony. "I was a Pharisee of the Pharisees." He told the story of
his own life. That was his favorite sermon. And yet everywhere this
strange man went, men's lives were transformed through contact with
him. And, paradoxically, they became devoted to Christ and not Paul.

Why? When he talked about himself so much? When Paul opened
his inner life, what was there? The living Christ was there. When we
committed Christians get vulnerable enough to open our lives in a natural

way, people see the living Christ at work healing and changing those lonely, miserable lives before their very eyes.

But we're terrified to open ourselves in the way Paul did, because other people can see Him in the brokenness of our circumstances, and in our lack of faith we're afraid they'll only see the truth about us and we can't risk it. Now what I think we're actually doing, we laymen and ministers, when we begin opening ourselves with our true needs and hopes and dreams to the rest of the world is that we're identifying with the problem instead of the answer, because we're afraid to express our dreams as much as we are our problems for fear they won't be fulfilled and then we will have failed.

For years as a Christian I have been trained — I do not know anyone who has not been trained — to identify with the answer. I was trained in seminary and church; and in all our planning meetings, like this one, somehow we represented in our minds the answer to the world's problems. The question was: how could we get the indifferent people in the world to sit still so we could drop it on them, this loving truth. Now that's oversimplifying, but they never would sit still and they're still not sitting still.

It was the late Richard Niebuhr who pointed out to me that Jesus Christ identified with the problem and not with the answer. As a matter of fact He identified so completely that the Sadducees could get away with mistaking Him for the problem and crucifying Him.

What do I mean identifying with the problem? It sounds as if you're denying your commitment or your identification with Christ at first. One night several years ago I was speaking to a group of laymen and we were stumped at this point. This was a men's group and one man finally said, "Fellow, we don't even know what you mean 'identify with the problem.' "

Alcoholics Anonymous found out a long time ago that only those who admit they are still weak and powerless to handle alcohol on their own can really help other alcoholics find new lives with self-respect. And the street workers have found out that only those who share the lives of those in the ghettos, who walk through the same garbage in the streets, are the people who are being effective in the ghettos and the Peace Corps. Those who become vulnerable enough to share the problems are those most likely to set men free from those problems.

I hope some of you will stay with me on this because I know what it sounds like. But Jesus Christ Himself, you remember, thought Himself not too great to be vulnerable, to taste, and feel, and reveal to us the struggling problems of our own lives. Now most people certainly don't think of Jesus Christ as one who talks about His own personal problems as a part of His ministry, but He did. He must have. As Bruce Larson has pointed out, if Jesus didn't tell His disciples about the specific nature of His dilemmas, His own temptations in the wilderness, then how did they find them out to write them down? No one was with Him but Satan and he probably wouldn't tell. Or in Gethsemane where He sweated blood. He must have told them something of what happened, how tough it was, how hard, and the agony of it, even though it isn't recorded, because they were all asleep part of the time.

In any case, here's a minister who shared His real life with His disciples, the pleasant and the unpleasant. An identifying power was released through the Holy Spirit: that we men can be unlocked, and be free to be the open, creative people God made us to be, in healing touch with people, and with Him, and with our true selves.

But how would one start? How would you start — after years of being careful *not* to be open — to *be* open? Please don't go home and take off the mask. I mean this is not what anyone's saying. I think there's a great mistake in the sensitivity training of ripping off people's masks, but I'm not talking about that.

But how would *you* start to be open? Well, it happened to me in an unexpected way. I made a commitment of my future to Christ. I said, "God" — at this time I was so "out of it" in my life I had no hope really and I turned to Him, I just backed into Him — "if you want anything in this stinking soul, take it." It was not much of a glorious commitment but He took it. I began to pray, I began to read the Scriptures, and I still do, almost every day.

When I get up in the morning they told me to say, "Lord, I love you," every morning, and I did whether I felt like it or not. One morning I got up and I felt terrible. I was tired of being good, I was sick of Christian meetings, and I had smiled till my teeth were dry. And I said, very hesitantly, because I thought it might be my last remark, "God, I don't want you at all. I wish you'd get off my back," and I lay there waiting for the lightning to strike. But, you know, no lightning. And so I told Him, "Hey, I don't want to feel this way, Lord. I really want to be your boy. Help me not to feel this way about the church and Christianity." For the first time I'd really leveled with God inside on the inner pilgrimage, when I didn't feel good about Him, and a strange thing began to take place on my inner pilgrimage. I began to accept my true feelings which I had pretended didn't exist. What kind of relationship can you have with somebody when you're hiding your true feelings?

I began to offer them when I could now see them, because I wasn't repressing them. I began to be able to offer all of these awful feelings for changing, and shaping, and forgiveness. I had never been forgiven. I had never been able to accept it because I hadn't been able to be a sinner. I began to find that I wanted, with a kind of growing excitement, to learn about this because all my life I'd wanted to accept myself inside. I began to see, as Tom did last night, that the Scriptures are filled with the ruggedness of actual life that would scare you to death if you read them without your evangelical glasses. We have sweetened them beyond recognition.

Jesus Christ talked about sex, drinking and crooked business deals all the time. Read the parables again when you go home. I began to see that, if we could only sweep away the accumulated sugar, He was talking about the restlessness of modern life in the inner pilgrimage where there is no color, where there is no rich or poor, where there is no barrier at all.

Out of this first honest, and therefore desperately personal, communication began to develop a new kind of personal relationship with God. I am convinced that honesty about one's self and personalness are highly correlated somehow. Now I'm not talking about just honesty. You know, I say, "I don't like you. I've never liked you." That just makes you vulnerable. That's a good way for Christians to work out their hostility which they've been repressing.

I'm talking about an honesty about me that is highly correlated with personalness. In fact, I'm convinced that we can only be personal to the extent that we can be honest. Think about it just a second. A personal friend is one with whom I can be most honest about myself and who still likes me. When the church loses this honesty from the pulpit, the Sunday School lectern, the deacons' meetings, and its prayers, then we're no longer personal in our congregation. Deep communication about the inner journey stops and we cannot speak to the world in its agony any more.

I think that's why this laymen's movement has been so fantastic, because these people are beginning to tell what they're seeing and hearing inside. But so far I've only told of being honest with God in my own room. And then came a miracle. One day, in a counseling situation, in order to identify with a man who was suffering from guilt like crazy, a Christian man, this inner honesty accidentally spilled over into my life with people. I told this guy I couldn't leave him and his misery because I had the same problem. I told him that I had the same problem of jealousy and resentment he did that same morning. I thought he would walk out of my office in disgust, and that I'd really fouled it up. Instead, he just sat there looking at me and in a minute he said, "Are you serious?" Then I wished I hadn't said it. When I nodded my head, he began to weep and he said, "Oh, thank you." He said, "If you've got this problem, and you're able to keep going, and you're a committed Christian, maybe I can one more day. I've been so lonely. Nobody else has ever had my problem." And I became like the priest Paul Rees talked about this morning who had a revival in a leprosarium when it turned out that people began to realize that he also had leprosy.

I began to experience a whole new dimension of communication and relatedness with people and with God — all kinds of people, because black people and white people all fuss, and you've got kids you're worried about. What difference does it make what color you are? Suddenly we've got the commonness in our agony and not, you see, in our humanness and not in our success, our attempts at divinity. We get together up here on this level, and our commonness is what breaks through all the bounds. I can cry about a black child and so can you, or a white one.

I had joined the men and women Christ lived with and came to heal, those who know they need a physician. And all it has cost me is my reputation with some of you Christians who don't have any problems.

How does this openness lead Christians out into the world to become involved with Christ in the social agony around us if this hypothesis is true? Now I don't know any rules for this and it's very experimental with us. But some of us started a small group at 6:30 in the morning, to begin to find out how to learn, in a safe atmosphere where nobody would hurt anybody else, how to communicate about the inner journey where we've been alone so long in our faith. It's a place where we begin facing openly the troubles and problems we have in living, working, praying with our families, with our jobs, with our cities, and being Christ's people, and doing His will. And we tried to help each other and do what we were talking about last night, go out in the community and see where the problems were. We didn't know what the problem was. We tried to find out what each guy's ministry might look like as a layman, as he moved out in the community. We had a couple of ministers in our group.

As we began to share this inward journey with Christ and with each other, some of us started being led beyond our own horizons in ways we could never have anticipated.

I'd like to end these remarks with one example of the way this has worked with one man in our group. His name is Walter. He's a successful home builder and real estate developer in our part of the country. Walter spent his youth in an orphan's home, though, and he knows what it's like not to have anything. Now he made a commitment of his life to Christ a few years ago. You might say this guy began to learn to live. One morning Walter came into the group and he was very thoughtful. He said, "Hey, you guys, I woke up at 4 o'clock this morning" (I have his permission to tell you this.) "and I couldn't go back to sleep. I was praying and I discovered an amazing thing." He's an old southern boy and he said, "I love niggers." And having been raised in the South he didn't see anything incongruous about what he was saying, besides he was crying. He said, "Listen, men, if I love them, I guess God would want me to do something about them, wouldn't He?" And we said, "We suppose so."

He said, "I'd like for you to pray for me that I'll know what I can do to help Christ with the race situation," and then he added something we seldom add, "here in our town." And we did pray that. The next week this crazy guy came to the meeting very excited but very uncertain. He said, "Listen, they've asked me to serve on the Human Rights Committee," he said, "and they want me to come out with a statement in favor of open housing." He said, "I went around to all the realtors in town the next day and none of them would go along." And we said, "We think you ought to go, Walter. Be good for you."

He said, "So I checked the National Realtors' Study and I found that in the price range of my homes, if a black family moves in the neighborhood the surrounding property goes down about 45 percent in the South." He stopped a minute and he said, "Hey, you guys, what I found out was that if I take a stand on open housing it might ruin me financially." We were playing with real bullets now, and he was just sharing his inner pilgrimage. We wrestled with Walter on this problem and we found out that these fellows — there were four ministers, and some social workers in the group — wanted him to make this statement. I said, "Hey, does anybody else on the Human Rights Committee have any property?" He said, "Not a stick." I said, "It seems to me you've got a different decision, Walter." And our advice to him was, "Don't do it out of guilt, do it because you feel as if Christ is leading you to do it."

The following week the whole business came to a head. Walter said he'd been looking into the problem, and praying about what to do, when he remembered a story Alton Trueblood had told our group the week before this thing started. It was a story about that guy, you know, who had the notion he wanted to push a wheelbarrow with a man in it across Niagara Falls on a tight rope. He set up two poles in his back yard and started practicing. He stretched a rope between them and practiced first with a balance bar, and then without it, and then with a wheelbarrow. He could run that thing back and forth, and finally he had 175 pounds of bricks in the wheelbarrow, and he never fell off the wire. His next door neighbor started watching every evening, the crowds got bigger and bigger, and the press picked it up as the time got nearer. A huge throng was on hand when they got to Niagara Falls. It was a clear day, just a little wind blowing that wire. And the fellow looked a little nervous as he stood looking at the wire. Finally the time had come and he turned to his faithful buddy, his neighbor Joe, and he said, "Hey, Joe, do you believe I can make it?" Joe looked at him, slapped him on the back and said, "Buddy, I absolutely believe you can make it. I'd bet a tenth of this year's income on it, $1,000." And the old boy looked back across the Falls and he said, "Joe, do you really believe?" And Joe said seriously, "I really believe." He said, "Great, you're my man. Get in the wheelbarrow."

Then Walter that morning said quietly to the rest of us in the group, "This week the Lord said to me, 'Walter, if you trust me with your future, get in the wheelbarrow on this race thing.' And I did."

Now this is not a happy ending story as evangelical stories are supposed to be. I talked to Walter. I was out of town a long time. When I came back it was about a year before I asked him about it and I said,

"Walter, how did that deal go on the race thing? Did that cost you anything?" He said, "Well, it cost me $100,000 last year." And we don't know how much more it's going to cost him. He went to the Chamber of Commerce, to which he belonged strictly on his ability. He'd never had a social standing because of his being from one of the old families, it was just because he was a sharp guy. And he went down there and he said, "Look, you guys, let's come out with a race statement that matches the national one. It won't be giving them a thing but it'll let them know we're thinking, we're trying." And it died for lack of a second.

So he said, "Okay, look." He was kind of embarrassed because he stammers, and he didn't know what to tell them. And he said, "I make a motion that we have a committee to study doing it." It died for lack of a second. Total rejection.

I prayed with him the next morning. He was just about to cry, a grown man, and it had cost him $100,000, and he had been rejected by the group he wanted to be his peers. Then I said, "Anything else happen?" He said, "Yeah. The last time I tried to get anything we had a little problem with money. Money tightened up." You know the money situation has been going like this for a couple of years. Money tightened up, the black man couldn't get his loan, and he thought Walter was trying to keep him from moving into that neighborhood. And the loan people said to the black man, "We're just not going to do it. Your situation's not so that we can." So Walter went down, didn't tell the man, but he wanted him to have that home for his family. Had a bunch of little kids and he was a nice guy, professional man. And you know the fact is that he would have been the kind who would have really helped the black population in that neighborhood. A fine man.

So Walter went, with nobody knowing about it, to this loan association and he said, "Look, give the guy the money." They said, "We can't, Walter. He doesn't fit the picture right now. We just can't do it." Walter said, "I'll co-sign for $25,000. Here's a $25,000 note." And Walter wouldn't have done that for his brother a year ago, because if the guy didn't pay, Walter was stuck for $25,000. And when Walter got back to his office he was feeling kind of good about it but kind of scared, and the telephone rang. It was the Race Relations Committee and they said, "Hey, Walter, I hate to tell you but a guy just turned you in for being a racist. Some guy that's trying to buy a house in your neighborhood, and he says you're trying to keep him from getting the finance money." And I said, "What did you think, Walter?" He said, "I thought, 'That black bastard.'" And I said, "Well, what do you think now?" He said, "Well, I prayed about it and do you know what the Lord taught me?" He said, "We hurt these people for so long they can't possibly believe us." He said, "We've got a real job on our hands of living with them, and loving them, and teaching them how to accept things. They don't even know how to take things when they're offered."

Now something happened about that time to some of us who watched this man struggle in his inner pilgrimage. Two ministers in the group have a big downtown church. They gave the educational wing for a Head Start program for the downtown kids. It didn't make any difference whether they were black or white. Suddenly something happened to the guys and now there's a free medical clinic in that same church, being run by an interdenominational group and, if anybody's got $10,000, we need it for medicine. The group is mostly Catholic, by the way. There are a lot of poor people that can't get any medical help, and we gave them prescriptions and they didn't have any way to get the medicine. So we've got to get the medicine for them now.

I began to speak to black groups. I've been haunted by this problem of the poor, and I've never been able to care. I'm still trying to find a way to find my place in it all, because a man shared with us the struggle of his inner journey against a lifelong prejudice. And we watched him alone, and afraid, and wonderful, as he climbed in the wheelbarrow for Jesus Christ; and for some black men and women and little children who will never know.

"YOU CANNOT QUARANTINE THE WIND"

Dr. Ford Philpot

> The wind bloweth where it listeth, and thou hearest the sound thereof, but canst not tell whence it cometh, and whither it goeth: so is every one that is born of the Spirit." — John 3:8

Jesus moves only by divine appointment, and I have that warm feeling that He has an appointment with someone here in Minneapolis this evening. All through the day we have been thinking about spiritual renewal. We have been asking questions; we have been giving answers. What can we do that we might see renewal come to the Christian church, that we might be able to see the Gospel preached to the whole world in which we live, that we might be able to see people everywhere come to know Jesus Christ as their Lord and their Savior? A study of the Gospels reveals the fact that Jesus did come into the world "to seek and to save that which was lost." His every move, His every act, His every word was directed in that direction. When He stood beside a well in Samaria it was for the specific purpose of talking to a woman of Sychar about the water of everlasting life. When He stood down in the city of Capernaum, He slowly edged His way up to the synagogue. As He watched the crowd draw near, He knew that among the crowd would come a man with a withered hand who was seeking to be healed. He was there to heal him.

When He walked beside the sea, He knew that Simon and James and John would be mending their nets, awaiting their life-changing call, "Follow me, and I will make you to become fishers of men."

Tonight, I want us to think together about one of the greatest interviews that Jesus ever had. It took place that evening when He stood on a moonlit street corner in ancient Jerusalem. He knew that a Jewish lawyer and leader, Nicodemus, was on his way to meet Him there. Jesus knew that He would use the occasion to publish His indispensable requisite for salvation, "Ye must be born again." He knew, too, that this would give Him the opportunity to speak the word about new life in Christ that He wanted you and me, and all before us, and all after us, to hear.

Nicodemus had evidently been watching the works of Jesus. No doubt he had listened to Him speak on these same streets before. Nicodemus began by saying, "I know that thou art a teacher come from God, for no man can do these miracles that thou doest except God be with him."

Jesus quickly answered him, "Except a man be born again he cannot see the kingdom of God."

DR. FORD PHILPOT, Evangelist and President, Ford Philpot Evangelistic Association, Lexington, Kentucky.

Nicodemus countered, "How can a man be born when he is old? Can he enter the second time into his mother's womb and be born?"

Again Jesus said, "Nicodemus, I say unto thee, Except a man be born of water and of the Spirit, he cannot enter into the Kingdom of God." He went on to tell Nicodemus that "that which is born of the flesh is flesh and that which is born of the Spirit is spirit." Then He said to Nicodemus, "Marvel not that I said unto thee, Ye must be born again."

This brought Him to the verse which I want us to consider this evening, "The wind bloweth where it listeth and thou hearest the sound thereof but canst not tell whence it cometh and whither it goeth. So is every one that is born of the Spirit." I like Phillips' translation, "The wind blows where it likes, you can hear the sound of it but you have no idea where it comes from and where it goes. Nor can you tell how a man is born by the wind of the Spirit."

Here we find Jesus comparing the activity of the Holy Spirit, in its life-changing ability, to that of the wind. The analogy can be traced throughout the Bible.

We all know that in both the original Hebrew and Greek the same word is used for "wind" and for "spirit." We know that God formed man of the dust of the ground and breathed into his nostrils the breath of life and man became a living soul.

We remember that after the resurrection when Jesus was giving His final instructions to the disciples in John 20:22, it is recorded, "And when He had said this, He breathed on them and saith unto them, Receive ye the Holy Ghost." And it was not just coincidental that one of the signs manifested on the day of Pentecost was "a sound from Heaven as of a rushing mighty wind that filled all the house where they were sitting, and they were all filled with the Holy Ghost."

The greatest need of the church around the world tonight is for a new infilling of the Holy Spirit. There can be no new life until the church itself is filled anew and afresh with the Holy Spirit.

Let us look at what is suggested in this comparison of the Holy Spirit and the wind:

I. First of all, notice with me that *the Holy Spirit is always acting.* Jesus said, "The wind bloweth." In other words, the Holy Spirit is always at work. His ceaseless action is denoted by this expression. We may be more conscious of His presence on some occasions than on others. Sometimes the wind blows like a hurricane, but at other times moves so gently that you can hardly see a leaf stir, but the Holy Spirit is acting. No human effort can produce any spiritual fruit or any results except as it is used by the Holy Spirit. Jesus evaluated the workings of the Holy Spirit when He said, "Nevertheless I tell you the truth; it is expedient (or necessary) for you that I go away: For if I go not away, the Comforter will not come unto you. But if I depart, I will send Him unto you. And when He is come, He will reprove the world of sin, and of righteousness, and of judgment."

Of Ezekiel's prophecy concerning the valley of dry bones, one writer said,

"Just so, after the dead bones had come together. After sinew and flesh and skin had covered them, after all the reformation had been effected that human preaching and moral influence could effect, God said, 'Prophesy now to the wind. Prophesy, Son of man and say to the wind, Come and breathe upon these bones that they may live.' It was all they needed now, and it was a need that only the Spirit of God could supply. In the Church that bears the name of Christ, we may have everything but the essential thing. We may have order, and decency, and reverence, and the appearance of fraternity. Bone may come upon bone and there may be sinews, and even the flesh and skin. And if there may be no breath of God there will be no mysterious and unifying life. We may have a congregation — but not a communion; we may have an assembly — but not an army; we may have a fellowship roll — but not of those who are counted alive and whose names are written in the Lamb's Book of Life. We may be just a crowd — and not the family of the living God. We may have prayers — but no power. We may have petitions — but no real intercession. We may have posture — but no supplication. We may have elaborate ritual — but no holy worship. We may have what men call a finished service — and yet there may be nothing of the *violence* of a *vital faith*. We may have benevolence — but no sacrifice. We may have the appearance of service — but no shedding of blood. The Church may be only an organized corpse. But when the breath comes, how then? The breath of God converts an organization into an organism. It transforms a combination into a fellowship, a congregation into a Church, a mob into an army. That breath came into a little band of disciples weakened by timidity and fear, and changed them into a spiritual army that could not be checked or hindered by the world, the flesh and the devil. And when the same breath of God comes into a man of many parts, of many faculties and talents sharpened by culture, drilled and organized by discipline, it endows him with the veritable power of an army and makes him irresistible."

Yes, the wind is always blowing. But organization without the Holy Spirit will never accomplish what we want to accomplish. One of our biggest problems today is that we are always trying to come up with *new* methods, *new* ideas, and *new* ways rather than to realize that the wind is always blowing, the wind of the Spirit. All we need to do is set our sails in that direction, that we might be able to be caught by the Spirit of God and be empowered by Him.

The Holy Spirit does work *in His* own way. The fires of revival can break out in the most unexpected places. The most humble church can suddenly become the center of spiritual awakening. The most unqualified man, according to human standards, can suddenly become the instrument that God's Holy Spirit uses to produce renewal. From the time that Jesus chose the fishermen and other ordinary men to be His disciples, He has chosen the most unlikely men and women and has made them spiritual dynamos in a world that needed to feel the renewing breath of the wind of the Holy Spirit.

Major Ian Thomas has a chapter in his book, *The Saving Life of Christ*, in which he describes the call of Moses through the burning bush. I think we might find help here — let's listen.

"Moses began by being a failure! That was the school from which he qualified! . . . Judged by purely human standards, you may be highly qualified for Christian service, and yet go out into the oblivion of spiritual uselessness. No matter to what distinction you may attain in this world, no matter how much you may be acclaimed by your fellowmen, no matter how gifted you may be, it is tragically possible for you to go down in the records of spiritual history as one of those who did not count, either for God or man — and do you know why? Because you never took time out to find the reason why God uses men!

"And as God called, Moses said, 'Here am I.' And (God) said, draw *not* nigh hither: put off thy shoes from off thy feet, for the place whereon thou standest is holy ground. Moreover He said, I am the God of thy father, the God of Abraham, the God of Isaac, and the God of Jacob. And Moses hid his face; for he was afraid to look upon God. God had something to say to Moses, and I think it must have been something like this: 'Moses, you have done a wise thing in making intelligent inquiry, for you thought that this was a very remarkable bush. You thought that there must be something about it at once peculiar and wonderful, something unique, that it could burn and burn, and burn, and go on burning, and yet not burn itself out. But you are wrong — you are *quite* wrong! Do you see that bush over there? That scrubby, scraggy-looking thing — *that* bush would have done! Do you see this beautiful looking bush, so shapely and fine — *this* bush would have done! For you see, Moses, *any old bush* will do — *any* old bush — if only *God* is in the bush! The trouble with you, Moses, is this: forty years ago, learned in all the wisdom of the Egyptians, mighty in word and deed, you admired your own foliage! You thought you were some bush! But you burned yourself out in 24 hours, and you have been a heap of ashes for forty years! If this bush that you have admired were depending upon its own substance to sustain the flame, it too would burn itself out in 24 hours; it too would be a heap of ashes like you. But it is not the *bush* that sustains the flame, it is God *in* the bush; and *any old bush* will do!' "

The wind of the Holy Spirit is blowing. He is acting in the lives of men, in churches, in nations. . .

II. *The Action of the Holy Spirit is Unpredictable and Yet Predictable.*
"The wind bloweth were *It* listeth."

No one has a corner on God's Holy Spirit. No individual, no denomination has God's Spirit bottled up for its own use alone. I know that many times it is hard for us to explain how and why God works as He does. Nevertheless Paul said, "God Has chosen the *foolish* things of the world to confound the *wise*, and God has chosen the *weak* things of the world to confound the things which are *mighty*: and *base* things of the world and things which are despised has God chosen, Yes, and things which *are not*, to bring to naught things *that are*, that no flesh should glory in His presence."

If this be true, I think the thing we need to do tonight is to find out what conditions are suitable and pleasing for the moving and blowing of God's Spirit.

1. First, there must be *unity*. On the day of Pentecost, they were all in one place and in one accord. For twenty years I have been in evangelistic work, and God has given me the privilege of preaching in nearly every state in the United States and in other countries around the world. The greatest revivals that I've ever been in have been in communities or areas where there was *unity* among the preachers and the people. If it's a local church, as I look back over my ministry, I am reminded that the greatest revivals have come where the pastor and the laity seemed to be unified with one great desire: and that was for a revival to sweep through their church.

In city-wide meetings, I would say that the *greatest hindrance* that we have to our work is in getting the ministers of the city totally united so that the Holy Spirit might be able to work through us as a unit in the area. Far too many times, we are unwilling to lay aside some of the small doctrinal issues that really do not count and unite behind a strong presentation of the power of Jesus Christ, whom we know to be "The way, the truth and the life."

I think this can best be illustrated by an experience out of my own life. Last year I was invited to Kinshasa, formerly Leopoldville, capital of the Congo. It is a city of perhaps a million and a half people. A city with tremendous problems, a city that has been torn with war and struggle for freedom. When we arrived in this city, we found there were 77 Protestant ministers, representing 50 denominations, in all of Kinshasa. Although I happen to be a Methodist preacher, there was not a single Methodist church in the city. There was one Methodist preacher and he had a mission where he preached to the Angolians. I met with these ministers on the day of my arrival. We had a time of fellowship and prayer together and I laid before them the plan that we had for the crusade. I had had an advance man in the area for about two months assisting and working with Rev. Willis Braun of the Christian and Missionary Alliance Church in preparing the city for the crusade. We were there for three weeks. Services were held in five areas of the city, three nights each. This was so we might reach most of the people of Kinshasa. They do not have modes of transportation as we have here, and we had to take the Gospel out to the sections of the city where they were. The average attendance at these evening meetings (at five o'clock each evening) was perhaps about ten to twenty thousand people. We closed with one giant rally in the soccer stadium in Kinshasa which seats 85,000 people. I didn't see how we could possibly see the soccer stadium filled. We rented what buses we could, did what we could to promote the crusade across the city and on Sunday morning, six hours before the service was to begin, I went out to see the stadium simply to check the rostrum from which I was to speak. I was amazed that at that early hour they were marching into the stadium. Some had been walking for four or five hours already. By 2:30 the soccer stadium was completely filled. These people sat there and listened, and at 4:00 when the invitation was given, approximately 15,000 of them responded to accept Christ as Savior. Then they made their way back toward their homes and their villages. This to me showed the hunger and the will of these people to know Christ. But the greatest thrill of my life was still to come. Two days later when the team went to the Kinshasha airport to board the jet to come back to the United States there were 77 pastors there waiting to see us off. When I went through Customs and started to make my way out to the plane, they gathered around me and began to sing. Then they followed me out to the plane and encircled me at the foot of the plane, some even climbing up the steps to the plane. They were weeping, they were saying, "Come back, Brother Philpot, come back. Come back, Brother Philpot, come back." There was unity. Every single pastor in the city giving all that he had, his whole life, his whole spirit. Now these people do not have big churches. The total population of the Protestant church in Kinshasha before the crusade began was about 18,000 people. They had no church buses. They had nothing. Nothing but themselves. But they had given themselves to unity, to prayer, to one great crusade and God had blessed. Approximately 28,000 souls had responded, in those 16 preaching days, to the Gospel of Jesus Christ. The church had more than doubled in 16 days. One pastor wrote me he had requests to baptize 782 people. I believe it was because they were in *one place*, in *one accord* and God honored them by pouring His Holy Spirit out upon them. What would happen in any city in America if all the Protestant pastors would come together and forget about their doctrinal differences, forget about salaries, forget about advertising, forget about promotion, and just go to their knees and say, "We're going to witness to our people and we're going to pray to God that He'll bring spiritual revival and renewal to our city." Yes, I'm convinced that the Spirit blows where it likes, and it pleases to blow where there is unity.

2. Then there must be *humility and prayer*. In 2 Chronicles 7:14, God said, "If my people, which are called by my name, shall humble

themselves, and pray, seek my face, and turn from their wicked ways; then will I hear from heaven, and will forgive their sin, and will heal their land." I do not think it was by accident that we are told in this verse that God said, "if *my* people, which are called by *my* name, shall," first of all, "Humble themselves, and pray, and seek my face, and turn from their wicked ways, then will I hear from heaven and *will forgive* their sin and *will heal* their land."

3. There must be a *desire*. In the 51st Psalm we find the word "renewal" connected with the Holy Spirit. We remember the tragic sin that had come into David's life. David knew that he had sinned. He was convinced that he had done wrong. He wanted forgiveness. And in this 51st Psalm, that we call the Penitent's Psalm, we hear David crying out, "Blot out my transgressions . . . and take not thy Holy Spirit from me." He cried that God would *renew him* and restore unto him the joy of His salvation.

David was not only pleading with God that the burden of his own guilt be removed that he might again know "joy" for himself, but he was realizing that the influence that he once had had with other people was *hindered by his own sin.* He knew that God could only use him effectively as a witness, when his own heart was clean.

This little poem came into my hands some time ago:

CLEAN HANDS

Once, in my childhood days long gone and dead,
I watched a supper table being spread
By busy hands; and eagerly I said —
Wishing to help — "Please, may I bring the bread?"
Gently, reprovingly, a kind voice said,
"Are your hands clean?"
Oft, when I see the multitude, unfed,
And waiting hungry for the living bread,
My heart and hands are eager to be sped
To bring the manna that they may be fed.
But One Voice says, e'en as a voice once said,
"Are your hands clean?"
    I only bow my head.
                                        —Mrs. Eddie Dunshie

David recognized the hindering influence of sin in his own life and prayed, "Restore unto me the joy of thy salvation; and uphold me with thy free spirit.

"Then will I teach transgressors thy ways; and (*then*) sinners shall be converted unto thee.

"Deliver me from bloodguiltiness, O God, thou God of my salvation: and (*then*) my tongue shall sing aloud of thy righteousness." Here is the key to renewal — it is repentance!!

III. *The results of the action of the Holy Spirit are very evident.* "Thou canst hear the sound thereof." You can hear the sound of the wind and you can feel its force. How much more powerful is the Spirit of God. The wind by its steady blowing turns the wheels of the mill, catches the sail of a ship, and by its violence in the form of a hurricane destroys great works, uproots trees, unroofs houses. But what is this as evidence of power compared with the effect wrought by the Holy Spirit in human hearts? The Spirit of God is the spirit of truth, of conviction, of holiness.

At this point I would like for us to remember one warning. *The Holy Spirit can be hindered.* The Holy Spirit can be blocked, just as the wind can be blocked or hindered. You know, you can set up a giant brick wall and the wind that blows against that brick wall will veer off to the left or to the right. You can build a fort that's strong enough so that it will check the wind until the wind either has to veer up, or to the left, or to the right. This is true in flying an airplane. In fact, this is the way an airplane is maneuvered.

Major Ian Thomas, using the principle of aerodynamics, said that we can be victorious by using the fact of God's Holy Spirit to soar above the law of gravity.

"I may wish to return to my home in England, and I stand in New York, but ever since I was born I have been bound to this earth by a law that I have never been able to break — the law of gravity. I am told, however, that there is another law, a higher law, the law of aerodynamics, and if only I will be willing to commit myself in total trust to this *new law*, then this *new law* will set me free from *the old law*. By faith I step into the plane, I sit back in the *rest* of faith, and as those mighty engines roar into life, I discover that the new law of aerodynamics sets me free from the law of gravity.

"So long as I maintain by faith that position of total dependence, I do not have *to try to be free* from the law of gravity — *I am being set free* by the operation of a new and higher law. Of course, if I am stupid enough way out across the Atlantic, I may decide that the cabin of the plane is too stuffy, and step out through the emergency window — but the moment I discard my position of faith in the new and higher law that is setting me free, I discover that the old down-drag is still fully in operation, and I am caught again by the law of gravity and plunged into the water!"

I am thoroughly convinced that there are many good reasons why the church needs to be careful not to check the moving of the Holy Spirit today, more than at any other time since God created man. Every person who deals with people, or who is in tune with what's happening in our world today, knows that this is an undisciplined spiritual age. Just two illustrations:

At the close of a service recently in one of our Southern cities, a man in his early forties asked if he could see me. Thirty minutes later we sat together in front of my motel. I asked him a question, "What's bothering you anyway? What do you think your real problem is?"

He said, "I am not sure that I can tell you, but I will try." He asked, "Do you have a tape recorder?" I said, "Yes." He said, "I feel like a tape recorder, where the tape has run out. Did you ever see a tape when it ran out and the tape just began to flip from one side to another?" I said, "Yes I have seen and heard one do that —."

He said, "That's the way I feel on the inside." What an imaginative description! This is the inner feeling of millions on our planet tonight. How are we to help men like this unless we are filled with God's Spirit of understanding?

The second illustration deals with the gap between our technological world and our spiritual nature.

Do you remember the Apollo 10 flight? While Charlie Brown was hovering somewhere over Snoopy, all of a sudden Snoopy went haywire. One of the astronauts at the controls swore, and the phrase that he used had to be later censored. Yet, at the same time he was able to "keep his cool," to remember what he had been taught, and to make the proper adjustments to straighten out as soon as possible. How true this is of us.

We know how to construct buildings and bridges and rockets, and how to perform heart transplants, but we still haven't learned the secret of how to control our inner emotions. What we need to learn is that *man* cannot — but that one of the world's greatest men discovered years ago that he could do all things through *Christ* who strengthened him.

Thank God, the Holy Spirit is acting, and He is acting where the proper conditions are met, and the evidences are always seen. He will continue to act in love and mercy, and — do not forget — in judgment, as long as it pleases God. Let this story sum up for us the ceaseless action of God's Spirit for all mankind.

A tragedy in the form of an outbreak of foot and mouth disease had a disastrous effect upon Britain's already ailing economy. Cattle by the tens of thousands had to be destroyed. As a result, drastic measures, including the strictest of quarantines were employed to try to check the spread of the malady. One farmer, in a desperate bid to save his animals, sprayed every building on his farm, every room in his home, moved his cattle into a building and padlocked the door. No visitors were allowed on the premises, groceries were ordered by phone, and left at the front gate, Even the daily newspaper was picked up from the front yard with sterile gloves and baked in an oven until thoroughly disinfected. But despite all of this, in only three weeks his first cows became ill and the entire herd had to be liquidated. The government of Ireland took harsh and frantic measures to keep the disease out of the country. They banned all meat imports, introduced a massive disinfectant plan for all of the little Island, and reluctantly began stringent measures concerning vacations and personal traveling plans of the population. One government official said, "I doubt if we could keep it out. Even if we created a complete police-state blockade, we have our doubts about stopping it. We're pretty certain that the virus can be transmitted by the wind for many, many miles." Then he concluded with this statement, "You cannot quarantine the wind."

"You cannot quarantine the Holy Spirit."

WHAT THIS CONGRESS CAN
MEAN TO SOCIETY

Dr. Ralph D. Abernathy

Thank you very kindly, Dr. Hoffmann, for these very kind and generous words of introduction. Dr. Thompson, Dr. Graham, delegates and honored guests, members of the U.S. Congress on Evangelism, my Christian brothers and sisters, my friends here assembled, and my soul brothers and sisters.

I need not pause to tell you how delighted I am to have the privilege and the honor of addressing you at this hour, of joining you in your magnificent and moving witness in behalf of the program of our Lord and Savior Jesus Christ. Please know that I understand very well that the ground I stand on at this hour is holy ground, and like Moses of old I should remove the sandals from my feet. This is an experience that I will cherish as long as the courts of memory shall allow me.

I regret so very much that my duties and responsibilities prevented me from being here sooner. I'm glad to be here even though I'm late, but I learned a long time ago that it is better to be Ralph David Abernathy late, than to be the late Ralph David Abernathy.

Honesty impels me to admit that I stand before you today, not as a civil rights leader — even though I am President of the Southern Christian Leadership Conference, and a leader of 40 million poor people, one-fifth of our population, who are left out of the mainstream of American life — but I come as a Christian minister of the Gospel, seeking to carry out the commission of our Lord and Savior Jesus Christ. In fact I come as both a priest and a prophet, filled with compassion for the countless numbers who are pushed out of the glittering sunlight of life's July, and left standing in the piercing chill of an Alpine November. As a priest, my heart is filled with love and understanding for those who are so weak, spineless and timid, that they dare not stand up for truth and righteousness. But my major role here today is not that of a priest, it is that of a prophet. God has sent me as a rugged Amos crying out to this battered and war-torn world, "Let justice roll down as waters and righteousness like a mighty stream." I come as a prophet in the tradition of Jeremiah and like him I weep for my nation as he wept for his Jerusalem. And I see the walls of brotherhood and understanding bombarded and torn asunder.

Yes, like Jeremiah, I weep today because I see my nation and your nation, the richest and most affluent in the history of mankind, denying necessities to the masses, only to give luxuries to the classes. I weep for my nation

DR. RALPH D. ABERNATHY, President, Southern Christian Leadership Conference, Atlanta, Georgia.

today and I weep for my society when I realize that those who control the destiny of America and western civilization, do not hear the voice of the Eternal God still crying out through the vistas of time, "Be not deceived, for God is not mocked, for whatsoever a man soweth, that shall he also reap."

I weep for my nation when I know that it does not realize the fact that righteousness "exalts a nation, but sin is a reproach to any people." Like Moses of old, today I stand in the courts of the Pharaohs of Egypt, the Egypt of the United States of America whose gross national product is fast approaching the trillion dollar mark, and I'm forced to cry out, "America, feed the hungry. America, clothe the naked. America, house your ill-housed. America, provide for those who are dying from malnutrition and from starvation. America, provide adequate medical and dental care for the poor, and for the disinherited of the land. America, educate your young and realize that your most precious resources are the human resources of this land — individual personalities, black and white, brown and yellow, Protestant and Catholic and Jew, believer and even non-believer. For we are the sons and daughters of the most high God. He is our Father, therefore, we are all brothers."

Yes, I come today to say to the Pharaohs of the nations of the world, to let my people go. I wish also to say to you that it is your responsibility to evangelize the world for it is only through evangelism that the nations of the world will be saved. I need not remind you, "Ye are the salt of the earth. Ye are the light of the world." Today there are mixed emotions in my heart, but I rejoice when I realize that through scientific and technological advancements and discoveries, we have been skillful enough to put a man on the moon. But through all of the religions of the world, with our many dogmas and creeds, our bishops, priests, preachers, and missionaries, our anthems and stirring hymns, we have failed to stand man on his feet right here on this earth. I have mixed emotions.

Let us take a brief look and examine some of the problems facing out nation, some of the problems facing Christians and men of religion in the world today.

The first problem that I wish to call to your attention is repression in the United States. We live in a time when the accumulated hopes of racial and cultural minorities are being met by the mounting fears and rising anxieties of the majority population. These hopes are issuing a strong demand, the fears are causing a nation of people to insist upon law with order, more than justice with strength. I need not remind you that Adolph Hitler came into power in Nazi Germany in 1933 after having campaigned for 11 years on the platform of law and order. There are parallels in this nation today that are similar to those found almost five decades ago in then powerful Germany. Repression is spreading across the land.

The law and order of the United States 1968 national political campaign, which was then read by certain radical and cultural minority groups as force and rigidity, has gained great political influence and has become increasingly hard in its expression. In early 1968 our society was described in official government reports as one that "would not listen." Since that time the deaf ears have been accompanied by heavy hands and tight fists. This may give aid and comfort to those who live in privileged places, with secure resources, and enjoy the advantages of a prosperous society, but it spells greater neglect, abridged freedom, and fading hope for those who have trusted in a rich nation to reorder its priorities and use its resources in bringing into being a new economic and social justice.

Priorities have been reordered but in the process the highest priority has been given to order seemingly regardless of the cost to liberty. A society can become repressive in nature with hardly a trace of consciousness by the mass of the people, particularly if that people is feverishly fearful and has developed the readiness to accept any measure that will offer a new form of protection. A society that is democratic in theory and structure can become repressive in policy and practice when it is faced with threats and exposed to dangers.

Out of fear, historic freedoms can be traded off for monetary security and the causes of liberty can be surrendered to the necessities for defense. We live in such a time, for the words "be compassionate" are being overshadowed by "get tough" and (like the visible poisons in the air we breathe) contaminate the atmosphere and subtly and swiftly alter the thinking of those who formerly supported the clear words of the Bill of Rights.

What do we have one year after the Kerner Report? We have nothing but another report on the Kerner Report. Not a single recommendation has been carried out by the Federal government, and we have an analysis of the report. All that happens in this country, seemingly, today is to make a study of the situation. Then we analyze what was studied, and we analyze the analysis. I say to you, my friends, that there is a danger in this country that we get bogged down in the paralysis of analysis.

We act out of fear but rarely can persons, or the people, recognize or admit that they are motivated by fear. Instead we find cloaks of righteousness to cover us, and to let us believe that we act for the good of society and for the protection of all people. There are grave dangers at hand but it is the responsibility of a free people, and particularly of a faithful church, to find responses that do not root in fear. "Perfect love casts out fear," says our Lord and our Master, and it is this love that must possess the church and influence a whole society.

The difficulty is that the church itself may be afraid, afraid for its future, afraid of it's own people who in their anxiety withdraw financial report from the church that pursues the goals of justice. A silent church, quieted by its determination to preserve itself, is a danger to the kingdom and a handicap to a people who look for moral leadership.

Even though it is difficult for the church to speak and the cost of speaking becomes ever so great, there is clearly the need for the church to be vigilant at a time that it has been counseled to be complacent. And in a nation in which repression had become the prevailing policy, the church was ultimately confronted with compromising the Gospel. When this was recognized too late, the influence of the church had little effect.

The church must be alert at this time, for the mood of the people, and, increasingly, the policy of a government is to use the power and the resources of the nation to put down those who after years of patient suffering, have risen up; to quiet those who after generations of being voiceless have spoken up.

The second problem is injustice and inequality. I said to you earlier, but please permit me to repeat, that we are sons and daughters of the most high God, yet after approximately 350 years, my people and poor people of all races in this wealthy land are denied their constitutional and God-given rights. Therefore, it must be the first item on the agenda of this Congress on Evangelism to call to the attention of America the fact that the world cannot be saved until all lost, black and white, brown and yellow, rich and poor, are saved. John Donne was eminently correct when he preached, more than a century ago, "No man is an island, entire of itself; but every man is a piece of the continent. He is a part of the main." And he went on to say that "One man's death diminishes me because I am a part of mankind, so send not to ask for whom the bell tolls, for the bell tolls for thee."

The Black man was brought to this country in 1619. Unlike the Pilgrim fathers who landed at Plymouth a year later, he was brought to these fertile fields and rich soil against his will. He came not as a person but as a slave — property — subject to the dictates of the white man, his owner. My people were snatched from their native Africa, robbed of their culture, stripped of their language, raped of their heritage, and upon their arrival they found no freedom at all.

Lerone Bennett in his book entitled *Before the Mayflower* says that thousands of Black men never completed the voyage across the Atlantic because mean and angry captains of ships unloaded their cargo — chained and shackled slaves — in the middle of the ocean by throwing their live bodies overboard in the angry waters to fierce and hungry sharks. Thanks be to God that a few did survive, and they made the journey.

In America, my people cleared the new ground, dug the ditches, cared for the sick, and carried the garbage away. They made cotton king for they were forced to work in the fields from sunup to sundown, or from can't to can't. They were taught by the white church in the Sunday School. They were given the message from the white minister as they worshiped in the balcony or down in the basement, "Servants, obey your masters." For almost two and one half centuries the Black man was loyal to his white master. He built the skyscrapers and the tall, gigantic buildings of the great cities of America, and he developed the backwoods and the plantations of the South. But the most magnificent thing was the fact that he never lost faith. For you see in

America, not only did the Black man discover a new culture and a more advanced civilization, but he also discovered the true and everlasting God. He discovered what I call "soul power."

Can't you hear them singing right now in the cotton fields of Alabama, the swamps of Louisiana, on the red clay hills of Georgia, and in the back hinterlands of Mississippi? "Keep inching and inching along, we'll get there by and by. I'm so glad that troubles don't last always. Soon we'll be done with the troubles of the world. You got shoes, I got shoes, all of God's chillun got shoes. I can't wear mine now, but when I get to heaven I'm going to put on my shoes; and I'm going to walk all over God's heaven."

If you will listen, listen with your spiritual ears, you can hear them crying now, "We will get there by and by." Oftentimes husbands were sold down the river, separated from their wives; babies, snatched from the bosoms of their mothers, and sold to the highest bidder, never to be united again in this life. Yet they could stand and see a land just beyond the river where the wicked would cease from troubling, and the weary would be at rest.

These were difficult years in the life of my people. Then came 1858 when Dred Scott, a Black man, took his case to the Supreme Court of the United States and the court said in essence that the Black man has no rights that the white man is bound to respect. The court ruled that he was property, subject to the dictates of his owner. But the Black man kept the faith and a few years later God spoke to Abraham Lincoln and said to him, "Put down your ax and lay your rail aside for I have a pronouncement that you must make from the White House through an Executive Order," which has become known as The Emancipation Proclamation. The 16th President of these United States of America etched across the pages of history his signature and freed 3 million Black slaves in these United States of America.

But soon after, we discovered that this was not freedom. It was merely partial freedom, that is physical freedom, for the system continued to enslave the minds of the Black people. In 1896, in the Plessy vs. Ferguson decision, the Supreme Court passed as the law of the land the so-called separate-but-equal doctrine. But God works in mysterious ways, and 58 years later, on May 17, 1954, the Supreme Court of these very same United States made the opinion of the minority of 1896 the unanimous opinion of the majority, and struck down the whole doctrine of so-called separate-but-equal.

About a year later Martin Luther King, Jr. — my dearest friend and closest associate, my predecessor — and I started a non-violent revolution in the nation by leading 50,000 Black people for 381 days in discovering that a walk for freedom is a little better than a segregated ride. This was the now well-known and famous Montgomery bus boycott of 1955–56, which gave birth to the Montgomery Improvement Association and now the Southern Christian Leadership Conference.

As we seek to carry on our duties and responsibilities in the field of evangelism, we must remind America of one or two things. We must demand that

America live up to her pronouncements and her promises. We must remind America that in 1776 almost 200 years ago, Thomas Jefferson and our founding fathers, etched across the pages of history, "We hold these truths to be self-evident that all men are created equal, and they are endowed by their Creator with certain inalienable rights; and among these are life, liberty, and the pursuit of happiness."

We must demand that these rights be extended, not only to the white man, but to all men, not only to the Black man but to all men, not only to Protestant men, but to all men, for God is not interested in the freedom of black, white, Protestant, Catholic or Jewish men only, He is concerned with the welfare of all men. We must remind this nation of the loyalty of the Black man to this country. We must make this nation aware of the Black man's contribution to the life and security of the nation, as well as to the development of the United States of America.

A Black man was the first to give his life on Boston Common to bring this country into being. A Black man was the captain of one of Columbus' ships when he discovered America. A black man discovered Chicago, the great metropolis of the Middle West. A Black man designed and laid out the plans for our nation's Capitol building in Washington, D.C. Booker T. Washington who said, "Let down your bucket where you are," was a Black man. Marian McCleod Bethune was a Black woman. W. E. B. Dubois was a Black man. Charles Drew, who saved millions of lives through the discovery of blood plasma, was a Black man. Tell the nation that the first successful heart operation was performed by a Black man. Tell the nation about Marion Anderson, a Black woman who was once denied an opportunity to sing in Congressional Hall in Washington, D.C., and was forced to lift her melodious soprano voice before thousands at the Lincoln Monument in Washington.

Tell the nation about Frederick Douglass and about Martin Luther King, Jr. and tell them about the godless, senseless, and unwinnable war presently in Vietnam where the blood of Black men is shed along with the blood of white men. Tell them that no longer will we be satisfied with injustice and inequalities. Tell them that we want our freedom, we demand our constitutional and God-given rights. We demand a more equal distribution of the wealth of the land. Tell them that we have paid our dues and we don't intend to lose. We have a date with destiny, a rendezvous with eternity, and we intend to keep it on schedule.

There is a cry in the land that comes no longer from the lips of Black and poor people, but it comes from our hearts and from the very depths of our souls, "Before I'll be a slave, I'll be buried in my grave."

The third and final problem is the failure of the church to be the church. When Jesus organized the church after having changed Peter from shifting sand into a solid rock, He gave the keys of the kingdom to the church, and informed us that the temperature of heaven would be regulated by the activities of the true church on earth.

But the church has failed to be the church. Too long we have been an old ambulance, moving along at the back of the battle, picking up the wounded, caring for the dying, and saving the perishing. The church must be a fire engine, a bulldozer, a tank, out front leading the battle so that every valley will be exalted, every hill and mountain made low. The church ought to be the church. We have become a taillight rather than a headlight. We've become a kind of social club, a middle-lower-upper class institution which serves as a thermometer registering the temperature of society, rather than being the thermostat that God intended that we be, controlling the temperature of the community.

If the church had been the church, there never would have been slavery for 244 years in this land. If the church had been the church there never would have been a doctrine of separate-but-equal for an additional 100 years. Had the church been the church in Nazi Germany and stood up, Hitler never could have murdered 6 million Jews. Rome never would have been burned while Nero fiddled, nor would Italy have crumbled while Mussolini vacillated and succumbed to the evil forces and the ungodlike powers of his time. When Norway was occupied by Germany and the orders came down that every Jew had to wear a star, the King of Norway was not a Jew, but he was a Christian. "Therefore," he said, "I will wear my star, and I call upon all of the Norwegian people to wear stars also." So it meant that if the Jews of Norway were to be destroyed by Hitler and his evil forces, then the whole nation of Norway would be destroyed. The church ought to be the church.

My friends, we are so busy trying to make a living, trying to make a name, trying to be popular, trying to make the headlines, trying to make the front pages, that we have forgotten about making a life. Remember Jesus said, "What does it profit a man to gain the whole world and then lose his soul?" And then He made it clear in one of those parables in the 25th chapter of Matthew that your reward shall be based upon the visits that you make to those who are sick, to those who are in prison, to those who are wounded for He says, "As often as ye do it unto the least of these my children, ye do it unto me."

I challenge you and I call upon you to take your evangelism beyond the four walls of our sacred sanctuaries. I challenge you to take the hymns and anthems beyond the stained-glass windows of our cathedrals. Take the Gospel of Jesus Christ, as the woman of Samaria did, out of the holy places, out of our churches, and our cathedrals into the alleys and the byways, the hills and the highways of life and tell all of God's children that regardless of your status in life, you're somebody. You have worth and you have dignity. You are a child of God. "For fleecy locks and black complexions cannot forfeit nature's claim. Skin may differ but affection dwells in black and white the same. And who are so tall to reach the pole, ought to grasp the ocean at a span. I must be measured by my soul for the mind, not the color, the mind is the standard of the man."

When the church decides to be the church it will teach all men that this is my Father's world, that "the earth is the Lord's, and the fullness thereof; the world and they that dwell therein."

When the church starts being the church, it will speak out against the fact that 90 percent of the wealth of the United States is owned and controlled by only 10 percent of the population. It is tragic that 90 percent of the 200 million Americans only control 10 percent of the wealth of this land.

There is another thing that the church must do. It must understand the frustrations of those who have lost faith in the orderly democratic process, and who have turned to a false theory of separatism and a misinterpretation of Black Power. The church must put its arms around these young people and these frustrated people, and help them to know that separatism is not the way. We must tell them that Black is beautiful and it *is* beautiful to be Black, but Black and white together are even more beautiful. We must teach them that violence never permanently solves any problem. We must teach them that there is still a voice that's crying out in this universe, " 'Not by might nor by power but by my spirit,' saith the Lord of Hosts." The philosophy of an eye for an eye, or a tooth for a tooth, if followed to its ultimate conclusion will end up with a blind society and a toothless generation.

I challenge you evangelists to become prophets of protest. Call for, demand an end, to the Godless, senseless, and unwinnable war in Vietnam. Call for the admission of Red China to the United Nations so that we may solve the problems of the world around the conference table, because they cannot be solved in the battlefields. Can't you hear Jesus saying right now to every repenting Peter, "Put down your sword, for he that fighteth with the sword will perish by the sword"?

I challenge you, fellow evangelists, to join hand in hand, and heart in heart, in solving the three great evils of our time: war, racism, and poverty. So "rise up, oh men of God. The day of march has come." Evangelize your community. Evangelize your state, evangelize our nation and our world, until every valley is exalted, the hills and mountains are made low, the crooked is made straight, the rough places are made plain, and the glory of the Lord is revealed. Evangelize, not only until Black and white shall live together as brothers, but the lion will lie down with the lamb, and the calf and fatling live together. Evangelize until repression is ended in America. Evangelize until injustice and inequality are destroyed and replaced with justice and equality for all men. Evangelize until the church becomes the church and its members do not necessarily, Mr. Chairman, *wear* a cross, but start *bearing* a cross. Evangelize until men can see Christ in you and you do not have to hang out your shingle, but men will know that you have been with God because you walk differently, and you talk differently. If you will do this, our nation and western civilization will not be destroyed. It will stand. If you will do it, Calvary may be waiting for you but I can assure you that jail cells will not hold you, because I've been there 27 times. Never for stealing, never for robbing, never for beating my wife, but always for standing up for my people. Every time I got behind the jail bars I discovered that Jesus was already there.

Evangelize until men will live together as brothers. I cannot tell you what will happen to you. I can tell you, however, what happened to Jesus. If you will be a Christian, it may be that you will be crucified on your Calvary, but eventually you will hear the words of the Eternal God, "Well done, thou good and faithful servant." If you will do it, you may not receive the praises of men. You may not win the popularity contest in the Harris or the Gallup polls, but unborn generations will rise up and they will call your name "Blessed."

I've been sued for 3 million dollars; my salary has been garnisheed; my home has been sold at public auction; my automobile has been taken away from me; 27 times was I jailed, beaten, and left by the oppressor thinking I was dead along the highway of life. Like the apostle Paul I bear in my body the marks and bruises of a soldier of the Cross and a follower of the Lamb. But I'm going through. I still feel like going on. Like Peter, I want to stay here on this mountain with you in Minneapolis. This has been a rich and moving experience just to listen to my fellow Baptist minister from the Calvary Baptist Church of New York deliver such a profound and eloquent message, to look into your faces and to see the light of hope, the love of friendship and brotherhood. Like Peter, I would like to stay here on this mountain except for the fact of the valleys of Alabama, Mississippi, Georgia, Florida, the ghettos of Chicago, the Bedford-Stuyvesant areas of Brooklyn, of Harlem in New York, the Watts of California. These are the valleys that beckon to me, and I must go to those valleys, but as I go, I want to leave with you the words of an old Baptist hymn. You wouldn't know these words for they are not found in your hymnal. Neither are they found in the hymnal of the Calvary Church, and they're not found in the hymnal of the Westminster Church. I learned them in the Black belt of Alabama at my mother's knee. Let me give them to you, Mr. Chairman, and to this conference, as I go.

"Beams of heaven as I go
Through this wilderness below
Guide my feet in peaceful ways
Turn my midnights into days.
When in the darkness I would grope
Faith always sees a star of hope
And soon from all life's heats and danger
I shall be free someday.
Harder yet may be the fight,

Right may often yield to might,
Wickedness awhile may reign,
And Satan's calls may seem to gain.
But there's a God, there's a God,
There's a God who rules above
With a hand of power
And a heart of love.
If I'm right He'll fight my battle.
I shall be free someday.
I do not know,
I said I do not know,
I do not know, I do not know
How long 'twill be
Nor what the future holds for me.
But this I know
That Jesus leads the way.
I shall be free someday."

REVIVAL IN OUR WORLD

Dr. Stephen F. Olford

I want to address myself to the theme that has been assigned me and that is "Revival in Our World Today." As my beginning point, I want us to turn for a moment to the Epistle of James, chapter 5, verse 16, "Confess your faults one to another, and pray one for another, that ye may be healed. The effectual fervent prayer of a righteous man availeth much. Elijah was a man subject to like passions as we are, and he prayed earnestly that it might not rain: and it rained not on the earth by the space of three years and six months. And he prayed again, and the heaven gave rain, and the earth brought forth her fruit."

Fellow-delegates, I am absolutely convinced after years of preaching, reading, and praying, that there is no problem facing us today which cannot be solved by a heaven-sent revival. We are living in a very unhappy world. It's a world of infidelity, growing infidelity. Whatever revivals have swept the earth in recent years, nothing has happened in recent times to stem the tide of evil, unrest, racism, hatred, and lust across the world, and particularly our own country. Infidelity as I say is growing apace. An author has written a book entitled "The Good Pagan" and has pointed out that more and more our nation is becoming a nation of pagans; and by pagan he means empty of those values and beliefs that once made us strong.

Carl Jung once said that the central neurosis of our times is a sense of emptiness. As a pastor of a city church, going to campuses, moving amongst the hippies in the park, going down to the ghettos and various other places where my ministry takes me, I sense this emptiness among men and women today. No longer is there conviction. No longer is there belief, no longer is there faith. Yes, and materialism is sweeping our land. A great thinker in Britain has recently stated that the realization of economic values is the prerequisite for the temporal things and eternity will take care of itself. Jesus Christ, the Son of God, stood upon this planet and said, "Seek ye *first* the Kingdom of God, and His righteousness and all these things shall be added unto you."

I never knew that materialism was such a power until I finished my nine to ten years in a city church and discovered that materialism is a spirit, a spirit that gets into people, a spirit that mobilizes and organizes, and (in terms of the spiritual) paralyzes. We are living in an hour not only of materialism, but of anti-Godism under the insti-

DR. STEPHEN F. OLFORD, Pastor, Calvary Baptist Church, New York, New York.

gation of Communism, anarchism, yes, and the followers of Herbert Marcuse. Across our campuses and our country there is a blatant and aggressive anti-Godism. Some of us are deeply concerned as we talk to people we once knew, who had a faith, who today are quite militant and blatant in their atheism. It is a growing infidelity. Somehow or other we've cut ourselves off from the only source of blessing, the only source of beneficence, even Almighty God.

It is a world of immorality, and by immorality I mean those inner ingredients that are in the minds of so many of us at this time, dishonesty, delinquency, dehumanization. Talk to sociologists, talk to religionists, talk to those who are in the streets, and you will hear of the dishonesty of our hour. Husband doesn't trust wife, wife doesn't trust husband, parents don't trust children, and children don't trust parents. Personal, social, spiritual, national, international, commercial pledges are broken with impunity. There is a dishonesty.

As one writer has put it, "When bribery becomes the way of life, when expense account-cheating is the common thing, our nation is in danger." But with that is the delinquency of the hour. Was there ever a time when crime has spiraled to such heights? What shall we say of the LaCosa Nostra, the Mafia? What shall we say of the crimes against the body, against the home, against the church that sweep our country today? We have been told that the American taxpayer today pays no less than $30,000 a minute for the crime of our so-called Christian country. Delinquency!

What shall we say of dehumanization?

One of the great psychologists of our time, Dr. Philip Zimbardo has pointed out that this hour is an hour of individuation — a word that he has brought out of the dictionary and filled with a new connotation. But the psychic pressures of great cities, the destruction of the family unit, the erosion of those moral standards which once made us great have made us capable as a nation of being potential assassins. This dehumanization has taken so many forms. There is the form of racism that hurts me and bruises my spirit. I see it across this nation, I feel it wherever I move. I see it in the faces of men and women. The hate, the lust, the exploitation, the incompatibility, the division that has come upon us are dehumanizations of the very dignity and nobility that God intended for man.

It is an hour of growing immorality in those kinds of aspects that are ugly, grim and sinister. Strangely enough, it is an hour and a world of insecurity. It is a strange thing that where man has walked on the moon and is now prepared to explore the far planets of our solar system, we are all afraid of the future, we are all afraid of tomorrow. There is the insecurity of resources. Isn't it an amazing thing that in affluent America today there is famine, there is starvation, there is poverty, there is the ghetto situation? Yes, not only famine and poverty, but even worse things that are going on in this so-called rich and wonderful society. And let me tell you, the countries in the East, the Communist countries have it no better.

I've just come back from Europe. And I remember just a few weeks ago being in a home of an official who has all the riches and all the valuable things that are acclaimed in this country — yes, by men and women who think that they are the great things, and unless I have them, I haven't anything. And in that same town in Europe, I went to hovels, I went to ghettos, and I saw poverty such as I hadn't seen in other parts of the world. Communism isn't the answer for that. We are in a state of insecurity in resources. Yes, and not only in resources but the insecurity of population altogether.

There is a physicist who has just stated that on the 13th of November, in the year 2,026 or thereabouts, "We're going to die not of starvation, but suffocation by population explosion alone."

What shall we say of the insecurity of civilization? By the splitting of the atom we have produced a situation now where we could face a holocaust that would destroy our entire civilization and reduce the planet to a cinder.

But you have heard, and you have heard again, and you have heard still again throughout these days of the terrible and dark situation we face in the world today, and in particular in our own country. The question — what is the answer? I am personally committed to the view that the answer is God, the answer is Jesus Christ, the answer is the coming of the Holy Ghost in revival. I repeat what I said at the beginning that there is nothing that revival couldn't solve in our country if we were prepared to pay the price.

As I read my Bible, the dawn of creation, the dawn of redemption is the sweep of revelation consummating in the coming again of our mighty King and Lord, even Jesus Christ.

But in the middle, in the history of the unfolding drama of redemption, is the story of the great prophets. I've been studying again the life of Elijah, and somehow or other I see a parallel between his time, his life, his ministry and ours as leaders in the Christian church today — we who are gathered in this very auditorium this afternoon.

I see Elijah called of God to face an hour of darkness, an hour of drought, an hour of death, an hour of famine, an hour of trouble in the history of Israel. Through this man God changed the entire course of things, the destiny of men, the history of Elijah's nation and time. I searched the Old Testament again and again to find out what was the answer to his life. What was the secret of this man's power? And I discovered it. It is found in the New Testament, it is found in the words we have just read together. James, this mighty apostle, this man of prayer, this man who has come, through tradition, to be known as a man of "camel knees" because of the great callouses on his knees caused by his kneeling so much in prayer, cites Elijah as his great illustration of prayer. James says, "The effectual fervent prayer of a righteous man availeth much." Elijah was a man of such passions as we are, and he prayed and heaven was shut. And he prayed, and heaven was opened.

I believe in that illustration we have what I am terming this afternoon "Revival Praying" — the greatest need of the hour, the greatest need of your life, the greatest need of my life.

I want you to notice what I mean by the ministry of revival praying. Elijah was a man subject to like passions as we are. He was a man who fled from a woman, a man who shrank under a prophet's yoke. He was a man who sat under a juniper tree and longed to end his life. He was a man who had his problems, but he was a man who knew how to pray. He was a man of obedience; it is the "effectual, fervent prayer of a righteous man," says James, and Elijah was such a man as that. As you go into the book of Kings and read his story we read, "He went and did according to the word of the Lord." A man of obedience. God has made it a principle that prayer can never find an answer, prayer can never move the hand that moved the world, prayer can never open the heavens to bring down the rain of revival until we know obedience in our lives, basic, radical, unflinching obedience.

The Bible says, "If I regard iniquity in my heart the Lord will not hear me." Jesus said, "If you abide in me and my words abide in you, you shall ask what you will and it shall be done unto you." Elijah was an obedient man.

And I want to say that the greatest need in the church of Jesus Christ at this hour among ministers and Christian leaders is obedience, total obedience to the Word of God, total obedience to the command of God. Elijah was a man of obedience. But supremely he was a man of vision, a man of observation, he was a man who could see what was happening in his country. He could say to a king upon the throne, "Thou and thy father's house have bowed to Baal and thou hast not obeyed the commandments of the Lord." A man of vision.

I believe with all my heart that when Solomon wrote those words, under inspiration, "where there is no vision the people perish," he was challenging the prophetic vision of his day, and the prophetic vision of men and women down through the centuries. Where there is no vision the people throw off all moral restraints. Where there is no vision the people go naked. Where there is no vision the people go wild. He was a man of vision, and as you see, so you pray.

Jeremiah said, "Mine eye affecteth mine heart." Observation leads to intercession. He was a man who was an intercessor.

I'm all for education. We need more of it. I'm all for legislation. We need more of it. I'm all for agitation. We need more of it very often, but I believe the greatest need for the hour is men of intercession, men who know how to pray. It was a ministry of prayer, but a manner of prayer that impresses me deeply. Yes, here was a man who knew how to pray. We are told that it was fervent praying — the effectual fervent prayer of a righteous man. The text tells us that he prayed earnestly, or he *prayed* in his prayer; so many of us *say* prayers, but we never *pray*. Oh, to know how to pray! Oh, to know how to echo the prayer that is in the heart of God, for all prayers start from heaven, not upon earth. Prayer starts in heaven you will see, if you study your eighth chapter of Romans. Prayer starts in the heartache of God and it is mediated to man by the Holy Ghost who indwells us, and when we know how to pray in the Holy Ghost we really know how to pray.

So few of us are prepared to give these bodies of ours, these lives of ours, over to the Holy Spirit and say, "Holy Spirit, whatever it costs in fasting, whatever it costs in sacrifice, whatever it costs, I want this body of mine to be a temple in which the Holy Ghost prays and prays and prays until that travail brings to birth the purposes of God." He knew fervent praying, this man Elijah. He knew more than that. He knew what it was to pray, and pray again. His was not spasmodic, intermittent, irregular praying. He was praying constantly. We read he prayed, and he prayed again, and he prayed again. His was focused praying. Here was a man who knew his God in such a fashion that he could say, "God, shut heaven," and heaven was shut. "God, open heaven," and heaven was open. This is the effectual fervent prayer of a righteous man which availeth much.

But my burden this afternoon, heavy upon my spirit, is what I'm going to call the miracle of revival praying. We've looked at the ministry of it, and the manner of it. Now look at the miracle of it. Had we time to go through the life of Elijah I could give you abundant emphasis on this matter of miracle. Revival is miracle, but let me choose two or three simple illustrations as I bring my address to a close, and let me put it this way. Here is a man who knew triumphant praying, miracle praying, and that miracle had an effect on three areas that are troubling us today. He had victory and triumph in this praying — revival praying — over the powers of darkness. It was when he took his prayer to Mount Carmel, built an altar before the Lord, and cried out to God, "Oh, God, let it be known that Thou art God, in this day" that God revealed His glory in such a visitation of fire that evil was slain with the sword. God was vindicated in the minds and hearts of the people.

We need to see the glory of God afresh. We need to see the vindication of the righteous judgments of our God, and the love and mercy of our God. We do need a new awareness of God again in this country that was founded on God. We need to see victory over the powers of darkness. But not only the powers of darkness. Because of Elijah's praying, he had victory over the drought. He knelt and he prayed and he said, "God, send the rain," and the rain came down, and his power over darkness illustrates the vindication of the glory of God. The rain falling on a plot of dry and thirsty land illustrates the revival of saints. Rain has always been a picture of revival, of refreshing, of renewal. Revival has always come through prayer.

If I've done any research and any reading in my lifetime, it's been on this theme of revival. I'm taken back immediately in my mind to the beginning of the eighteenth century. Britain was never in a worse mess. We talk about dark days today but you should read your history and see what Britain was going through at that time. What was God's answer? God's answer was to raise a man named Wesley, to raise a man named Whitefield. As those men joined hands together and crossed the country and started prayer groups all over — especially John Wesley with his classes and his prayer groups — a wave of prayer swept through that land and God rained righteousness from heaven.

You know, my friends, the impact of that revival has been described by historians down through the years. Samuel Green says, "The temper of the English people seemed to be transformed overnight." Lecky, the historian, said, "Wesley saved Britain from a revolution of blood." The Right Honorable Lloyd George, writing as Prime Minister of Britain, said, "Wesley changed the history of the British Isles."

I want to tell you everything was cleaned up. There was such a cleansing in that country that crime was dealt with, evil among the workers was dealt with, trade unions in their proper sense were instituted, the bloody games of cock-fighting and bear-baiting were exchanged for the green fields with their cricket and football. All emerged out of that mighty awakening of the Spirit of God.

Come to our own country here in 1857 when revival swept this country. At its height, prayer meetings were held all over this country. Two thousand men gathered for prayer in Philadelphia at noon. Another 3,000 in Chicago. At the height of that revival 50,000 men and women were being swept into the Kingdom of our Lord and Savior Jesus Christ every week. I want to remind you that it is out of that revival that anti-slavery began with all its force in this country — in New England, and then down through the South. Whatever else has happened, let me tell you that the beginnings of anti-slavery came out of revival, came out of a heaven-sent revival. It touched not only that area of life, humanitarianism, and the uplift of men and women, but I want to remind you that it touched education.

Out of the nine colonial colleges of those days, six of them were born out of revival. Later that tradition was followed. Some of you may not know, but that Christian school we call Wheaton College was instituted as an anti-slavery school, an institution of learning against anti-slavery and oppression. Revival, heaven-sent revival, produced it. New researchers have discovered that the Welsh revival in 1904, which men and women popularly have limited to the principality of Wales, not only swept Wales, but also Scotland, England, Ireland and came over to this country, where it brought to birth the greatest movement and the fastest growing church in South America that we know today. It went right through to India and South Africa. In my years in Wales I have sat hour after hour at the feet of some of those men who went through the revival. I have looked into the face of Evan Roberts who cried after hearing a sermon, "God, bend me, God, bend me." God bent him, and God broke him and made him the spearhead of revival throughout Wales.

I've heard the story from, and seen the faces of, men who told of the great cleansing that swept the country of Wales. Do you know there is an expression in Wales today "the magistrate's white gloves"? "The magistrate's white gloves" stems from the revival of 1904, because the judiciaries across the principality of Wales were given white gloves, since the judges had no crimes to judge. Revival swept through the land. The very donkeys in the mines ceased to work, we're told. Why? They were unused to kindness. The great valleys of Wales echoed and re-echoed with the song of revival. From morning until night men and women met to worship God, to testify. Gambling was cleaned up. Crime was cleaned up. Horrible things that were happening in the churches were cleaned up, and God swept through that entire land in a mighty, sweeping revival.

Can God do it again? I believe He can. "Jesus Christ the same yesterday, today and forever." Our God is unchanging and faithful, the mighty Spirit of the Living God is waiting, brooding over this land to pour out another refreshing before the coming of the Lord. I believe our Savior in heaven waits for that latter rain until the harvest is complete. The latter rain of revival is that for which I pray. I want to tell you that in my own personal life — and I want to say it very humbly — I've never seen anything happen either in my evangelistic work or church work that hasn't come out of revival. I am ashamed to have to own the fact that when I came to New York City ten years ago, I came to a church that was segregated. But I thought it was a challenge. I felt it was an opportunity to prove the releasing power of the Gospel. Although many pressures were put on me to force the issue, I maintained my stand that through the preaching of the Word of God and through a moving of the Spirit of God, the situation would be resolved.

I remember talking with Dr. Martin Luther King, Jr., for two or three hours as we flew down to Rio de Janeiro nearly nine years ago to the great Baptist Convention and conference down there. I told him this story, and it moved him very deeply. I said I took a poll of our church and discovered just how many there were who would not accept integration. And to my astonishment I discovered it was a high proportion. I could have split the church. I could have ruined my ministry. I could have left, possibly in disgrace. But we began to preach.

We began to pray and revival came to Calvary, a moving of the Spirit. I sensed the hour in which to put to the church the challenge of the Scripture — so clear, that God has made us all one in Christ Jesus — so a person is not a black man or a white man but a Christ-man. Let's unite in Him. I put the challenge to the church, and we held the most famous church meeting I suppose ever held in Calvary Baptist Church. The amazing thing about it is, having finished speaking and answering questions from the floor, we took the vote and the vote was absolutely overwhelming — only 11 against. The church *had* been almost 99 percent against integration. Now only 11 were against integration. Four of those came to me and confessed their sin. Seven of them are dead. God's judgment fell. Every one of them buried. We had the happiest fellowship at Calvary Baptist Church.

I was born in Africa. I love my black brethren. I love the wonder of that glorious wisdom of God, the oriented wisdom of God, the variegated wisdom of God which sees all colors, all personalities, all dispositions — making up the great jewel with all its flashing facets of the manifestation of the person of Jesus Christ. And the church is only a miniature of that. That is the local church. Thank God we can enjoy the happiest fellowship, the happiest joy in these years of ministry. I wouldn't have exchanged this experience for anything. But what did it? God in revival.

Now I don't believe any healing, any cleansing, any righting of wrongs in our country will ever come about merely by legislation, merely by education. God must work through revival. But we've got to pay the price. We've got to be men like Elijah, ordinary men, obedient men, observant men, who are prepared to give themselves to fervent, frequent, focused praying and pay the price for revival. But being rebel hearts as we are, we will try everything else, write the church off, explain everything away rather than paying the price for God to move in, and God won't work until we come on His terms.

God is calling for repentance. God is calling for obedience. God is calling for faith, for revival. Are you ready for it? Are you prepared to enlist? Are you prepared to do the hardest work God has ever called us to do? It is unpublicized work. You won't read about it. It won't be in the press. It's work behind closed doors, it's work on our knees, it's the work of prayer, but it's the work that brings revival.

If you really mean business, and you mean to say yes to that, here is this simple challenge to your heart. I am going to ask those of you who mean business with God and are prepared to go back to your study to pray, back to your church to get your church to pray, back to your organizations to lead them into revival praying, I am going to ask you to stand for a closing prayer.

THE MAKING OF DISCIPLES IN A SECULAR WORLD

Dr. Myron S. Augsburger

"The Kingdom of Heaven suffers violence, and the violent take it by force." "If any man will come after me, let him deny himself, and take up his cross daily and follow me."

These words of Jesus have a strange sound in today's world. They speak of an urgency, a desperation about the meaning of faith which we have rarely seen. Yet all about us are persons who are desperate, activists, revolutionaries, determined to bring about change in our world. The activist would do it by reforming our structures, the revolutionary would do it by destroying them. We must ask, "Why, with the Kingdom of Christ as a most revolutionary force is it not seen as a real option?"

We have met in this Congress to help one another clarify what it means to be the people of God in a modern world. As His people we are called to a life of discipleship, abandoning power, wealth, status, and influence in order that men may know the mystery and power of divine love. As disciples we will live among the downtrodden and oppressed, minister to the broken, and reach a hand of fellowship into the life of one who is different from ourselves. We will not rest until all men have the privilege of knowing Jesus Christ as Lord, of sharing His life and love.

That this is a day of revolution introduces new responsibilities and opportunities for the church. Let us not forget that while a violent revolution was breaking in Russia, the clergy were arguing about the form of vestments and liturgical order! It is for us to seize this opportunity of showing that Christian faith is more than American cultural religion, that the true church is not a gathering of affluent Americans with white skins who have achieved status in our materialistic society. The nature of our times calls us to a reassessment of the quality of our involvement in the Christian faith. Dr. Elton Trueblood has said, "One of the most heartening features of the Christian religion is its capacity for reformation and renewal from the inside."

All about us people have developed a deep concern. In his book, *The Social Conscience of the Evangelical,* Dr. Sherwood Wirt quotes a young lady who wrote in the 1964 school paper at Arizona State University:

DR. MYRON S. AUGSBURGER, President, Eastern Mennonite College, Harrisonburg, Virginia.

"I'm tired, tired of puppets instead of people. Of persons who drop soliloquies carefully labeled 'intelligence.' I'm tired of cynics who call themselves realists; tired of minds rotting in indifference, of people bored because they are afraid to care. I'm tired of people who have to be entertained, of girls proud of knowing the score and snickering about it. I'm tired of sophisticated slobs. Tired of people with nothing better to do than to glue their days together with alcohol. I'm tired of people embarrassed at honesty, at love, at knowledge. Tired, yes. . . . very tired."

It is my thesis that the mission of the Christian Church has been seen too narrowly by both right and left wings of the church, too often obsessed with their attacks on each other. The mission which Jesus outlined for us was that of making disciples of *all* men.

Evangelism with this goal means the Christianizing of the thought and life of society. Among other things this involves: (1) making faith in Christ a clear option, (2) judging and correcting those social structures which warp and blind men's lives, and (3) enlisting men and women to follow the will of God in the total life.

It is probably the last of these three in which the Christian Church finds its greatest failure. The evangelical-minded Christian majors on introducing people to Christ, while the more humanistic Christian majors on interaction with social structures, but both appear to fail in showing how the total life of the Christian is to be brought under the will of Christ. The lordship of Christ is no mere credal concept, it is to be the marching cry for Christians the world over.

Martin Luther once said:

"If I profess with the loudest voice, in clearest exposition, every portion of the truth of God except precisely that little point which the world and the devil are at the moment attacking, I am not confessing Christ, however boldly I may be professing Christ."

The point which not only the world and the devil, but also a secularized church, is attacking, is the call to bring the total life under the lordship of Christ. It is not that what we have said about saving souls is wrong, but that we have not said enough! When we speak of God's transforming grace, our perspective is too small. We have too often limited God to the inner aspects of the individual's life, until in helping individuals to a personal faith they have concluded it is a private faith. As a result, we lack a profound sense of Christian community, we lack a vision for the transformation of the human scene of action, and we fail to Christianize the leaders of society — to evangelize the landowner, the housing authorities, the Chamber of Commerce personnel, and the national thought-makers.

When the Church becomes ingrown, it fails to communicate with its world. When it becomes acculturated, it has nothing truly unique to communicate. The team-meeting is important for sharing together as disciples, in keeping the quality of its work at the proper level, but the team-meeting in itself is not the purpose of the team. The church is called by Christ to exist for those beyond itself, by being an exhibit of what God wants the human community to be like.

Because of the human element in the church, it tends toward idolatry — an idolatry of faith, of system, and of symbols. But the answer is not to replace the structure of the gathered community, and the discipline, and refinement of worship by structures of social action which lack a spiritual center. When men reject institutionalized religion, it does not follow that they thereby must reject Jesus Christ! The answer for society is in the full character of the work of Christ, who makes all things new. He came to save us from problems, — not just the problems we have, but the problems we are!

Having set forth the thesis that our mission is to make disciples in the twentieth century, we look now at the basic premises by which this is achieved.

I. *We Must Acknowledge the Priority of the Kingdom of Christ Today.*

From the days of Caesar to the present, the Kingdom of Christ has stood against the empires of the world. Jesus said, "My Kingdom is not of this world." It does not find its character nor takes its direction from the world. But He also said, "The Kingdom of God is within you," and again, "The Kingdom of God cometh not with observation." In sharing the Kingdom of Christ, in being citizens of heaven while we live here on the earth, the Christian commitment finds its basic structure. This is not to say that we are not a part of the world, for Jesus Himself said, "As the Father hath sent me, even so send I you." Christ loved the world. He bound Himself to it in the Incarnation, and in redemption. Consequently, His followers are bound to this world as extensions of the work of God today.

Few people in our society are convinced that a kingdom of Christ actually exists. Few recognize that Christians have an absolute loyalty to Christ when they read us through our acculturated religion. We need to regain a consistent witness of righteousness, of God-given holiness or wholeness. When our personal involvement with Christ is "visibly" expressed in our social relations with others, they can be convinced of the reality of His Kingdom. This is the work of the Holy Spirit — to glorify Christ today. The Kingdom of Heaven will suffer violence and the violent will take it by force when they see its grandeur in the lives of persons who live Christ-like — in joy and assurance, in Christian brotherhood — by Christian ethics in business, by taking an active part in correcting the problems of poverty, of race, and of war.

This priority of the Kingdom of Christ confronts us in the realm

of Truth. Jesus Christ said that He is the Truth, to know Him is to
know the Father. Knowing God is more than knowing something
about Him. You do not know another person without trust and commitment. Furthermore, a person can be known only if he reveals himself! God as Person can be known only through His own self-revela-
tion. Jesus Christ stands in the stream of history as the revelation of
God; as such He must be given priority in our conversation about God.
While other religions of the world may seek to merge into one universal
humanitarian — even ethical — religion, Christianity stands as a declaration that Jesus Christ is God.

But at this point the Christian Church may be guilty of its greatest
hypocrisy. The evangelical groupings of the Church are no less guilty
than the rest. To confess Christ as God means that one acknowledges
His lordship in the total of life. Christian faith calls us to let God be
God in our lives. We have been guilty of using Jesus as one aspect of
God's program by which we have salvation and have refused to follow
His Word and will as a way of life.

The Kingdom of Christ must be given priority in the realm of
ethics. Jesus Christ taught us the will of God in life and love, and the
Christian Church must discover what this means in actual experience.
As "very God of very God," He revealed God's will in what He said,
in what He did, and in what He was. We must accept the whole Christ,
and face our guilt of accepting a partial Jesus.

We would like to have the sweet Jesus of subjective piety, and
reject the bitter Jesus who calls us to the way of the cross. We would
like to have the Jesus who offers assurance of salvation by telling us
that we may abide in Him, while we reject the Jesus who calls us to
relate the sacred to the secular experience of life as He outlines it in
the Sermon on the Mount. We have chopped-up His revelation, saying that
His demands for discipleship in His Sermon of sermons was prior to Pentecost, and thus not applicable to the church age. Can we any longer avoid
the fact that the Church is built on the foundation of Jesus Christ — the
total Christ!

The Kingdom of Christ stands at the center of history, it is the
key to its interpretation. Because of Christ's work, history is real. Time
is of the essence, for God is doing something. The symbol of life for the
Christian is a road — life is not static, we are on the march with the King
of kings! The coherence of life in its ultimate purpose and unity lies not
in the human mind, nor in systems of rational thought, but in the Divine
Reality which unifies the whole. History, not mystical experiences, is the
is the scene through which God has revealed Himself. When one takes history seriously, he will take God seriously, recognizing that His Kingdom is
among us.

II. *We Must Actively Participate in a New Kind of Brotherhood.*

The people of God share a fellowship which centers in Christ. This is our unity — one in Him. In our urbanized, mobile society we must discover the meaning and dynamic of the covenant community. As a Christian one is called to be his brother's brother, to share a covenant of grace which transcends all earthly divisions. This spirit of community is a gift of God, it is a work of the Holy Spirit. In the covenant community we share with the Spirit in disciplined lives, in "binding and loosing," as we seek to behave our beliefs. The congregation can itself experience a fellowship of belonging, and partake of a group therapy which has a spiritual center. In our fragmented age one of the greatest things the Church can offer the man of the world is brotherhood.

The meaning of history centers in the people of God, not in the empires of the world! The Christian Church is to be God's exhibit of a new kind of humanity. The Christ who makes all things new, who makes each of us new, wills to create a brotherhood that is bound together in covenant community. This is a new kind of people for the world to behold. It is a covenant community in fellowship, a people who relate to one another in and through Jesus Christ. It is a people who confess that their identity and relationship is not built on ethnic characteristics, but on their common fellowship in Jesus Christ. It is a people which knows no racial lines nor class structures. It is a fellowship which transcends the lines drawn by nationalism. Its ministry must follow needs of men on roads that lead to Somalia and Saigon, to Montgomery and Mozambique, to Kingston and Kabul, to Detroit and Delhi, to Philadelphia and Peking. Our prayer and our goal must be to invite all men to become our brothers in Jesus Christ.

We must overcome the temptations to feel secure in affluence, to build financial empires, to measure values by financial status, and we must seek daily the larger will of Christ. We must reject the struggle for power and status in relation to our fellowmen, finding the way to serve men rather than seek to dominate them, to be friends to those in need rather than to be involved in destruction.

The English poet, Auder, has expressed this dilemma in a few lines: "The expert designing his long-range gun, To exterminate everything under the sun, Would like to get out, but can only mutter, 'What can I do? It's my bread and butter.' "

The Christian Church in this hour must become a conscience among mankind. Especially must the evangelical church repent and seek peace in the world — for if our evangelistic claims are true, then we cannot condone the destruction of lives which we actually want to redeem through Jesus Christ.

The faithful church is God's new work in the world. Dr. Paul Rees has said, "If the Church today is awake to the full authority and splendor of her evangelizing mission, she must realize that her evangelism consists as truly of what she is, as it does of what she says. She is Christ's holy presence in the world of the unholy, different from the world because delivered from it, yet all the while redemptively linked with it. If the Pharisees' superior glint is in her eye, she is useless. If the slave's apron is wrapped about her for service, she is authentically fruitful."

III. *We Must Affirm the Place of Christ's Lordship in Judgment on Social Evils*

Jesus Christ is not a hero figure of the past, but a living Person, present in His world and in His church. He is inescapable, and calls us to follow Him in life. Today He confronts us in the social dimensions of life where our compromise of His lordship is the most obvious. He calls us to relate our ethics to Him as clearly as we relate our salvation to Him!

Our society is looking for leadership in moral and spiritual matters. Someone has paraphrased a popular song, "Where Have All the Flowers Gone?" by asking, "Where have all the heroes gone?" National leaders cannot act irresponsibly in areas of moral behavior or economic impropriety without being called into judgment by Christ's ethics. Parental inconsistencies, lack of fidelity, and broken homes which rob children of a normal and decent life, must face Christ's judgments. Those youth who are dropping out, tripping on LSD, and destroying the structures which could be transformed, cannot dodge their responsibility to thousands of other youth who are asking for something better from them. The churches which have become clubs for the sophisticated religious rather than servants of the Master must answer to His judgment. The self-satisfied, who measure their status by the level of affluent white suburban communities in which they share, and who disregard their responsibility to be a brother to their black neighbor, must answer to the judgment of Christ.

Each of us is inescapably bound up before the gaze of the world with affluent Americanism. For example, the Far East sees America's moral and social failures as the failure of Christianity. India reads America's moral failures as the failure of Christianity. As Christians we should call our nation not to rule the world but to serve the world. If we could bring the nearly 500,000 troops back from Vietnam and send one-fifth that many to overcome poverty, hunger, and illiteracy, we could enrich their country rather than destroy it. The Christian Church must ask in all seriousness, "What is Christ's way to serve Vietnam? the Far East? the Middle East? South America?"

Our world now faces the possibility of its final destiny through the valley of starvation. The millions with empty stomachs cry out to us for help now! Abraham Lincoln said, "No nation can exist half-free and half-slave." Our world cannot exist half-surfeiting and half-starving! If Jesus Christ is our King, we will operate by a new ethic, by a love that reaches its hand around the globe. But this is costly, and there are too few disciples who are willing to pay the price. G. K. Chesterton once said, "It is not so much that Christianity has been tried and found wanting, as that it has been found difficult and not tried."

In this age of technological advance, we are responsible to bring our moral and spiritual development to an even higher level. Man's footprints on the moon leave us now with the larger question — will the conquest of space be used for enriching or destroying mankind? Every advance of science focuses more attention upon the men who will use the achievement. The Christian Church is not only a servant in society but must be its conscience as well. We must call our nation to a better role than a military economy and a program of conscription which turns us into an armed fortress.

Nobel Prize Winner, Dr. George Wald, professor of biology at Harvard, quoting former President Eisenhower's warning against what he called a military-industrial complex, said, "I don't think we can live with the present military establishment, and its eighty-billion-dollar-a-year budget, and keep America anything like the America we have known in the past. It is corrupting the life of the whole country. . . .

"Our business is with life, not death. Our challenge is to give what account we can of what becomes of life in the solar system . . . and, most of all, what becomes of men — all men, of all nations, colors, and creeds."

IV. *We Must Aggressively Permeate All Strata of Society with the Gospel*

The early church turned the world upside down without even talking about it. They simply shared the good news of God's redemptive work in Jesus Christ. Everything that is Christian derives from its origin in the Gospel of Christ. Evangelism is really the love of God in action. It is introducing persons to the meaning of life and inviting them to become disciples of Jesus Christ. Evangelism is the demonstration that we care about the whole man, that we want to bring his total person to the quality of life which Jesus Christ provides. Dr. Lesslie Newbigin has said: "Preaching which is divorced from deeds of love is without power to evoke belief. Deeds of love which are permanently disconnected from witness to Christ evoke belief in the wrong thing."

The Christian Church exists not for its own sake but for the sake of those who have yet to be introduced to Jesus Christ. It has well been said that, "The Church exists by mission, as fire exists by burning." Jesus said to His disciples, "I chose you and appointed you that you should go and bear fruit," and that fruit is new disciples, men and women converted to Christ. The Christian Church is not a static institution but is a dynamic reality, men and women who flesh-out in daily life the meaning of faith, the reality of the risen Christ.

The Holy Spirit calls every member of the Church to be witness to the resurrection life of Jesus Christ. Where there is no witness, no evangelism, that person or church group is not true to the mandate of its risen Lord. In fact, where evangelism is absent, it may be concluded that the freedom and dynamic of the Spirit is also absent.

Christ calls us not to live selfishly but to live for others. As we save souls, we are actually saving persons, families, communities, people. We need to interpret the commission of our Lord vocationally as well as geographically, carrying our Christian witness into our occupational associations. We must not assign the evangelistic work of the church to a select group of professionals, but must all share in the meaning of Christ's words: "While going about in your personal worlds, make disciples of all men."

The Christian Church today needs a program for evangelistic social action! Such a program will serve to make us relevant in a secular world.

(1) It will show how Christian experience can change our lives now, can change our conservatism on social issues, and make us into a transforming force in society.

(2) It will show how our evangelistic concerns can take seriously the whole life and plight of our fellowmen, and involve us in helping them in their dilemma.

(3) It will show us where redemptive action in the world brings human concerns and Christian concerns together for common action.

(4) It will show us how spiritual ideals and character can enrich and judge the limitations of the secular, improving rather than destroying secular orders.

(5) It will show us how to be citizens of Christ's global Kingdom, and how to be good earthly citizens without supporting the idolatries of nationalism.

Such a program in Christian action can awaken our society to realize the relevance of the Christian faith and of the Church. It can make clear that love is not a word, but a way of life. It will exemplify that all peoples of the world can be one in Christ. It can hold service and evangelism together and demonstrate as Dr. Lesslie Newbigin has said, that the two "are not to be separated, neither must they be wrongly related." He interprets the relation for us.

"Service must not be subordinated to evangelism. The Christian works of love should be as Christ's were, a spontaneous outflowing of the love of God from men, not a means to something else. . . . At no point, therefore, is it sufficient for the church to point to its own good deeds. It must always be penitently aware of the fact that even the best of its good deeds cannot mediate for man the ultimate judgment and mercy of God. For that there is no place where we can go but to the Cross. The Church has therefore to preach Christ afresh to every man of every generation. There is, and there can be, no substitute for telling the Good News. Evangelism, the activity of telling men by word of mouth or by pen the story of Jesus, is a necessary and indispensable manifestation of the new reality in action."

What does this mean for us who have gathered here? What good will come of these words on which we have thought? What does the Spirit of God want to accomplish through this meeting that will be a part of His ultimate goal and purpose?

The Church as it is generally known in the Western world is a fallen church. No doubt the God who shatters idols is needing to raise up a stronger church so that the world will meet *Him*, rather than simply meet American cultural religion. We must today seek a spiritual renewal that will transform the Church, rather than give ourselves to defend it.

We are called to be God's people, scattered through society as the "salt of the earth" and as "a light in the world." This calls for a radical change in the Church's life, for it is not prepared for the task of discipling men and women. This means a rediscovery of first century Christianity, both in terms of experience and of extension. We must recognize our place on the unbroken continuum of the followers of Christ.

Evangelism for the twentieth century is more than ever discipling people. It is calling men and women to "the Jesus way" of life and faith. Our mission calls for a deep awareness of the unity of Christ's mission, a rejection of the polarization of evangelism and social action, engaging us in a service which brings the whole man to Christ. While good deeds are good in themselves, and are not bait to enlist a man in spiritual exercises, we must recognize that a deed is not a good deed when its humanitarian service is inconsistent with man's essence as a creature made in the image of God. A truly good deed serves the highest level of man's nature — mind, faith, fellowship, and decision.

People are not rushing into churches where the programs are solely humanistic, for they can find all that such churches have to offer in secular programs. Nor are people rushing into conservative churches where they see no answer to the known and felt needs of their lives. Furthermore, the Kingdom of Heaven is not suffering violence in America because people are not desperate about the most revolutionary aspects of life!

Our task is to shatter man's complacency, destroy the comfort of his apathy, expose his limited securities, so that, either in desperation or in new understanding, he will come to the Kingdom of Christ! Such discipling of men cannot be done in armchair comfort! We must go where the people are, be where the action is, stimulate a new awareness that commitment to Jesus Christ is the most revolutionary experience a man can have.

Modern man, secular man, claims to be able to deal with life without God. His is a stance of intellectual autonomy, and a claim that we have seen the end of the metaphysical, and a resolve to save man by man's own technical genius. If we would stimulate urgency on the matters of Christian faith, the character of our discipleship will need to do it in today's world. Persons caught in the despair of our times may recognize that faith is a real option when they see twentieth century exhibits of Christ's kind of men and women. We must give ourselves to the life of discipleship, no matter how costly, lest our world die without knowing that the Kingdom of Christ can actually be experienced.

COMMITMENT TO SERVE

Dr. Billy Graham

Dr. Hoffmann, Dr. Fryhling, Dr. Ockenga, Dr. Lindsell, and all of the others that are on the platform, Dr. Judd, I wanted to yell, "Amen" at everything I heard this morning from these speakers, and I would like us to stand one more time and give our appreciation to the greatest chairman of any conference or congress that I've ever been associated with, Dr. Oswald Hoffmann.

I was rather hoping he would come here and speak so I wouldn't have to.

Now I'm not going to say anything worth applauding so please don't applaud and take the time that I have left because I'm supposed to be finished in just a few minutes. And I'm not going to try to give the message that I have prepared because I don't think the moment calls for that. You're tired, many of you have to go and catch planes. About a third of our delegates have already had to go back because they're pastors with churches, and the pulpits need to be filled tomorrow. Many of them had to go to the West Coast and the East Coast and get what planes they could get. But this has been, what Dr. Judd said, "a soul-stretching, mind-expanding" conference for me, and I'm sure that my ministry and my work will never be quite the same after this week in Minneapolis.

It has gone beyond all expectations of my own, and my expectations were high. It has gone in different directions than I had anticipated, and I'm deeply grateful.

How we all got together as evangelicals is an amazement to almost everybody. It reminds me of Jesus when He called His disciples. He called Simon, the zealot, who was a revolutionary. He wanted to go out and fight and use violence and change the whole thing. And He called Matthew into the same little group who was a member of the "establishment," and they worked together with Jesus. We've had a diverse group here in Minneapolis and we've worked together, we've prayed together, and we have all felt a developing koinonia, a fellowship, among us.

The Executive Committee that has planned this Congress has had hundreds of suggestions about the program, as to what they should do, I'm sure. I sent some suggestions that they didn't accept, and I think they were right in not accepting as I look back.

It was my privilege to go up to the Redwoods, a week ago, with

DR. BILLY GRAHAM, Founder and President, The Billy Graham Evangelistic Association, and Honorary Chairman, U.S. Congress on Evangelism.

former President Johnson and President Nixon. On the plane I sat with them going and on the way back. President Johnson said something that I don't think he would mind my quoting. I never quote the President of the United States but he's no longer President. He was describing the Presidency and I thought it was the best description of the Presidency I ever heard. He said, "Every President likes to escape the responsibilities of the White House as much as he can. He likes to go off to Texas, or to California, or somewhere. But," he said, "I soon learned that you just had to sit here in the White House like a jackass in a hailstorm." And I think that's one of the best descriptions of the presidency I ever heard, in Texas language.

I heard about the lady that was concerned that she had no husband and she went to her pastor, and he said, "The Lord has a plan. One man for one woman. That's the Lord's plan. You cannot improve on that." And she replied, "I don't want to improve on it. I just want to get in on it."

Well, I'm glad I've been in on this conference this week.

Cardinal Cooke was in Vietnam at Christmas and it was my privilege to be there as well. He told a little story that perhaps most of you know but I never heard it. He said a Catholic priest in a certain community played golf every Monday morning with three Protestant clergymen, and they made up a foursome. Christmas was approaching and he said to his three Protestant friends, "We're going to have a Christmas Eve service at our church. We're going to have a Mass. Have you ever been to one?" They said, "No." He asked, "Are you having a service in your church?" They said, "No." He said, "Would you accept my invitation and come to the Christmas Mass at our church?" And they said, "Why, yes, we'd be honored to come." So that night the church was packed, the priest and his two assistants were conducting the service, but the Protestant clergymen hadn't shown up, and the priest was disappointed. About halfway through the Mass he looked in the back and he saw them there in the door standing, and he whispered to his assistant, "Set three chairs for the Protestants." The assistant stood there and shook his head and grew red. About a minute or two passed, and he said a little bit louder, "Three chairs for the Protestants, I said." The priest stood there and shook his head, and the senior priest was getting angrier by the minute. In the middle of his service he said, "I said three chairs for the Protestants." And the assistant held up his hands to the congregation and he said, "Ladies and gentlemen, I do not know what our minister, our priest means, but he wants us to give three cheers for the Protestants." I say three cheers for the evangelicals.

Now in the talk that I had prepared, which I won't give, I had taken another passage of Scripture, but following Dr. Ockenga I would like to take a different passage and make personal what he said. Because I want to talk for a moment on the personal life of the minister. That's what I've been asked to do and I want to abbreviate it. I have eight points. I'm going to give only the first two points I think, because time will not permit.

But in the 22nd chapter of Ezekiel, God is speaking about Jerusalem. God enumerates the sins of the people, idolatry, immorality, oppression of minority groups, social injustice, greed, lust, gluttony, and then He comes to the prophets. He says this about the prophets, in the 25th verse of the 22nd chapter. "There is a conspiracy of her prophets in the midst thereof." Then He goes a little bit further and says, "Her priests have violated my law, and have profaned mine holy things: they have put no difference between the holy and [the] profane, neither have they shown difference between the unclean and the clean, and have hid their eyes . . . and I am profaned among them."

And then He said in the 30th verse, "And I sought for a man among them." Among the priests, among the preachers, among the clergy, among the prophets. "I, the Lord God of heaven, am looking for a man to stand in the gap and make up the hedge before me for the land, that I should not destroy it."

Now Jerusalem was the holy city occupied by God's chosen people and God says, "I'm going to destroy it. Jerusalem is no longer my pet. Judgment is coming, but if I could only find one man to stand in the gap and make up the hedge, a man of courage and conviction, a man of dependence on me, and of humility and prayer, a man filled with the Spirit, it might turn the tide."

Dr. Ockenga is exactly right. We live on the edge of judgment. What we see in Vietnam today is only a side show compared to what's building up in the Middle East. The Middle Eastern situation could drive the whole world into war within the next two years because the Soviet presence is tremendous there, the American presence is tremendous, the Chinese presence is growing, and the Arab/Israeli conflict seemingly has no answer except more bloodletting. The United Nations are paralyzed and helpless to do anything about it, and the world at this moment is moving toward what could be a gigantic Armageddon.

I asked John Steinbeck before he died, "John, what is the hope of America," and he gave me a strange reply. He said, "The hope of America is that we have a catastrophe." He said, "That's the only thing that will save this country is a catastrophe."

I didn't agree with him but the catastrophe that hit Mississippi two weeks ago, with all of its terrible and tragic suffering, had one aspect to it that the newspaper writers made a lot of. It did more to bring the races together in lower Mississippi than anything that's ever happened.

One of my associates, Walter Smyth, was in Prague on the Sunday before the Russians invaded Czechoslovakia last summer. He said in the church service there was a Czech soldier, strong, handsome, straight in his uniform, who came up to him after the service and said, "Dr. Smyth, do you think that the commitment to Jesus Christ is greater in America where you have all those freedoms, or is it greater in Czechoslovakia where we have no civil rights?" Dr. Smyth thought for a moment and he said, "I believe that I see a deeper commitment to Christ on the part of the Czech church, with all of its problems, than I do the American church." And then the Czech soldier gave a very interesting reply. He said, "Then why do we need all these freedoms?"

I was in Vienna three weeks ago and I spoke to 650 Czech leaders. When I walked into the auditorium they all burst into tears. They sang and they cried. The next day they were going back into Czechoslovakia and back to all their problems. While I talked they cried and wept, many times audibly, and when I finished speaking they came up with a great big vase so big that I could hardly carry it that had cost them $300 at the factory, to present to me as a gift, and the average salary of the average Czech pastor is $20 a month. They bought that to give to me.

I stood there and Bob Denny who is the secretary of The Baptist World Alliance was there, and he is here, and I said to Bob Denny, "This to me is the real church."

Brethren, we are in the middle of a revolution and things are going to change, acceleration is going to be tremendous. Where does the Christian stand in the middle of it? Unless we have those spiritual resources in Christ, many a clergyman is going to throw up his hands in despair. The despair of the existential philosophers of this hour is going to grip you, and you're going to think that life has no meaning and the world makes no sense.

Paul said, "Do the work of an evangelist." Ralph Abernathy said yesterday, "I say evangelize, for it is only through evangelism that the nations of the world will be saved." Where does this word "evangelist" come from? I'll tell you where it comes from. The first time it's ever used in history, so I'm told, was in 490 B.C., the battle of Marathon, when the Persians had moved their great force toward Athens. The outnumbered Athenians met them 25 miles from Athens and fought them and won the battle. The people of Athens were locked in their city, frightened and trembling, and they sent a messenger to give the good news to Athens. The messenger traveled, running every step of the way, and his message was this, "Rejoice, we have conquered," and he fell dead from exhaustion. That's the first time in history that the word "evangelist" was used. Good news, even if it means death. Do the work of an evangelist.

We're going back to our parishes, back to our communities, back to our towns, to do the work of an evangelist.

Now in order to do that several things will have to characterize you. First, the man that God uses in evangelism will have to have an experience with Christ. We hear a great deal about the word "experience." Have you bought the new LIFE magazine supplement on Woodstock? Well, you go get it. It will cost you $1.50 but you'll see I don't know how many pages of pictures of the gathering of those 400,000 young people in New York in the mud the other day. And if you ever saw a group of wistful, wonderful young people standing there as though they were searching for something they hadn't found, you'll see it in those pictures that LIFE magazine has taken. I wanted to go there and shout the Good News to those people, because we haven't heard much about the student world in this Congress. I want to tell you the young people and the students are searching for something, and they're searching desperately. They're trying to find in drugs, they're trying to find in sex experience, they're trying to find in their "things," and their "happenings," an experience that they will really only find in a personal encounter with Jesus Christ.

Now I wonder if you, as a Christian worker and minister, have had an experience with Christ. I said "with Christ." Now you can have an experience. Every neurotic has an experience. Neurosis is now called a private religion. But I'm talking about an experience with Christ, so that Christ is yours.

The old rabbis used to say, "First be trained thyself and then adorn thy brother. The hand that means to make another clean must not itself be dirty."

Charles Spurgeon once said to his students, "Conversion is a 'must' in a minister." John Wesley said, "What a dreadful thing it would be for me if I should be ignorant of the power of the truth which I am preparing to proclaim."

Have you ever read what Martin Luther had to say about his own conversion? I'm sure that most of you have, but I want to remind you of it again. You see Luther was a priest, a monk, a professor of theology, and yet he felt a great sense of hypocrisy and failure and sin in his life, frustration and depression. Like many of you. You came to this conference. One minister said, "If I don't find the answer here, I'm going to leave the ministry." In 1545 Martin Luther wrote this, "For however irreproachably I lived as a monk, I felt myself in the presence of God to be a sinner with the most unquiet conscience. Nor could I believe that I pleased Him with my works. I did not love, indeed I hated, God. If not with open blasphemy at least with huge murmurings and complainings, for I was indignant against God saying,

'As if it were really not enough for God that miserable sinners should be eternally lost through original sin and oppressed with all kinds of calamities through the law of the Ten Commandments, now God must add sorrow to sorrow and even by the Gospel bring His wrath to bear.' Thus," said Luther, "I raged with a fierce and most agitated conscience and yet I continued to knock away at Paul in this place, thirsting to know what Paul really meant."

Then Luther had his crisis and here's what he said, "At last I began to understand the justice of God as that by which the just man lives by the gift of God and that is to say by faith, the just man shall live by faith. At this I felt myself to have been born again and to have entered through open gates into Paradise itself."

I want to ask you, have you ever had an experience like that? Depressed, discouraged, despondent, seemingly not getting through to God, bewildered by all that's happening in our world, have you ever gotten on your knees and had such a crisis experience with God that you felt that you were entering Paradise itself?

I have had several experiences like that. I had one when I was first converted to Christ. I've had them since then as a clergyman, as a minister. John Wesley was a missionary to Georgia, and on the way back to Europe he was afraid in the storms. He watched the Moravians, who were not afraid, and he became attached to them. But Wesley was convinced that he lacked that faith whereby alone we are saved. On Wednesday, May 24, 1738, he went to a society meeting at Aldersgate Street where Luther's preface to the epistle of Romans was read, and you've all heard it a thousand times. But let's listen to what Wesley said again.

"About a quarter before 9, while they were describing the change which God works in the heart through faith in Christ, I felt my heart strangely warmed. I felt I *did* trust in Christ and Christ alone for my salvation, and an assurance was given me that He had taken away my sins, even mine, and saved me from the law of sin and death."

Have you ever had the experience of the warm heart? You know we seem to be so afraid of a crisis, we seem to be so afraid of conversion, we're so afraid of infilling of the Holy Spirit, we're so afraid of emotion, and yet our young people are screaming and crying for a little bit of feeling. And that's one of the reasons why they're turning away from the church. And on the part of the young people today, they are revolting against the institution called the church, but they're not revolting against Jesus. They make a big distinction. They even call the boots that they wear "Jesus boots." And they wear long hair and beards many times because, some psychologists have said, they subconsciously want to be like Jesus. We have a great open door to them if we approach them right, and when we talk to them in our crusades, something remarkable is happening. Anywhere from 60 to 80 percent of the audiences every night are under 25 years of age, and on the nights I speak to young people, 80 percent of the audience will be under 25. And when I give the invitation they come by the hundreds, and the thousands. But when I stand there to give them the little instructions afterward they follow me until I say, "You must follow Christ to the church," and I see many of them turning off at that moment.

Now maybe we've learned something here this week about our church structures and even our services, that may have to be adapted to receive this new, modern, "now" generation.

And I'm going to skip my second point, but I think I will go to one other point, because that is very important. The man that God uses will be a faithful steward of the Gospel.

Brethren, I have been preaching the same message for nearly 30 years, for 22 years in mass evangelism. I have preached it at Harvard, I have preached it at Cambridge, I have preached it at Oxford, I have preached it at Berkeley, I have preached it all over the world. I preached it in Africa, I preached it in India, I preached it in every country in Latin America, I preached it in every part of the world. I have preached the same message, exactly the same. I have a different text and use a few new illustrations if I can find them, but it's the same message. When I had preached for 16 weeks at the Harringay Arena in London, an Anglican clergyman came to me and said, "I was here every night and you preached the same sermon every night." Well he was complimenting me because you see there's only one Gospel. And I want to tell you that I don't intend to compromise it, to change it, to tamper with it, to water it down in the slightest, in the future. The framework, the approach, the methods vary and change, but not the Gospel.

The apostle Paul said, "The preaching of the Cross is foolishness to them that perish. It'll always be foolish to a secular world. When the apostle Paul went to Corinth it was pagan, it was immoral, it was intellectual, but what did he preach? He was the only Christian in all of Corinth. What did he preach? He said, "I determined to know nothing among you save Jesus Christ and Him crucified." He said, "I didn't use enticing words of men's wisdom." He said, "I could have done it." Paul was an intellectual but he didn't do it. He deliberately turned from it and he said, "In fear and trembling I stood up and talked about Jesus on the Cross and Jesus raised from the dead."

And that in itself had a built-in power that transformed individuals and societies. It's called the everlasting Gospel and the same Gospel that was preached in the first century is the Gospel that Wesley preached in the 18th century. It's the Gospel that we preach today, and it's the same Gospel that will be preached a hundred years from now. It will work then, it worked before, it works now.

But then Paul said something that ought to frighten us a little bit. He said, "But though we or an angel from heaven preach any other Gospel unto you than that which we preached unto you, let him be accursed." Let him be accursed. If you're preaching any other Gospel than the Gospel revealed in this book, it would be better if you never preached again, because you're under a curse and under the judgment of God.

My third point, it was actually my fifth, the man that God uses will have a compassionate and sensitive social conscience. You know there have been some erroneous views held about this business of evangelicals and social responsibilities. There have been some that held the view that we have no social responsibility. Just get people saved, that's enough. We don't need to think about the race problem, the poverty problem, and all these other problems, that's for other people. We forgot how much of Jesus' teaching had to do with the salt, and the light, and the ministering to the whole man.

Then there were those that said that evangelicals had no social conscience. Well, a few might not have, but many, and most, of the great social movements in history had their roots in the evangelical Gospel. And somehow we've allowed people to become brainwashed into thinking that evangelicals had no social burden, when actually we did. But I think Dr. Ockenga is right. In the '20s and '30s, in the reaction against the liberalism of that day, there began a period when we over emphasized the vertical, and we forgot the horizontal.

Then there are some who say that we do not need to get personally involved. You know it's easy to sit on a committee and it's easy to make great sweeping statements and go back to our air-conditioned hotel rooms, back to our homes in the suburbs, and think we have done our social work. But what about getting down and getting our fingernails dirty, and maybe getting a scar on our back?

I was playing golf one day with the President of one of the great liberal seminaries of the country. He said, "You know," he said, "I admire your father-in-law, Dr. Nelson Bell, but you know he's a fundamentalist," and he said, "he doesn't really have a social concern." I stopped and I was just about to swing a golf club, not at him, at the ball. I said, "Now wait a minute. No social concern?" I said, "He was a pitcher in professional baseball and had been sold to a big league team and was one of the most promising young pitchers of that year. He quit professional baseball to go study medicine because God had called him to be a medical missionary. And he took his little family and went out to China before they ever had modern drugs and modern sanitation and things as we have them today. He went way back in the interior of China and did for 25 years, in actual social work and social involvement, what you *preach* about from your air-conditioned pulpit on Sunday."

That's the kind of social involvement we need. We need something that's personal. I remember I was convicted about this. I began to search my own heart, for example, in the race question. I think all of us have been on a pilgrimage at this point. I said, "Now is my concern based upon guilt," as many of our modern psychologists are saying, "or is it an escape from anxiety, or is it because I want the approval of men, like the Pharisees when they liked to parade up and down and show their good works in front of people? Or is my concern based upon a burden and a Christian compassion placed upon our hearts by the Holy Spirit?" When I got my motives right, and it took me a long time to do it, then I said, "I want to get personally involved." Drew Pearson wrote me a letter about that time, and the first big crisis we had in America in the race problem was Clinton, Tennessee. And he said, "Billy, the White Citizens' Council are in charge down there. Have you got the guts to go down there and preach your Gospel?" I said, "Mr. Pearson, I'll do it, if you'll sit on the platform with me." He said, "I'll do it." We went down there and I wish you could have been there. Half black and half white, the auditorium jammed to capacity, and I preached the Gospel; and the first man forward was one of the leaders of the White Citizens' Council.

One of the Presidents of the United States called me to the White House and said, "Billy, the crisis in Alabama is reaching major proportions. Will you go and preach from one end of Alabama to the other?" I said, "Yes, sir." I bet you didn't read about it in your newspaper, but every major stadium in Alabama was packed from Birmingham, one whole week in Montgomery, in Dothan, in Tuskegee, in Auburn, city after city, and most of the time it was about half white and half black, all sitting mixed up. The choir totally integrated — in the middle of the crisis — and as far as I know it never was on any national television network.

Some of the Klu Klux Klan people had gone and put all their smears on the signs and the advertising. So many threats came to me personally that the police had to go with me everywhere I went. We have it all on motion picture. We took our own films, because we knew people 10 years later wouldn't believe it.

The New York Times sent a man. They wrote it up pretty faithfully but that was about all. Because you see there weren't any riots and nobody was killed, and it was just the demonstration of the love of God that two races could sit down together and worship God in Alabama.

Now, my eighth point and my time was gone 10 minutes ago but they told me that I wouldn't be limited, and Dr. Hoffmann hasn't yelled at me yet.

The man of God, the man that God uses, must have a Gospel of hope. Brethren, the despair in this country in intellectual circles is beyond anything I've ever seen. I talked to a professor at Cornell University. I went there right after they had their problem. This professor said that all the theories and ideas that they held one year ago have come crumbling down and he said, "My God, we don't know which way to turn."

I've talked to leaders in Washington who say the same thing politically. I've talked to leaders in every realm and they all seemingly have this terrible sense of despair as Camus had it, as Sartre had it, as Marcuse has it. Despair! At this hour, what a moment to stand up with the Gospel of Jesus Christ and offer them hope.

I'm an optimist. Ours is a theology of hope. God has a plan for this world. There's a future. And let me tell you this. We're not going to bring Paradise to earth by our own efforts. You see our whole world system is based on the cracked foundation of human nature, and you're never going to — let me repeat this — you're *never* going to have permanent world peace by the efforts of men. We're to work for it, we're to pray for it, and I'll do all that I can, and so should you, but it's not going to be accomplished. It'll only be accomplished when the Prince of Peace is reigning as King of kings and Lord of lords. That's when peace is going to come. And that will come by the intervention of God once again in history in supernatural power, when Christ comes back.

Brethren, we ought to be preaching that. The world is crying for our eschatological message. The despair! They don't know which way to turn. The only alternative that seems to have a little ray of hope to some of our intellectual leaders may be the eschatological aspect of Communism. And that's where we can learn. They're saying, "All right, let's change the world. We've got a program, we've got a system. We don't believe it can be done voluntarily."

You see, the Communist, the real Marxist, accepts our view of man that something is wrong with man. So they say that all they need is to control the world for about 30 years, because all the different problems of the world can only be solved by compulsion. By compulsion!

Even that wouldn't do it unless the "compulsors" were absolutely just with love, compassion, mercy, and justice. And all the statements that Dr. Abernathy read yesterday and all that Martin Luther King, Jr., said in his great speech, "I have a dream," is going to come to pass because the one that's going to reign and rule is the Lord Jesus Christ. He is our hope.

Shall we bow our heads.

You've sat here all week. You've been disturbed. You've been convicted. You've been challenged. You've been made angry. But you've not been apathetic and deep down in your spirit and in your heart, God has been speaking to you. You know that. You don't want to go home the same man or the same woman that you came here. This whole week would be wasted. Some of you've gotten a new glimpse of the Gospel. Others have gotten a new glimpse of your fellowman, and your neighbor, and your responsibility to him. Others of you have gotten a new glimpse of God. You've gotten a new glimpse of what it means to be filled with the Spirit. You've gotten a new glimpse of what it means to have love, as Harold Lindsell told us yesterday, and of prayer. You feel in your own life a great sense of need, and frustration, and failure, and before you leave Minneapolis you want God to touch your life.

I don't want people to do what I'm going to ask en masse. I want you to do it one by one, slowly and thoughtfully. I want to ask some people here today to receive Christ into your heart. Maybe you were like Luther, or maybe you were like Wesley. I don't want to put it into theological terminology. But you need an experience with Christ. You want to have the experience of the warm heart. You want to have the experience of entering God's spiritual Paradise, that we can have even in this world of trouble and difficulty. You'd like that experience this morning. You want God to touch your life and touch your ministry in every way that He wants to touch it. You're willing to commit yourself this morning and say, "God, you said you're searching for a man to make up the hedge and stand in the gap and, O God, I want to be that man in my community, in my area of service. I want to be God's man."

If you will say that, and you want God to touch you and fill you this morning, I want you to stand up with bowed heads. Stand up deliberately, and slowly, and thoughtfully, because this is recorded in heaven and it would be a terrible and tragic thing to make such a commitment to God and not mean it with all your heart. As Dr. Abernathy reminded us, the cost will be tremendous, but the joy will also be tremendous.

And I want to tell you something. I need in my life and my ministry a new touch from God. I really do. I sincerely need it. I want to stand up this morning at my own invitation and say, "O God, I want the experience of the warm heart."

You may have to have Luther's experience. All of us may have a different experience, but we want Christ to touch us. Maybe He needs to touch your mind so that you will have more faith in His Word. Maybe your heart, so that you will put your intellectual comprehension together with a warm heart. Whatever it is that God is speaking to you about, you stand up now and keep standing.

I want us to sing together as a prayer "Spirit of the Living God Fall Afresh on Me," then I want us to kneel where we are for just about two minutes, and pray your prayer of consecration, and ask God to come into your life and heart in a new way, as I shall kneel on this platform. Maybe it's impossible for you to kneel but you can sit if you cannot kneel. It would be wonderful if we could all kneel. Then I'm going to ask after that, that we have a prayer by Dr. Paul Fryhling, and then after that I'm going to ask that we sing "O For a Thousand Tongues," as we leave this place to go and evangelize.

Now let us sing "Spirit of the Living God."

(Everyone sang "Spirit of the Living God.")

Mr. Graham: Let us kneel for two minutes and pray our prayer, a personal prayer. Don't pray for the other person now, this is your prayer before God for yourself.

Dr. Fryhling will come now and pray for all of us.

Dr. Fryhling: O God, not my brother, nor my sister, but it's me, O Lord, standing in the need of prayer, and in the need of the touch of your hand, of your Spirit. Feed us, Lord, as you have done so wonderfully. Break us, as now we feel broken. Melt us, as now indeed by thy Spirit and by the warmth of your love we now sense ourselves melted together. The unity of the Spirit in the bond of peace, the unity in thee, O Lord. Melt us. Mold us, O Lord, forgive us for having constructed so many molds that we thought, sometimes very sincerely, were the need of the hour that should make the structure what it should be in order to do what the world needs. We pray that you will mold us. What you want of me, what you want of the church, the local church, the denomination, the church of Jesus Christ, the body of Christ, will you mold it? No, let us be yielded, pliable in your hands, still poured out into the mold with no direction from within ourselves, but as clay in the potter's hand, not asking Him, "Why will you make me thus?" Make us what you want us to be to fill the places, to fill the needs, to carry out the responsibilities. Whatever, Lord. Those who must wait aside in ineffectiveness because of physical handicaps to be in the chamber of prayer, as well as those that must be out on the ramparts, sounding forth. Whatever, Lord, mold us, and fill us. We know that we shall be used then.

O Spirit of the living God, fall upon us and come within us. Thy enabling, blessed Holy Spirit of God, we wait for that. We need that. We want it personally. We want it in the church of Jesus Christ in America today, and around the world.

Spirit of God, we thank you that again we know that you have answered the prayer of old, "Take not thy Holy Spirit from us." Glory be to thee, O God. May our lives bring glory to thee. For whatever we ask, and in this prayer that we are asking today, you said, blessed Savior, that will you do if it's asked in your name, that the Father may be glorified in the Son.

Glory be to thee, O God, Father, Son and Holy Spirit, we are thine. Take our lives and let them be consecrated to thee. Amen.

Dr. Graham: We're going to stand and sing "O For a Thousand Tongues," and then Dr. Oswald Hoffmann will close this great Congress on Evangelism.

(Everyone sang "O For a Thousand Tongues.")

Dr. Davies: In the light of the consecration of this hour, let us sing the stanza that goes, "He breaks the power of canceled sin, He sets the prisoner free, His blood can make the foulest clean, His blood availed for me." Let's sing.

(Everyone sang another stanza.)

Dr. Hoffmann: In response from you to Dr. Graham, I say what one of you said to me this morning as we walked quietly over here. I don't know who he is because we just fell in with each other on the street, and after some thought he said, "I came here because I've got some obstreperous people in my congregation and I didn't care whether they went to heaven or hell." And he said, "Now I care, and I'm going back to care for them."

That's why we came. This is a churchly meeting and the church is back there waiting for all of us, pastors and people, and the Lord has a word too for each of us. It's one of His own words in His own language and it is, "Maranatha," the Lord has come, or the Lord will come, or better still, the Lord is coming. "Maranatha," and the grace of our Lord Jesus Christ, and the love of God, and the communion of His Holy Spirit be with us. Amen.

The Lord goes with you. Go with Him, my brethren, and have joy.

A CONGRESS RESUME'

Dr. Oswald C. J. Hoffmann

I'm going to give you a little report tonight on what happened here in this city during the last week. We felt that we owed that to you people of Minneapolis, because you've been such wonderful and generous hosts to all of us. I'm going to make this report on the basis of a little verse that was written by St. Peter a long time ago when he said, "Thanks to the God and Father of our Lord Jesus Christ who by the greatness of His mercy has brought us to life again, to a hope that is genuinely alive through the resurrection of Jesus Christ from the dead."

Thousands of people came to Minneapolis this week from 93 denominations and they met in the auditorium of your city. The original idea for this meeting came from the evangelism committee of the American Lutheran Church which has its headquarters here in Minneapolis. As a result of their action, the people of Minnesota, headed by the Governor of Minnesota, appointed a committee of 100 which in turn appointed a national committee of church leaders, both clergymen and laymen, who could organize this United States Congress on Evangelism. They did this because a World Congress was held three years ago in Berlin, and it was felt that a United States Congress would be the logical thing to follow upon that World Congress.

The national committee then appointed an executive committee from this city and that executive committee was headed by Dr. Paul Fryhling, pastor of The First Covenant Church. I'm going to ask him and his committee to rise one after the other as I call their names, and please don't applaud until I have finished calling the roll of that committee. I thought you people in Minneapolis ought to know who your fellow citizens are who arranged this magnificent event.

All right, Dr. Paul Fryhling, the chairman of the Executive Committee, please rise. Dr. Victor B. Nelson, of the Billy Graham organization, who served as the executive secretary and did an awful lot of the work that was necessary. Dr. Conrad N. Thompson, who is the Director of Evangelism of the American Lutheran Church and was chairman of the Participation Committee for this Congress. George M. Wilson who has been treasurer and general factotum of the whole committee and I would be surprised if he's on the platform. He's probably running around downstairs trying to rig up loudspeakers for those thousands of people ouside this evening. Then there's Mel Larson, the editor of the official publication of the Covenant Church,

DR. OSWALD C. J. HOFFMANN, Speaker on The Lutheran Hour, St. Louis, Missouri, and Chairman, National Committee, U.S. Congress on Evangelism.

who I don't think is here because Mel has been rather sick lately, and I don't think he's going to risk entering a large auditorium like this tonight.

Then there's Dr. William Berg of Augustana Lutheran Church who wrote and directed the black light presentation which was such a sensation the other evening. There's Dr. C. Philip Hinerman, pastor of the Park Avenue United Methodist Church and I don't know whether Phil made it either this evening. And then Dr. Carl H. Lundquist who is the President of Bethel College and Seminary in St. Paul.

These men did the work that resulted in that magnificent meeting which has sent people today on their way singing the praises of Minneapolis and St. Paul, and now you can recognize your fellow citizens.

Oh, Mel Larson, you remember I told you he's been under the weather a little bit. I do want Mel to rise and take your response. You can applaud him yourselves.

It was a free and open meeting that we held here in Minneapolis. No one told anyone else what to say at this meeting. I want to say also that it was a disciplined meeting, for which the chairman was extremely grateful. It was not the iron discipline of regimentation but the free discipline of a people who are accustomed to discipline themselves, the self-discipline of committed Christians. That's the kind of thing it seems to me that the world needs today, and for which the world is looking in this age.

It was a church meeting. These people came from their churches. Most of them were invited by their churches to come here, and they're going back to their churches. It was a meeting that was associated deeply with the church and with the congregations who form that church.

It was a practical meeting, interested not merely in the profession of the faith but in the practice of the faith. One layman said to me, "I've been told for years that I should go out and speak for Jesus Christ," but he said, "no one ever told me before just what I can do to speak for Jesus Christ. How, for example, do you talk to a man whom you never met before, and start talking to him about Jesus Christ?"

Well, there were 40 meetings in the afternoons, Christian activity meetings where men who knew how to do this and have practiced it for years, indeed have refined it down so that they know exactly what to do, shared their experience with people like that. And this layman went away and said, "Now I know. In one half hour I got the idea, and I can go back now and talk about Christ to people whom I was afraid to talk to before."

And I want to add one thing. There isn't a Christian who can't talk to people about Jesus Christ. Don't ever believe that you can't talk to people about Him. Anyone can speak about Jesus Christ if he knows just how to go and talk to people about Him.

The centrality of the Gospel was the heart of this meeting. There's nothing musty about the Gospel and nothing misty about it either. People here just assumed that people knew in that day what the Gospel is all about, and then they went ahead and told them what it is. The Gospel is the good news of Jesus Christ sent by His Father to be a man for every one of us men. That man, in whom dwelt all the fullness of the Godhead bodily, lived His life — the kind of life we have to live — and died His death — the kind of death that we are destined to die — and He gave all of that for all of us. Because He laid down His life in all obedience, for us disobedient sons and daughters of our heavenly Father, God has given Him a name which is above every name, that at the name of Jesus every knee should bow. There is forgiveness in Him and there is life in Him.

That is the Gospel and the Gospel was central to this meeting. Also central to this meeting was the destiny of people — black people, white people, red people, yellow people, and an awful lot of green and scared people around the world. I noted something that was said by a Minneapolis man who happens to be a black man, "We feared this would be just a continuation of the tradition that has seen evangelism divorced from social action. The two have been like the steamer trying to cross the English Channel, when it moved it couldn't whistle, and when it whistled it couldn't move. But here we have experienced a renaissance in our understanding of evangelism. For that reason I'm grateful to be a part of it."

Archbishop Loane came all the way from Sydney, Australia, to lead the Bible Study the first two days and Harold Lindsell, of "Christianity Today" magazine conducted the Bible Study of the last three days. Leighton Ford, who is the brother-in-law of Dr. Billy Graham, delivered a really key address in one of the first days of the meeting on "The Church and Evangelism in a Day of Revolution." Tom Skinner followed that same evening with a talk on Jesus Christ and the black revolution, and Tom is a black man who follows the Lord Jesus Christ.

Then there came Keith Miller who is an Episcopalian layman, and he talked about how necessary it is that Christians lay themselves open to the world so that the world may come and hear what they have to say. He said Christians have to allow themselves to become vulnerable to the world.

Then there was Senator Mark Hatfield of Oregon, and Dr. Paul Rees of World Vision, who used to be a pastor here in Minneapolis. And Harold Ockenga who used to be pastor of Park Street Congregational Church in Boston and now is the new President of Gordon and Conwell Seminary up in Massachusetts.

And then there were evangelists like Ford Philpot, and then there were Baptists like Dr. Ralph Abernathy and also Dr. Stephen Olford whom you heard before. There were so many people that I'm not going to begin to mention them all. They all contributed like the Rev. D. James Kennedy of the Coral Ridge Presbyterian Church in Fort Lauderdale which has such a great program of parish evangelism.

I want to say also that there was a certain mark of humility in this meeting that was very encouraging. As one man said to me, "People here seem to be shaken." They were not so sure they knew the answers to every question and that's a mighty healthy attitude. There is One who knows all the answers, but He's the One in whom we believe. We who follow Him are not equipped to know all the answers and that's why we follow Him. We follow Him in faith and He will show us the way. As Leighton Ford said that evening, "I believe in God the Father Almighty, maker of heaven and earth, and I also believe in God the Father Almighty, shaker of heaven and earth." And He's shaking it a good deal these days.

The young people, I think, got a good deal of attention in this meeting and they gave us a good deal of attention last night too when they turned out in such numbers. The Sergeant whom we called at the Police Department to get an escort to the meeting here tonight spent 10 minutes talking to us about the youth meeting last night and what a great thing it was, while he was waiting for the captain to give him authorization to send a squad car out here with me to the meeting. That's what happens when young people turn out this way. He said that the psychedelic groups never get a crowd such as the Gospel got last night from the youth of Minneapolis. I guess we can take our hats off to some of the older people who have such a heart for youth that they give of their time for something like this. People like Billy Zeoli who organized that "Turn On" last night, and Pat Boone and all those youth groups that came out, and everybody else who participated in this whole Congress.

There are three things that move us you know. Faith in the Lord Jesus Christ. It is by faith that we are saved. "We . . . conclude that a man is . . . justified by faith without the deeds of the law." It is Christ who saves and it is faith which accepts Him.

There is also hope and Dr. Billy Graham closed the meeting out today by saying, "The world is looking for hope and here we Christians have hope. How dare we refuse to offer hope to this world? There is hope in Jesus Christ and that hope is like an anchor that holds the soul fast in a restless and troubled sea."

And then, my friends, there's another great thing and that's also in Christ. It's the one thing that is most notable about Him and that is love, compassion. When He saw the multitudes, the masses, "He was moved with compassion on them." And how can we who follow Him not be moved by what we see today?

If anything is going to happen from this U.S. Congress on Evangelism— and I'm persuaded that a great thing is going to happen because the people went away more enthusiastic than I've ever seen them go out from any church meeting that I have ever attended in my whole lifetime — it's going to be because the love of those people is going to move them, and the love that they have is something like the love of Christ. The love of Christ compels us.

Men and brethren, even though we have tongues of men and of angels (and we don't have that), we are just as sounding brass or a tinkling cymbal. Though we have the gift of prophecy and understand all mysteries

and all knowledge and though we have all faith, great as it is, to move mountains, and don't have this one thing, we are nothing. And though we have
all the social welfare in the world, and though we bestow all our goods to feed
the poor and though we give our body to be burned, and we don't have this,
this great quality of Christ, love, it doesn't mean a thing. Love suffers long
and is kind. Love envies none, love vaunts not itself, is not puffed up, does
not behave itself unseemly, seeks not her own, is not easily provoked,
thinks no evil, rejoices not in iniquity but rejoices in the truth, bears all
things, believes all things, hopes all things, endures all things.

Fathers and mothers, sons and daughters, remember it please. Love
never fails. Whether there be prophecies they shall fail, and whether there be
tongues they shall cease and whether there be knowledge it shall vanish
away. For now we know in part, and we prophesy in part, but when that
which is perfect is come, that which is in part shall be done away. When I
was a child I spoke as a child, I thought as a child, I understood as a child.
When I became a man, I put away childish things. Now we see as through
a glass, darkly, but then face to face. Now I know in part, but then shall I
know even as also I am known. And now abide faith, hope, love, these three,
but the greatest of these (probably because finally it is the proof of the
whole pudding), the greatest of these is love. Amen.

THE MESSAGE FOR OUR TIMES

Dr. Billy Graham

Our Father and our God, we pray that Thy Holy Spirit will apply the Gospel to our heart and we pray that Thou wouldst draw by Thy Holy Spirit all of those whose hearts Thou hast prepared for this hour. For we ask it in Christ's name. Amen.

I want you to turn with me to the twelfth chapter of the book of Hebrews, if you have a Bible. If you don't I'll read it to you from the new American Bible Society's translation called *Good News for Modern Man* that I believe is the best seller of all Bibles at the moment.

"His voice shook the earth at that time, but now He has promised, 'I will once more shake, not only the earth but heaven as well.' The words 'once more' plainly show that the created things will be shaken and removed, so that the things that are not shaken will remain."

Now the writer of the book of Hebrews says there are two kinds of things in the world, things that are going to be shaken, and things that will not be shaken. He said God is going to shake the world and is going to shake the heavens at some future point of history. Let us be thankful then, because we receive a kingdom that cannot be shaken. The kingdom of God, he said, cannot be shaken. If the kingdom of God dwells in you, it can never be shaken by whatever the circumstances may be in our world.

Let us be grateful and worship God in a way that will please Him, with reverence and fear, for our God is indeed a consuming fire.

Then the eighth verse of the next chapter, "Jesus Christ is the same yesterday, today, and for ever."

During this past week, in this conference we've heard a great deal about revolution; and the word "revolution" means change. We've heard a great deal about the political changes in our world in the past few years and Jesus made an interesting statement in the 21st chapter of Luke. He said, "And there shall be signs in the sun, and in the moon, and in the stars; and upon the earth distress of nations."

What did He mean? Think of it now. Jesus said 2,000 years ago there's going to come a generation when there'll be signs on the moon. Well, I thought when Neil Armstrong set his foot down there, that was a sign. Signs on the moon. And then God said there'll be signs in the stars. Wernher von Braun said this past week that by 1982 we will have landed a man on Mars.

Jesus said that while all that's going on in space, on the earth

DR. BILLY GRAHAM, Founder and President, The Billy Graham Evangelistic Association, and Honorary Chairman, U.S. Congress on Evangelism.

there's going to be distress; and that word "distress" means to be pressed from all sides. Then He said "with perplexity" and that word "perplexity" means no way out. You ask our modern philosophers today what's the way out. They don't know. Albert Camus and Sartre say there is no way out. Sartre wrote a book entitled *No Exit*. There is no hope. There's no way out of our dilemma. Our problems are too great.

Many of our philosophers are saying that life means absolutely nothing. It doesn't make any sense at all, and that's what Jesus warned about. He said we will be pressed from all sides and there'll be no way out. He said men's hearts will fail them because of fear, fear of the population explosion, fear of the hydrogen bomb, fear of all that is going to come upon the earth. He said the powers of heaven shall be shaken.

And then it's a period of great social changes, and I want to tell you that when a black man can be elected mayor in a town in Mississippi, social change is taking place. The problems of poverty, race, war, disease — all of these — drugs, the youth rebellion.

It's a period of scientific change. If my grandfather were to awake today and see a color television, listen to the blaring of the radio, watch a jet airliner pass overhead, and see a rocket shooting up from Cape Kennedy, I think he would ask to go back to the grave. I don't think he could take it psychologically. It's hard for us in the older generation because I remember back when we didn't have telephones, and I remember back when we had just got radios. I remember the time my father fixed up an old crystal set and we had the earphones on when I was a little boy; there was only one station on the air anywhere in the eastern part of the United States, KDKA in Pittsburgh. My dad heard a bunch of static and he said, "I think I've heard it." That's in my lifetime.

I remember going to the New York World's Fair in 1939 and they talked about television. They had a little set there. I don't know whether they had a wire, or what they had, but it was called television. We all laughed and said, "How absurd. Couldn't be." Never would happen. Never would come.

I remember the first time I got in an airplane, a DC3, to take a trip. We went all the way from Chicago to Detroit and it only took us three hours. I thought, "Man, this is traveling." Now you can do it in 30 minutes.

The changes that have taken place in our lifetime! And the religious changes! My goodness, look at the religious changes. Lutheran and Baptist together in Minnesota. And since the coming of Pope John the tremendous revolution within the church of Rome. What a change!

The other night I was in Brussels, Belgium. I went there at the invitation of, and was received by, the Papal Nuncio, Archbishop Silvio Oddi one of the most brilliant men in the Roman Catholic world.

We walked into his little chapel. He said, "Let's have a prayer," and he sat there and told me about his own spiritual experience, and his own spiritual pilgrimage. That couldn't have happened even 10 years ago, but it's happening today.

Something's happening. The world is changing. The earth is being shaken in every area of life, but the Scripture says there are some things that will never, never, never change. Some things you can count on if all the stars in heaven fall, if the moon turns to blood, if the sun is shining, if the whole thing blows up, there'll be some things that remain. What are they?

First, the nature of God will never change. The Lord said, "I am the Lord. I change not." The Scripture says, "Whatsoever God doeth, it shall be forever." Nothing can be put to it nor anything taken from it. The Scripture says, "There is no variableness, neither shadow of turning with God." The Scripture says, "Holy, holy, holy, Lord God Almighty which was and is and is to come." God is unchanging in His holiness and righteousness.

You and I may change. We may change our philosophies, we may change our style of dress. I saw a strange thing. I've been in California four times in the last three weeks. Our next crusade is in California, and when I was out there last year the girls were wearing micro-miniskirts. But up on the north beach, in Haight-Asbury, on Sunset Strip, and Westwood Village where I walked, I noticed they were wearing skirts down to their ankles. I don't know whether that's the new style or not. I don't know what they call them. Styles change, attitudes change. But there's one thing that never changes. God never changes.

God is a righteous and a holy God and He demands righteousness in you. God also is unchanging in judgment. The Bible says the Lord shall judge the ends of the earth. I want to tell you there's a day of judgment coming. The day has been appointed, and God is going to judge the world by that man Christ Jesus.

We don't like to hear about judgment today. We want preachers to tickle our ears, and tell us about all these wonderful things; but when it comes to judgment and hell, we don't want to hear it. I want to tell you judgment's coming and you're going to be there. If you're outside of Christ you're going to be at the great white throne judgment, when God's computers get to rolling.

I was shown a computer the other night, and I asked the computer a question. I said, "I'd like to have all the dates of Easter for the next 2,000 years." In a matter of about, oh quicker than I could tell it, they were all there, the dates of Easter for 2,000 years. That's a fact. If you don't believe it, go to our office. We've got the computer. It'll tell you. And they've got computers now that'll talk back to you. Now we don't have that one. I just read about that one.

But everything is being computerized. Well I want to tell you, if man can build computers like that, what do you think God has? God is keeping an account, and every moral choice that you ever faced in your whole life is computerized. The alternative that you could have taken, the option that you didn't pick up, will be there and it'll all be unraveled at the judgment. That's why the Bible says that the whole world will declare that God is just. Nobody is going to say, "God, you're unjust. God, I don't deserve it. God, I don't deserve this judgment, I don't deserve hell." Nobody's going to say that because it'll all be there; all the thoughts and the intents of your mind and heart will be there. The day of judgment is coming.

God is unchanging in His love. "Yea I have loved thee with an everlasting love," says the Scriptures. God loves you, everlastingly. Right to the gates of hell itself God's love goes with you. I don't care what sin you've committed. I don't care how dark and ugly and black it is and how wicked you've been. God loves you. He loves you with an everlasting love, so much so that He gave His Son on the Cross to die for you and to shed His blood for you. "God who is rich in mercy for His great love wherewith He loved us."

Not only is the nature of God unchanging and He will never be shaken, but the Word of God has not changed. The Bible says, "The grass withereth and the flower fadeth, but the Word of our God shall stand forever." The Bible says, "Heaven and earth shall pass away, but my Word shall not pass away."

Our views of the Bible may change from generation to generation but this book is the revealed Word of God; and from Genesis to Revelation, it is God's Word and it will never pass away. The commandments in this book are forever. The love expressed in this book is forever. Unchanging is the Word of God, and when you read the Bible, it's more relevant today than it's ever been.

I was sitting on a plane sometime ago beside a professor of psychology at one of the universities in California, and we got to talking a little bit. He said, "I don't believe the Bible." He said, "I'm an agnostic. There may be a God, there may be a supernatural presence, but I'm not sure about it. The Bible is way out of date." He said, "I've listened to you on television and," he said, "you're just out of date. I turn you off when you come on."

And so I just sat there, I didn't say much more. I thought, "I've been turned off, I'll just go ahead and read." Well, I was reading Phillips' translation, and I was reading the first, second, and third chapters of Romans because I was preparing a little talk on it. It didn't look like a Bible, he didn't know it was a Bible. It looked like a regular book. He said, "What are you reading?" I said, "I'm reading a very interesting book that analyzes the situation today better than anything I ever read." He said, "What is it?" I said, "Read it for yourself." He read it, he said, "Man, you know that's tremendous. That's one of the greatest analyses of the present situation I've ever read." He said, "Could you get me one of those?" And I said, "Yes, sir."

The Word of God is relevant today if you'll take time to read it and study it. It speaks to your problem, no matter how young you are or how old you are.

And then thirdly, the moral law has not changed. "Till earth and heaven pass," said Jesus, "one jot or one tittle shall in no wise pass from the law." Oh, we don't like law and we don't like discipline, but I want to tell you it's just as wrong to tell a lie tonight as it was 2,000 years ago. It's just as wrong to commit immorality tonight as it was 4,000 years ago when the law was given. And we may have a lot of people coming along preaching a new morality, and they may say that it's all right if it's meaningful. Well, all of those rationalizations and all of those arguments don't count with God. God is unchanging. His law is unchanging and there are certain moral laws, just as in the physical universe there are physical laws that God put there, that we're now discovering. So much so that we can send a man up on the moon and he lands at the precise spot that's picked out for him to land, going by law that God has placed in nature. God has moral laws just as precise. And the Bible says you and I have broken them. We've "come short" and that's what sin is. It's coming short of God's law. It's coming short of God's moral requirements, and the Bible says, "All have sinned and come short of the glory of God."

I'm a sinner and you're a sinner. That's the reason every one of us needs redemption. Every one of us needs forgiveness. Every one of us needs salvation. Every one of us needs to come to the Cross and acknowledge our sins, and repent of our sins, and receive Christ.

And then human nature has not changed. It's still the same. Cain killed Abel and men are still killing each other tonight. Hate, lust and greed rule in our world. Jeremiah the prophet said, "The heart is deceitful above all things and desperately wicked. Who can know it?" It hasn't changed. The mugging, the raping, the knifing, the social injustice, the greed, the lust — it's all here, as it was all there when this book was written. Man is the same in every generation, and that's why the Gospel is relevant in every generation because the Gospel meets human need.

And then God's purpose for the world has not changed. Yes, God has a purpose. We're heading somewhere. Where are we heading? I'm going to tell you right now. We're headed for judgment. There's

going to be a judgment in this world, but at the end of the judgment
the kingdom of God is going to come, in the person of Jesus Christ.
He's going to set up His kingdom, and the utopia that you dreamed
of, and the utopia that you and I have caught glimpses of through
science and through what the world could be and ought to be, is
actually going to come. God has a plan and none of the things that
are happening in the world take God by surprise. God doesn't wake
up some morning and scratch His head and say, "Boy, oh boy, it looks
like that Middle Eastern thing is getting out of hand." God doesn't
do that. You see, everything is in the eternal present with God.

It's a very interesting thing to me that we have broken the sound
barrier, and now scientists tell us that we might be able to break the
light barrier. When we break the light barrier and are able to travel
at the speed of 186,000 miles a second, you know what happens? Time
ceases to be. If an astronaut left Cape Kennedy and went at the speed
of light — a little faster than the speed of light — it would take him
10 years to get to the nearest star and back. Five years there and five
years back. When he got back and you met him at the airport, you'd
be 10 years older but he would only be a few *hours* older, because
he would have approached the point in space where time ceases to be
and that's precisely what the Bible says. God is from everlasting to
everlasting. There's no past with God and no future with God. It's
all present and science now says that's right. *We've* just found it out.

I don't know much about science but you can take books of
science today, and statements by scientists, and take the Bible and
science is just confirming the Bible almost every day. It's happening
so fast it's going to take a computer to keep up with it.

Then, lastly, the way of personal salvation has not changed.
The Scripture says, "Neither is there salvation in any other, for there
is none other name under heaven given among men whereby we must
be saved." There's no other way. There's no other way in the Bible
that you can have your sins forgiven. There's no other way that you
can be saved. There's no other way that you can go to heaven. There's
no other way that you can have permanent peace and joy in your
heart except coming the way God has outlined in the Bible.

The Scripture says that there's a way that seemeth right unto
man but the end thereof are the ways of death. Oh, there are other
ways, other roads that seem more acceptable to my intellect, more
rational, more logical. They seem to be good. They seem to be right,
but Jesus said the end is death. The Scripture says the end is death.
There is no other way except through Jesus Christ. "He that believeth
on the Son hath everlasting life, and he that believeth not the Son shall
not see life but the wrath of God abideth on him."

Now, ladies and gentlemen, God is not going to change that formula. There's no use for you to look any further trying to find some other way. There is none. Jesus said the gate to heaven is narrow, the road is narrow; and He said the road that leads to destruction is broad and wide is the gate and He said many go therein.

Now I want to ask you tonight which road are you on? Are you on the broad road that leads to destruction, or are you on the narrow road that leads to eternal life? You're on one or the other tonight. Which is it?

I'm going to ask you tonight to change roads. I'm going to ask you to leave the broad road and start through the narrow gate and say, "Tonight I want Christ to forgive my sin. I want to know I'm ready to meet God. I want to know I'm going to heaven."

You say, "But what do I have to do?" You must repent of your sin. You say, "Well, what's that?" Repentance means to change, to change your mind, to change your attitude, to be willing for God to come in your life, and make a big change in the way you live. That's repentance. It means that you acknowledge, "Oh God, I have sinned. I'm sorry. I'm ready to change my way of living."

Secondly, not only must you repent but you must believe. Notice I said it's by faith. But as many as received Him, to them gave He power to become the sons of God even to them that believe on His name. It's by faith. As Dr. Hoffmann said, it's not by works. It's by faith alone. You cannot come intellectually and sit all alone and just reason it all out. Very few come that way. You come with a simple faith in Jesus Christ. Not understanding it all. You can study the Bible the rest of your life and not understand it all. Come just as you are.

You say, "But my faith is so small." Jesus said if it's the faith of a mustard seed it's enough. If it's faith in Him. How many of you are members of the church? You may be Catholic or Protestant, you may be Jewish, you may not have any church background. Some of you are members of the church, but you're not sure that you're ready to meet God. You're not sure that Christ really lives in your heart. Some of you are Lutheran and you've been confirmed. You need to make real your confirmation and renew the vow that you took at confirmation. Some of you are Baptist and you were baptized and you made a vow. Some of you are Presbyterian or Reformed. Your parents made a vow. You need to renew that vow and make sure for yourself, because there comes a moment in your life when you must exercise your own choice.

And you must confess Christ openly. Jesus said, "If you're not willing to acknowledge me before men, I'll not acknowledge you before my Father which is in heaven." That's why in my crusades I call people to come forward, because every person that Jesus called in the New

Testament He called publicly. Somebody said, "Oh, no. What about Nicodemus?" Remember He never called Nicodemus. Nicodemus made an appointment to come and see Him at night. But the people that Jesus called, He called publicly. There was a reason for that.

Then you must be willing to obey. That means that you're willing to go back to your community, back to your home, back to your business, and back to your school and witness for Christ even if it means persecution. In many places today it means a certain type of persecution. You're laughed at, you're sneered at, you're called a square. When you say, "No" to certain things that you know to be wrong, when you take a stand for Jesus Christ in high school and in the university today, it costs many young people a great deal. That's exactly what Jesus meant when He said, "Take up your cross and follow Me." He said, "I'm going to die on a Cross, I want you to die to self and I want you to follow me, even if it means death to your ambitions and death to your popularity and death to everything." And He said, "If you're willing to die, I'll give you my life, and my joy, and my peace, and you will have something that cannot be shaken, no matter if the whole world blows up."

I'm going to ask you to receive Christ publicly tonight. I cannot ask you to come forward. There's no room. But I am going to ask you to stand where you are. Then an usher or a counselor is going to bring you some literature that I want you to have. Take it home with you and in there will be a little place for you to fill out your name and address. You mail it back in. You'll see an address to mail it to and we'll send you some more literature. But if you are willing tonight to say, "I shall repent of my sin. I receive Christ as Savior and Lord by faith. I confess Him, I want to obey Him, I want my name written in the book of life, I want my sin forgiven," I want you to stand up. And I want all of our heads bowed in prayer — no one leaving, no one moving. All over this place there are hundreds of young and old alike. You've been waiting a long time to make a public commitment of your faith in Jesus Christ and you'd like to settle that right now.

I want you to stand up where you are, all over the place. You may be in the choir. You may be the best person in your church, or you may not have any church background, but God has spoken to you tonight, and you want to receive Christ into your heart as best you can. You stand up quickly, everywhere, hundreds of you that God has spoken to. Everywhere, all over the place.

Many people are standing. Just keep standing. I'm going to ask that no one leave. The ushers are moving up with literature. Back here many people are standing. God has spoken to you. You stand. We're going to wait.

I'm going to ask that we sing a verse while others think it over and while others stand. Sing a verse of "Just as I am, without one plea, O Lamb of God, I come to Thee." The choir will sing it softly while you stand.

Keep standing. We're going to have a prayer. That's it, God bless you.

(The choir sang "Just As I Am.")

Stand up, remain standing for the prayer that we're going to have in a moment. Is God speaking to you now? This is your moment with Him and it may never come again quite like this. You stand.

If you're already standing in that crowd back there, just raise your hand and an usher will come and bring you your literature if you're standing way in the back.

And now for all of you that are standing, here's what we want you to do. You take that Gospel of John that you have in your hand and read it. You may not understand all you're reading but read it anyway, because it speaks to you. It's a living Word. Just the reading has its impact on you. It feeds you and you cannot grow as a Christian unless you're reading the Scriptures every day.

Then you'll find the beginning of a Bible study in there. You'll find all the instructions in there. The second thing is to spend time every day in prayer. That's our communication. That's where our power comes from to live the life. Thirdly, witness for Christ. You ought to tell somebody tonight that you've received Christ, and you witness in the community and in the home by your love. And then fourthly, get into the church, and get to work for Christ in the church.

I'm going to ask that we bow and I want you to pray this prayer out loud wherever you are. Pray it out loud after me.

O God, I am a sinner. I'm sorry for my sin. I'm willing to turn from my sins. I receive Christ as Savior. I confess Him as Lord. I want to follow Him in the fellowship of His church. In Christ's name. Amen.

Now you take that little card that's in there. Tear it out sometime tonight or tomorrow. Drop it in the mail to let us know about your commitment. You may be seated.

AN EVALUATION: WHAT THE U.S. CONGRESS ON EVANGELISM MEANS TO THE FUTURE OF THE CHURCH

Dr. W. Stanley Mooneyham, Dr. J. Sherrard Rice, and Dr. Sherwood E. Wirt, Chairman

The first U. S. Congress on Evangelism can best be described, we believe, in the words of Acts 4:31: "And when they had prayed, the place was shaken where they were assembled together."

During these five days past we have seen the church in microcosm. We have seen her radiant in the splendor of her united witness to the Lord Jesus Christ. We have seen the frailty, impotence and sin of her daily walk. We have joined in the church's struggle to carry out her ministry of healing and redemptive love right here on Grant Street. We have beheld the church rocked, challenged, and even exposed by the humanity around her; and we have sought to learn all over again what it means to follow Jesus.

We believe that what has happened this week in Minneapolis has not happened before in our lifetimes. We thank God for the experience. We believe that evangelism in America has had a new birth of freedom: freedom from old clichés, freedom from narrow loyalties, freedom from restricted fellowship, freedom in Christ to proclaim the Gospel in love to the family of mankind.

We shall go from this city in the strong conviction that we shall never be the same, and we are carrying with us a message that will make sure that our churches will never be the same. Our fervent prayer and desire is that we shall be empowered to win men and women to Jesus Christ in such a fresh and appealing way that God the Holy Spirit will be pleased to send spiritual awakening to our land and to the world.

As the Word of God has been preached in full power from this platform, we have tasted the new wine of God's liberating spirit, and the old wineskins seem strangely inadequate to contain it. The wind of the Spirit has blown through our assembly. Together we have undergone a baptism of love, and we covet it for our churches. We do not believe, as Karl Marx did, that men can change the world; but we believe that God can. We dedicate ourselves to be His instruments, available to the moving of His Spirit, and responding in obedience to His command with the word of the prophet: "Here am I, send me."

Dr. W. Stanley Mooneyham,
Dr. J. Sherrard Rice
and *Dr. Sherwood E. Wirt,* Chairman

INDEX OF SPEAKERS